Museum Politics

Museum Politics

Power Plays at the Exhibition

Timothy W. Luke

University of Minnesota Press
Minneapolis
London

Early versions of chapters 1 and 6 appeared in *The Australasian Journal of American Studies* 15 (December 1996) and 16 (December 1997). Earlier versions of chapters 2 and 3 appeared in *ARENA Journal* 8 (1997) and 6 (1996), respectively. Portions of chapter 4 appeared in an earlier form in *Art Papers* 13 (1989) and *Strategies* 12 (1999). Portions of chapter 5 appeared in an earlier form in *Art Papers* 21 (January/February 1997). Earlier versions of chapters 7 and 8 appeared in *Organization and Environment* 13 (September 2000) and 10 (June 1997).

Published by the University of Minnesota Press
111 Third Avenue South, Suite 290
Minneapolis, MN 55401-2520
http://www.upress.umn.edu

Library of Congress Cataloging-in-Publication Data

Luke, Timothy W.
    Museum politics : power plays at the exhibition / Timothy W. Luke.
        p.   cm.
    Includes bibliographical references and index.
    ISBN 0-8166-1988-3 (HC : alk. paper) — ISBN 0-8166-1989-1 (PB : alk. paper)
        1. Museum exhibits—Political aspects.   2. Popular culture—Political aspects.   3. Culture conflict—Political aspects.   4. Culture diffusion—Political aspects.   5. Nationalism—Social aspects.   6. Political correctness.   7. Social influence.   8. Museums—Political aspects.   I. Title.
    AM151 .L85   2002
    069'.5—dc21   2001007532

12 11 10 09 08 07 06 05 04   10 9 8 7 6 5 4 3 2

For three outstanding teachers:
Bonnie Owen, Fay Logsdon, and Gene Wolff

Contents

Acknowledgments   ix

Introduction: Museum Exhibitions as Power Plays   xiii

ONE
Politics at the Exhibition:
Aesthetics, History, and Nationality in the Culture Wars   1

TWO
Nuclear Reactions:
The (Re)Presentation of Hiroshima at the National Air and
Space Museum   19

THREE
Memorializing Mass Murder:
The United States Holocaust Memorial Museum   37

FOUR
Signs of Empire/Empires of Sign:
Daimyo Culture in the District of Columbia   65

FIVE
Inventing the Southwest:
The Fred Harvey Company and Native American Art   82

SIX
Museum Pieces:
Politics and Knowledge at the American Museum of
Natural History   100

SEVEN
The Missouri Botanical Garden:
Sharing Knowledge about Plants to Preserve and Enrich Life   124

EIGHT
Southwestern Environments as Hyperreality:
The Arizona–Sonora Desert Museum   146

NINE
Superpower Aircraft and Aircrafting Superpower:
The Pima Air and Space Museum   165

TEN
Strange Attractor: The Tech Museum of Innovation   186

ELEVEN
Channeling the News Stream:
The Full Press of a Free Press at the Newseum   203

Conclusion:
Piecing Together Knowledge and Pulling Apart Power at
the Museum   218

Notes   231

Index   259

Acknowledgments

Museums often are ignored by political analysts, especially in the United States where the "high culture" of museum exhibitions ordinarily is not brought into everyday politics by public figures. The 1990s and early years of the twenty-first century have been somewhat exceptional in this regard, because they have been marked by unusually heated discussions about the impact of museum shows on American society. While these debates have proven quite acrimonious, they chewed over the significance of only a few controversial exhibits whose curators dared to question some unspoken assumptions about America's national identity and historical development. Sometimes called the "culture war," "history war," or "science war," these battles attracted a great deal of attention over the past fifteen years. Becoming distracted by such bursts of rancor, however, leads us to overlook the continuous cultural combustion that is stoked every day with each museum visitor seeking amusement or enlightenment at America's many museums. Whether it reduces personal independence or refines collective solidarity, I want to argue that the discursive struggle waged at museum exhibitions can have a profound effect on the body politic. While some see important wars of movement being won or lost at the Smithsonian Institution in the aftermath of the *Enola Gay* exhibit or "The West as America" show, I believe the ongoing wars of position, which are being waged every day for smaller gains or losses, make museums truly interesting venues for political analysis.

This book then sets a course away from the methodological mainstream in contemporary American political science by approaching museums as significant sites of ideological controversy and political conflict. While I examine a couple of shows at art museums, my analysis focuses upon the politics of culture, history, nature, and technology exhibitions. If museums succeed at serving as places of awakening, enlightenment, or renewal for their visitors, then they are operating very concretely as normative theories-in-action, imparting new values and spreading different perspectives with their displays. Whether it is the Mapplethorpe show in Cincinnati during 1989 or the "Sensation" exhibit of 1999 in Brooklyn, these cultural battles illustrate how broadly power plays in and out of the didactic scripts of museum shows. Continuing to ignore this reality is futile. The terrorist attacks at the World Trade Center in New York and the Pentagon in Washington, D.C., on September 11, 2001, have introduced the violent destruction of a real war into the everyday life of ordinary Americans in the United States. Up against these events, the issues at stake in culture wars of the past ten or fifteen years may seem insignificant. Yet, there also is another sort of culture war at the core of the recently declared transnational war on international terrorism. Consequently, the character and conduct of culture warring must be given closer consideration, if only because some culture wars easily can flip over into wars between cultures.

Some of these studies have appeared previously in slightly different versions, more of them include much new material, and some of them are found only in this book. Chapter 6 had a fairly interesting reception in the larger world. In its initial form, it was an invited keynote address at the Third Annual Arlington Humanities Colloquium at the University of Texas-Arlington in April 1997. After being published in *The Australasian Journal of American Studies,* it was celebrated almost simultaneously as in the Antipodes, first, a prize-winning "gem" in *Philosophy and Literature*'s "Bad Scholarly Writing" contest at the University of Canterbury in Christchurch, New Zealand, along with pieces by Judith Butler and Homi K. Bhabha. It was then selected by the Australian and New Zealand American Studies Association as the winner of the Norman Harper Award for the Best Article published in the *Australasian Journal of American Studies* in 1996 and 1997. These very contradictory recognitions undoubtedly reveal how the culture war is a transnational conflict, but they also position the chapter, and by implication this book, out on the terrain of the culture wars in a certain fashion.

Over the time I have been writing this book, many people have freely given me their insights and encouragement. This sort of critique is not typical fare for those who now work for universities in the United States, especially in American political science departments. Still, I have found a few like-minded individuals who agree that we must pay much more attention to museums as places that are worthy of political analysis. Here I would like to thank Ben Agger, David Barzilai, Keith Beattie, David Campbell, Patty Catto, Cynthia Enloe, Suzi Gablik, Glenn Harper, Byron Hawk, John Jermier, Doug Kellner, Brad Klein, Bradley Macdonald, Brian Opie, Gearóid Ó Tuathail, Michael Peters, Christine Sylvester, R. B. J. Walker, and Stephen K. White. I also have benefited greatly from the assistance of Lisa Freeman and Carrie Mullen at the University of Minnesota Press. Kim Hedge and Maxine Riley in the Department of Political Science at Virginia Polytechnic Institute and State University provided, once again, expert word processing with great skill and endless patience.

INTRODUCTION

Museum Exhibitions as Power Plays

Even though the electronic media are acquiring tremendous clout, and entire television channels are devoted solely to culture, history, nature, and technology programming, museums today are still critically important educational institutions. In playing this role, they also possess a power to shape collective values and social understandings in a decisively important fashion. This book is my attempt to highlight this reality, because most American social scientists are not especially open to considering the workings of cultural power, institutions, or conflict in museums. Indeed, most are shocked when they find truly heated political struggle at museums, and even then they do not take these conflicts seriously. In fact, museums rarely are regarded as affording rich opportunities for political analysis, and those that do exist are, all too often, consigned by professional prejudice to cultural studies departments at best or to the style sections of big urban newspapers at worst.

I see this blindness in mainstream political science as a tragic flaw. Today museums are venues where many key cultural realities are first defined; and, in this process of definition, the personal becomes political, and the political cannot be divided easily thereafter from the personal. Different social forces—to the left, on the right, and at the center—all are intent on defining what reality is, will be, or has been, and major museums quickly can become embattled bastions of resistance or threatening outposts of invasion in the cultural war that these social forces wage against each other. What is accepted as knowledge, and the power to which many accede, are both easily articulated and constantly affirmed in the exhibitions museums produce for their visiting publics. Therefore, the continuous struggles to define power and knowledge at museums often can be intense, as the cultural wars of the 1990s and the early years of the twenty-first century illustrate.

This conflict is not new, and its frontlines fall back or move forward every day in many museums scattered across the country. Museum displays may quickly change, but their cultural effects can linger indefinitely. This fact has become more evident during the debates over multiculturalism, public morality, and postmodernism during the past decade. The tensions behind that controversy, however, never abated, and this enduring set of fractures in the body politic has intrigued me for many years.[1] My analysis here is a series of critical probes, which reassess the power plays of knowledge as they have reticulated deeper political contradictions and ideological pressures in culture, history, nature, and technology exhibitions at a number of major American museums.

Many major museums were founded in the nineteenth century as vital outposts for the civilizing mission of that time's "pedagogical state." The upper and middle classes of the Victorian era believed museums could cultivate the scientific outlook and cultural sensibility needed by modern industrial democracies among the urban masses coming into the world's growing capitalist economies. By the end of the twentieth century, museums came to be widely regarded as modern scientific society's "secular cathedrals," "guardians of shared history," or "storehouses for national treasures." As institutions with such secular significance, museums also have become high-profile places for heated struggles over many exhibitions as sites for moralizing memorials, highly politicized polemics, and ritualized reflection.

My study focuses on symbolic politics, but such analysis should not be dismissed because it deals with symbols. The politics of symbols are quite powerful, because they invoke ideals, recast realities, and manufacture meanings. Museum exhibits may not change public policies, but they can change other larger values and practices that will transform policy. New York mayor Rudolph W. Giuliani plainly recognized this fact when he assailed the Brooklyn Art Museum for its "Sensation" show of new British art from the Charles Saatchi collection in October 1999, and Gertrude Himmelfarb obviously was leveraging such values during the winter of 1999–2000 in her call to arms for another culture war during the 2000 presidential elections and beyond. The conservative and corporate cast of President George W. Bush's cabinet appointees as well as the culture-warring voice of Vice President Dick Cheney's spouse, Lynne V. Cheney, who served as chair of the National Endowment for the Humanities from 1986 to 1992, point toward a continuation of these cultural battles in the coming years.

When we learn that there were more than seven thousand museums of various types open and operating in North America during the 1990s, and one or two more opened every week, the battles fought in culture wars at museums become much more understandable.[2] Museum attendance at this time in the United States is the highest that it has ever been, and in comparative terms more Americans visit their museums than the residents of Asian, Australasian, or European nations do in their countries. More than twenty exhibitions of art and culture at American museums drew more than 200,000 visitors each in 1998, but only seven exhibits had this sort of traffic in all of Europe.[3] Most American museum visitors, as Robert Sullivan, the associate director for public programs at the National Museum of Natural History, observes, "think of the museum as a social, educational experience."[4] At the same time, it is precisely those numbers of people showing up with such regularity in search of social meaning and educational value that made museums into contested ground in the *Kulturkampf* of the past decade.[5]

Actually, the much-touted culture wars of the 1980s and 1990s are simply the most recent flareups in conflicts that never end, particularly in multicultural, multiethnic, multisectional states, like the United States, where many warring cultures and people have always been engaged in struggles to renew and redirect this nation's republican institutions. Indeed, conflicts between established cultural blocs and insurgent countercultures have been part of the daily life in the United States all the way back to its colonial period.[6] To believe these recent fights are somehow different, new, or unusual, I would argue, is a feeble conceit wholly unsupported by even the shallowest reading of the nation's history. With little else to unite it, cultural values have played a vital role in forging a single country out of immigrant communities, subjugated indigenous nations, and a slave population at different turns in the development of the United States. Today is no exception to this trend. Indeed, during 2000, a widespread distrust of the Clinton-Gore administration among most American conservatives and an intense dread felt by many American liberals about the incoming Bush-Cheney administration both stemmed from two very different cultural understandings of what the United States is, has been, and should be. Inventing the American nation has always been an open-ended experiment. So cultural controversies over independence, suffrage, abolition, equality, industrialization, language, work, religion, urbanization, race, and family life typically are a piece of many ruling and rising elites' campaigns to maintain or gain authority. Museums are, like neighborhoods, schools, or churches, a place where Americans first learn, and later reassure themselves, about their culture, history, environment, or technology. Lynne V. Cheney complains that this reality has changed completely when she suggests that "museums used to be places that invited visitors to learn about great works of art, to understand their society, and to know more about the course of history. Today, like so many other cultural institutions, they appear instead to be in the business of debunking greatness, Western society, and even history itself."[7]

Cheney overstates how much contestation occurs in many museums and overestimates how many of the traditional functions played by museums have been changed. In fact, for many museums in most places, the public still goes seeking to learn more about art, culture, history, nature, science, and technology. Because museums are valued sites, community activists, new social historians, local pundits, and anyone else with a stake in an exhibition's topic all rightly feel that they are part of a larger community with the right to have some say about the exhibits. Consequently, museums are frontline emplacements for competing classes, groups, or regions, as Cheney's culture-warring complaints suggest, to either declare or defend their hegemony and then conduct culture battles in defense of their visions of reality. I came to my first awareness of this tendency at the museum in my small hometown in northern Arizona when I was younger. Of course, some will scoff at this admission, but it is when and where my concerns about museum politics begin.

I was raised in the 1950s and 1960s out in the American Southwest, in Kingman, Arizona, quite far away from most big cities and all bright lights. At that time, it was a very small place, but it is much easier to see in such places how political the personal can be or why the personal can never be easily divorced from the political in the racial, class, and economic conflicts of its recently settled frontier society. The county seat of Mohave County, this settlement of what was then about 3,000 people was founded in 1882 by the Atlantic and Pacific Railroad near an old

U.S. Army outpost, Camp Beale. A railroad town, a ranching town, a mining town, and finally an airbase town during World War II, it was becoming a well-known Route 66 tourist town when my parents moved there in 1955. Its fortunes were tied to servicing the thousands of travelers and truckers who streamed through every day on their way west to Los Angeles, north to Las Vegas, east to Albuquerque, or south to Phoenix. Even though it was barely eight decades old on the calendars used by its Anglo-American settlers, there was a genuine sense of real history about the place. Because of "the Old West" mythos in which this new western town was saturated, a small circle of local women, the Daughters of the Mohave County Pioneers, began organizing the Mohave County Pioneers Historical Society in 1958. They incorporated in 1961, and by 1965 they had built a good-sized museum building on Beale Plaza at the intersections of Route 66 and Highway 93.

One afternoon during the last days of my summer vacation in 1965, I rode past their new museum building on a long bicycle trip with my best friend. We stopped there to rest, and then stared in the museum's front windows, transfixed by a full-size, working replica of a muzzle-loading, frontier-era, U.S. Army field piece that belonged to the museum's new curator, Kermit Edmonds. Not long after, we were equally mesmerized at a display booth he built at the county fair, which was festooned with old U.S. cavalry uniforms, and frontier firearms. For the next three years, we spent many of our Friday afternoons and Saturday mornings working at the museum, doing anything we could to stay around and maybe help.

One of the most impressive aspects of the museum at that time was an incomplete, but nonetheless quite striking, mixed-media mural. It ran around the walls in the main exhibit hall and through a series of well-organized display cases, weaving together painting, sculpture, poetry, illustrations, photos, and artifacts in a fabulous narrative collage. Painted by Roy Purcell, a local artist and poet who later served as the museum's director from 1967 to 1970, it sought to depict the history of Mohave County from creation to the 1960s. And in some ways it did. Yet in many other ways it could not, because of the contradictory gaps that any narrative also bears within its figurations of reality. Purcell's metaphysically charged images and captions express a quite romantic concern for the earth, guilt over the dispossession of Native Americans, and anxiety about the false promises of technology. Those motifs, however, rise in subdued counterpoint against the celebration of material progress and popular freedom. These contradictory qualities in one display have moved me to think long and hard over the intervening years about the rhetorical properties of museums, as well as to question the proper rhetorics that so many museums purport to uphold.

What I slowly recognized then, and realize more fully now, is how much museums remain the commanding heights of many ongoing battles over what is accepted as "reality." Their display halls can be seen, in part, as polemical fortifications meant to hold, through the artful presentation of words, pictures, sounds, and objects, the hearts and minds of visitors. Creating and then maintaining any sort of sophisticated knowledge of culture, history, nature, or science always is a struggle. Efforts to define and defend these social projects easily can become skirmishes in ongoing culture wars, history wars, nature wars, or science wars. The Mohave County Pioneers Historical Society mostly was recruited from the first and second generation of Anglo-American settlers whose ranches, mines, and shops had tamed this part of the Old West from the 1880s to the 1960s. In writing this book, I returned to an old pamphlet published to commemorate their museum's opening in 1965. In it, the Pioneers spoke directly about how they saw their museum working for them as well as the many visitors who would enjoy its displays:

> The museum will be based on the modern concept. It will reflect the significant experience in this county and also will reflect the attitudes and policies of the pioneers who directed its destinies. Articles will be exhibited only if they reflect the human processes, past and present, of our county. To meet this objective, a full-time professional director-curator has been employed. It will be his duties to supervise all activities of the museum, and to catalog, preserve, and exhibit items that will present an accurate panorama of Mohave County.
>
> The museum will be a permanent tool to supplement the educational system for adults and youth of the community. It also will serve the thousands of tourists who pass through Kingman daily.[8]

These sentiments are simple, and the wording is plain, but it would be difficult to be more succinct about how most museums function. That is, they piece together knowledge in accord with the reigning power in specific localities "based on the modern concept" as a permanent tool to shape the lifelong cultural learning of people living in or passing through those communities.

The panoramic accuracy that this museum created also represented the history of white pioneer society in Mohave County as being consciously pitted against, and distinctly privileged over, the histories of others—the now-subjugated natives, since-departed non-Anglo settlers, and later-arriving immigrants from around the world. Those other "human processes" could be included, but they obviously were presented as being less important. Kingman was, for example, the boyhood home of Andy Devine, the movie and television actor, and the Mohave Museum of History and Arts has devoted about as much space to celebrate both his younger days and acting career as it has to document the cultures of the county's Native Americans. To work as "a permanent tool" that could supplement the educations of both the young and old, the museum chose to articulate a concrete rhetoric that reflected the most "significant experiences" of the county as they complied with attitudes and policies of the pioneers who directed its subsequent destiny. Being Andy Devine's boyhood home is far more important than exploring all of the complexities of its Native American communities.

From within this discursive fortification, the Pioneers also saw their museum as a normative engine, capturing the energy of objects in the artful displays of the museum and transmitting their theoretical torque to teach others how to make certain critical economic, political, and social decisions after this studied cultural instruction:

> Visitors to the museum will have the opportunity to see and understand the objects that once played a part in our colorful past. A firsthand contact with former events will contribute to the better understanding of the origins and growth of present community interests and activities, and may assist in decisions or current problems. The very functions of the museum will make it potentially capable of becoming an important and influential public service organization.[9]

Once again, the assertions are bald-faced, but, as the Mohave County Pioneers Historical Society asserts here, museums always have served as subtle agencies of political persuasion. Museums deputize the muses of knowledge to instruct the masses who, in turn, visit them to learn about deeper realities, even as those realities are being written and wrought by elites around them in museums.

A generation later, it would appear that the pedagogical purposes of preaching progress at this museum have worked very well. The population of Mohave County in and around Kingman has increased nearly tenfold, and many new, albeit somewhat dangerous and dirty, industries have relocated in and around the city. Nonetheless, the economy and society of the Kingman area are not entirely sound. Many tourists who once flooded through town on Route 66 now bypass the city's merchants and motelkeepers as they blast through at 75 mph on Interstate 40's controlled-access right-of-way. The local mining industry is virtually dead, and ranching no longer is as profitable as it once was. Always a head-banging blue-collar town, much of Kingman now has a more tired, working-poor quality, which is aggravated by the close proximity of a new gambling mecca in Laughlin, Nevada, where busloads of retirees from Los Angeles, Phoenix, and Tucson travel daily to test their fortunes at the quarter slots and blackjack tables. It is no surprise that Timothy McVeigh and his coconspirators in the 1995 bombing of the Oklahoma City Federal Building spent many weeks here at a motel on Hilltop and then found willing confederates for their terrorist acts on the dusty double-wide lots of Butlerville out on Kingman's east side.

To recharge the battered tourist base of the town, today's city fathers are returning to the original wisdom of the Mohave Pioneers Historical Society, which recognized that its museum would serve the thousands of tourists who once passed directly through Kingman daily. On the one hand, millions of people have traversed old Route 66, and once may have stayed as children, young marrieds, or working people in Kingman's old 1950s-style motels. And, on the other hand, there still is a tremendous aura around Route 66 thanks to Bobby Troup's classic song, Nelson Riddle's instrumental tune, and the much-repeated *Route 66* television series of 1960–1964. Consequently, Kingman is, like many fading old Route 66 towns, transforming much of its original business district into a Route 66 nostalgia center for people from around the world seeking to find something in the mythos of Route 66 as "The Mother Road" of America. In turn, those who would not have even stopped for gas in Kingman a decade ago now motor into town for a few hours in their old Corvettes from Chicago, new Moto Guzzis from Milan, or classic Bentleys from Birmingham to see the places Bobby Troup's lyrics mention or create a time trip back into an old *Route 66* episode soundtracked by Nelson Riddle's orchestra.

Clearly, if these larger social forces are at play in a very small place like Kingman, Arizona, then similar relations of power and knowledge must underpin the major institutions of cultural production and social reproduction everywhere else in the United States. Museums are where art as well as culture, history, nature, and technology can be put to work as useful knowledge. What some still believe to be an autonomous realm of aesthetic contemplation for disinterested satisfaction or spiritual re-vitalization increasingly is now drawn, as the sociology of art suggests, into the instrumental relations of commodity exchange that are "simi-lar to, if not identical with, the structure of other institutions, that is, as a system of social interaction"[10] embedded in more enduring economic and political practices. Instead of artists producing works for royal, mu-nicipal, or ecclesiastical patrons, new relations of consumerist exchange between mass publics and artistic producers develop in museums, gal-leries, publishing houses, theaters, bookshops, major newspapers, schools, magazines, and concert halls. Moreover, many of these interactions also occur thanks to trained specialists, privileged experts, famous critics, and prestigious markets that propagate these developments in and around museums.

The social functions of art—as well as artful representations of cul-ture, history, nature, and technology—in this institutional context can produce shared meanings, cultural capital reserves, and aestheticized lifestyles that promote social cohesion, economic growth, and political stability, particularly under the increasingly global guidance provided by transnational firms, professional-technical associations, and mass me-dia networks. All of these institutions, as Raymond Williams argues, generate "a central system of practices, meanings, and values" that are not "merely abstract but which are organized and lived" as a "whole body of practices and expectations,"[11] whether it is how one plans a va-cation out in Arizona or what one believes the meaning of the United States of America should be. This colonization of the private sphere by museum practices to produce and circulate cultural capital simply rearti-culates some of the necessities of bureaucratically controlled consump-tion in the ongoing transformations of today's entertainment industry. As Baudrillard maintains, mass consumption becomes

> a productive force required by the functioning of the system itself, by its process of reproduction and survival. In other words, there are only needs because the system needs them. And the needs invested by the individual consumer today are just as essential to the order of produc-tion as the capital invested in the wage laborer. It is *all* capital.[12]

Once all these relations become capital, all other modes of knowing also can become integrated into the same institutional networks of social reproduction.

Even a minor local historical society in a small town far removed from any major urban area expresses these imperatives, as the Mohave Pioneers Historical Society illustrates in its frank admissions about what its museum could be and how it should operate for its publics. Like art, collective understandings of culture, history, nature, and technology have been transformed into clusters of aestheticized practices, meanings, and values that are mediated by expert producers, interpreters, and critics among mass publics through museums, schools, publishers, bookstores, and the media. Like art museums, culture, history, nature, and technology museums are now outlets to organize larger practices and expectations to be lived by their visitors. Cultivating comfort, clarity, and consensus, such museums round out the aestheticization of consumer lifestyles by turning the ordinarily less aesthetic realms of culture, history, nature, and technology into artful displays for a society that increasingly imagines itself through such mediated spectacles.

Once they are invested in the same networks of social reproduction as art, the domains of culture, history, nature, and technology also undergo their own thoroughgoing canonization in curatorial celebrations and public perceptions. With regard to art, Bürger claims,

> Canonization always brings with it a restorative element. However much interpretation seeks to lead art into the universality in which it ideally participates, interpretation nevertheless forces art into institutionalized conceptions. The discourse subjugates art to the principle of utilization.[13]

The same dynamics pertain to culture, history, nature, and technology as their interpretation in museums strips them of whatever transcendent meaning they might otherwise have in order to render them more useful. Cultural otherness, historical freedom, natural purity, and technological possibility can be ignored. When they are, this facilitates the effortless circulation of ideas about moral consensus, uncontroversial histories, instrumentalized views of nature, and unthreatening approaches to technics, which provides a restorative sense of useful practices and shared meanings to museum publics. The museum visitor's acceptance of new behavioral expectations and ethical practices at entertaining museum exhibitions, or the secondary recirculation of theses outcomes in bookstores, galleries, newspapers, magazines, schools, and colleges, only underscores the important role played by museums in shaping personal identities and collective purposes.

The Mohave County Pioneers Historical Society sought to spread its stories as "history," and this group commanded enough authority, clout, and wealth at this one locale to build a museum with enough "art" to serve that end. It, in turn, transmuted a hard-won power over the land and its original inhabitants into highly didactic displays that have created, perpetuated, and validated their shared understandings there as useful true knowledge. Clearly, it was power that constructed these truths, and such truths were meant to express, justify, and occlude the cultural, economic, and political power that enabled it to operate in this manner. Believing that power should shape this institutionalized knowledge, and wanting that knowledge to match the many-layered conceptions of this institutionalized power, that museum—now named the Mohave Museum of History and Art—is still there, more than thirty-five years later, operating as an important educational tool for all the adults, youth, and tourists still passing through its doors. At the same time, its Andy Devine displays and tie-ins to *Route 66* episodes indicate how even small museums in out-of-the-way places are fully invested in the aesthetic assumptions of the global entertainment business.

From those days spent with the Pioneers Historical Society, in Kingman only a parking lot away from Route 66, I have been fascinated by museums and their rhetorics of instruction and memorialization.[14] My approach to museum exhibitions here asks us, as Jameson suggests, to accept museums as rich opportunities for engaging in sustained political criticism, because "everything is 'in the final analysis' political."[15] This approach works on two levels. First, it acknowledges that normative impulses and ethical commands are integral components of any museum's display of art works, cultural artifacts, historical chronicles, nature studies, scientific activities, or technical devices. And, second, it recognizes that all exhibits of such materials can become events, places, or arrangements with their own normative effects and ethical agendas. These cultural experiences, in turn, often have many more normative effects on their visitors than all of the great books that go unread by the same people.

My analysis, then, does not accept the restrictive guidelines of contemporary political theory that still understand normative texts much more narrowly as formal treatises of article or book length written by philosophically inclined experts intent on carrying on small conversations with each other in search of great truths.[16] Such paralyzing beliefs follow more from the professional presumptions of an academic guild than they do from any clear sense of how ordinary moral instruction actually works in everyday cultural reproduction of the larger society. Museums must be taken more seriously as cultural texts and polemical locales, because political discourses have more voices in them than those coming from thick theoretical treatises propounding the writings of moral philosophers.[17] We must focus museums as sites of finely structured normative argument and artfully staged cultural normalization. Art works, historical expositions, nature interpretations, and technological exhibits, as they are shown in museums, are products of an ongoing struggle by individuals and groups to establish what is real, to organize collective interests, and to gain command over what is regarded as having authority. Consequently, this book works out a style of interpretive criticism that articulates how fully political knowledge and power can be, in fact, propagated in images and narratives other than those developed by philosophical treatises. And I want to direct others toward museums to think about how many of every society's most accessible normative truths and effective normalizing events are relayed through museum settings.

Finally, it is difficult to disconnect these internal culture wars from the global war between two cultural systems during the Cold War. That struggle shaped most of the issues and many of the people who are at war over American culture in the twenty-first century. Indeed, the initial support for agencies like the National Endowment for the Arts (NEA) and National Endowment for the Humanities (NEH) derived from the Cold War's ideological conflicts between the USSR and the United States. As the NEA's current chairman, Bill Ivey, observed at a February 2000 symposium held by the John F. Kennedy School of Government, the Office for the Arts at Harvard, and the NEA,

> In the 1960s rhetoric surrounding the creation of the NEA extolled the overarching, universal value of the arts, while at the same time promoting the American artist as a symbol of America's democratic freedoms.... It is no accident that the notion of the artist as a unique symbol of democracy faded with the Iron Curtain.[18]

In this context, Ivey argued, cultural promotion was an integral part of the Cold War fought in the music, publishing, film, writing, and dance worlds from the mid-1940s to the early 1990s. To deny this influence, as many cultural conservatives often do, is to distort the realties that have been at work here.[19] The following chapters, in turn, illustrate some of these discursive dynamics in greater detail.

This introduction and overview positions my analysis in the political controversies of the culture wars, while emphasizing the importance of museums as sites of public instruction and collective imagination.[20] If culture can be understood as the conventional understandings common to specific social groups, which are made manifest in their shared acts and artifacts, then it is no surprise that museums become flashpoints of struggle. Because they preserve, and often define, the changing conventions of social understanding, museum exhibitions cannot escape cultural turmoil. Any views that doubt existing conventions or endorse new unconventional interpretations will be challenged. Similarly, museums are storehouses of treasured artifacts, and if some question the worth of those valued objects or expose them to unconventional forms of understanding, then the shared understandings and specific conventions of the larger culture quickly will come into dispute, as they have in the culture wars.[21]

Chapter 1 returns to the notorious "The West as America" show at the National Museum of American Art in Washington, D.C., during 1991 to discuss how the conventional understanding of the Old West became such a point of contention in the culture wars. It develops another perspective on this controversy by contrasting this exhibit with a much more comforting vision of the Old West at the Gene Autry Museum of Western Heritage in Los Angeles, California. Chapter 2 continues this focus on cultural controversy in the nation's capital by reexamining the infamous 1995 National Air and Space Museum show for the fiftieth anniversary of the bombing of Hiroshima, which showcased the restored B-29 bomber, the *Enola Gay*. Chapter 3 looks at another high-profile Washington, D.C., cultural institution—the United States Holocaust Memorial Museum—to reconsider how it approaches the Holocaust in comparison with the treatment given to the same issues at the Museum of Tolerance in Los Angeles. Chapter 4 also stays in Washington to reexamine two different shows of medieval Japanese art and culture at the East Building of the National Gallery of Art ten years apart in 1988 and 1998.

Chapter 5 moves outside the nation's capital city to look at the Heard Museum in Phoenix, Arizona, and a show that it hosted in 1995 on the influence of the Fred Harvey Company in the shaping of the popular imagination of Americans about the Southwest. Chapter 6 turns the focus away from history, culture, and art in chapters 1 through 5 and begins a discussion of nature, science, and technology at major American museums. Chapter 6, in particular, takes up the disposition of nature at museums by rethinking how natural history has been represented at the American Museum of Natural History in New York. Chapter 7 continues this analysis in its study of the Missouri Botanical Garden in St. Louis, while chapter 8 closely reevaluates the Arizona–Sonora Desert Museum in Tucson. Chapter 9 reevaluates another fascinating museum located in Tucson, namely, the Pima Air and Space Museum. A recently expanded high technology celebration of high-technology in California's Silicon Valley, The Tech Museum of Innovation, is discussed in chapter 10, while chapter 11 returns to the greater metropolitan region of Washington, D.C., to explore the exhibits at the Freedom Forum's Newseum in Arlington, Virginia. The conclusion pulls together some final reflections about museums as sites of political conflict over cultural meaning, and there I close my bid to interest others in the critical interpretation of museum exhibitions.

CHAPTER ONE

Politics at the Exhibition: Aesthetics, History, and Nationality in the Culture Wars

As Richard Bolton recounts in *Culture Wars,* the public debate in the United States over how museum exhibitions can exert deleterious moral effects on either individual citizens or the nation's culture began in May 1989. Once Senator Alphonse D'Amato (R-NY) ripped up a photograph, *Piss Christ* by Andres Serrano, and tossed the pieces on the Senate floor, decrying the image as "a deplorable, despicable display of vulgarity," a whole generation of artists ran afoul in the politicization of public art funding by the National Endowment for the Arts (NEA): Robert Mapplethorpe, Mel Chin, Annie Sprinkle, Karen Finley, Holly Hughes, John Fleck, Hans Haacke, to only name a few.[1] Many would dismiss the subsequent six-year running battle over federal funding for the arts through the NEA, which came to a head during 1995 when the newly GOP-dominated Congress drastically cut all cultural, art, and science program funding in the national budget, as a small squabble over a tidbit of pork for the cultural elite. There are, however, larger issues at stake here, namely, the cultural ties that get drawn in museums between aesthetics, memory, and political identity.

The cultural right's fixation on artworks that allegedly depict pornographic, homoerotic, sadomasochistic or other "unnatural" behaviors already has received considerable attention, so I will not retrace those controversies here. However, there have been other comparatively tame art exhibitions (tame in the sense that they display only cowboys and their horses in natural positions) that have touched off equally explosive reactions, because they too have used art to question the foundations of Americans' political identity and collective subjectivity. In this chapter, I explore some political dimensions in the culture wars of the 1990s, first, by revisiting one of their major battle sites, namely, the controversial 1991 "The West as America: Reinterpreting Images of the Frontier, 1820–1920" exhibition at the National Museum of American Art, and, second, by contrasting that exhibit to the ongoing displays at the Gene Autry Western Heritage Museum, which also is known officially as the Autry Museum of Western Heritage, in Los Angeles. This museum show in Washington, D.C., sparked a series of major controversies about museum displays as public culture events that still have not ended, because it was, in large part, not how many believed the West should be seen. In counterpoint, that "correct" vision of the American West is the sole focus on the Autry Museum.

The exhibition in the nation's capital pressed the envelope of acceptability as it contested the nature of collective identity in the United States with displays of artistic and historic artifacts unusual for a major public museum exhibition. By repositioning famous artworks and historical curios in problematic angles, questionable poses, and perhaps even quasi-sacrilegious stances, the exhibition sought to raise moral qualms in its viewers, contesting what many might otherwise regard as utterly uncontestable. In thinking about this exhibition, and especially its reported public reception, I want to reconsider how politics works, or does not work, at the exhibition when museum performances probe a nation's individual and collective political identity with challenging displays.

In this chapter, then, I undertake three tasks: First, I explore why artistic displays can affect political identity, by indicating how aesthetic objects are used in museum performances to guide individuals and groups through political discourses of self-recognition and self-activity. Second, I provide an interpretive overview of "The West as America" museum exhibition. And, third, I consider why this exhibit drew protests from the political right, suggesting that it violated the current practices of governmentality as "entertainmentality," which are adhered to almost religiously at the Autry Museum. These normative expectations increasingly denominate the operations of all cultural institutions, but, more

importantly, they now mediate many institutionalized means for forming political subjectivity in the United States.

"At the Museum" or "That's Entertainment"?

History exhibitions formalize norms of how to see without being seen
inasmuch as the curators pose as unseen seers, and then fuse their vision with authority. In the organization of their exhibitions' spaces, the
enscription of any show's textual interpretations, and the coordination
of an exhibit's aesthetic performances, curators are acting as normative
agents, directing people what to see, think, and value. Museum exhibitions become culture-writing formations, using their acts and artifacts
to create conventional understandings that are made manifest or left
latent in any visitor's/viewer's personal encounters with the museum's
normative performances. Simply by entering display spaces, all visitors/
viewers learn something about how they must act or should regard their
artifacts. Historical displays, then, do operate as power plays in which
plays for power circulate with the movement of viewers through their
curated spaces. Seeing historical objects, witnessing historic performances,
encountering interpretations of history are all behaviors that can alter
people's attitudes in relation to certain political values associated with
particular cultural things. As the educational means of helping people
to "im-personate" more easily the ideal person valued by their nations,
history museums also can be recast as exercises of governmentality in
which disciplinary discourses, the order of things, or specific intellectuals
redirect the consciousness and behavior of museum visitors to advance
various governmental goals. In contemporary cultural mediascapes, the
agendas of governmentality often compound themselves with systems
of entertainment. The contrast between Gene Autry's highly entertaining "Western Heritage" Museum and the United States of America's National Museum of American Art typifies these conflicts.

This split becomes significant inasmuch as history displays are being
redefined to complement, if not fit into, the larger orbits of the entertainment industry. Like many terms, "entertainment" as a word carries
a potent semiotic charge for its current semantic deployments from its
early linguistic origins. From its late Latin *intertenēre* to its Middle English *entertene* or old French *entretenir* roots, one sees that "to entertain" means "to hold" or "to keep among." Thus, the idea of entertaining

already has powerful carceral implications that suggest a practice of containment and confinement. Plainly, "entertainments" are arrangements to keep one occupied, to engage one in a specified manner, or to maintain one as such. To speak of entertainment, one already moves rhetorically into spaces of an "entertainmentality," or practices that keep us held in some mutually prespecified manners. An entertainment industry is in business to keep its charges occupied, to hold them together, to engage their time and attention as a psychosocial means of furthering their containment. Of course, at the same time, one can admit to other semantic charges in the term: an entertainment also will be an agreeable engagement, an amusing occupation, or some interesting diversion that helps constitute the experience. Even so, entertainmentality creates and maintains an occupation, which like all occupations is designed to hold its charges in some peculiar form of mutual containment to keep them both together and apart. Any museum constructs a very concrete rhetoric for entertainment in the spaces of its built environment. The preoccupations of museum-borne entertainmentalities are aimed at keeping everyone occupied by the same reality, which might show how one, "in his being, can be concerned with the things he knows, and know the things that, in positivity, determine his mode of being."[2]

From "The West as America" to the Autry Museum

The ferocious political combat over depicting America's past at the National Museum of American Art can be chalked up, in part, to the prestige of the venue. And, in part, it can be traced back to the use of artworks to illustrate an account of America's culture and history rather than art per se. As a major institution receiving public monies to display cultural truths in the nation's capital city, this museum is expected to appear "objective" or "nonpartisan" by being entirely "subjective" and "partisan" in a highly nationalist fashion, just like the Autry Museum in Los Angeles is. Yet it was precisely such rhetorical assumptions about objectivity or partisanship that the curators of "The West as America" show sought to contest.

Rereading the Old West

"The West as America: Reinterpreting Images of the Frontier, 1820–1920" was organized by the National Museum of American Art with the full support of the Smithsonian Institution and assistance from the Getty

Grant Program. After running in Washington, D.C., from 15 March to 7 July 1991, the exhibition was scheduled to travel to the Denver Art Museum from 3 August to 13 October 1991 and then close out its run at the St. Louis Art Museum from 9 November 1991 to 12 January 1992. Because of the tremendously negative response in the mass media and Congress, however, "unforeseen difficulties" in local funding arrangements led the Denver and St. Louis art museums both to cancel their hosting of the show's national tour. Consequently, the exhibition ran for only a few months in Washington, D.C.

On one level, this exhibition was unique in that as it explicitly posed as a reinterpretation of "frontier images" as they had been invented, produced, and consumed for nearly four generations of Americans from the 1820s through the 1920s. As the public brochure for the exhibit noted: "Works of art don't always mean what they seem to say. The exhibition has been organized with that idea in mind. . . . we have come to doubt our former understanding of western scenes. The doubt rests not on a sure knowledge of what did happen, but on evidence sufficient to show it did not happen as the pictures suggest."[3] Consequently, the curators' selection of images and the explication of their reception in historical context aimed to contest what the images might have meant to their producers, how they were received by their consumers, and why they should not be treated as neutral documents of the West for America today. Indeed, the exhibition's on-site visitor's guide, book-length catalogue, and on-the-wall captions were all brimming with didactic reinterpretations of all these variables as they reappraised how the West as America—gauged as a part defining a whole—has worked within the civic religion or collective mythos of Americanism. A few of the on-the-wall captions soon were sent up by cultural conservatives as being off-the-wall, politically correct diatribes against America; hence, they were discreetly reworded and changed a month into the exhibit's public run, but not before a major debate was launched about the show's ideological credibility.

On a second level, much of the exhibition actually was not particularly remarkable artistically. Big dramatic paintings—like Emanuel Leutze's *The Founding of Maryland* (1860), with bare-breasted Indian maidens and noble Indian braves presenting a bounty of foods and handshakes of peace to European settlers as they are all blessed by a priest, as well as his *The Storming of the Teocalli by Cortez and His Troops* (1848), with conquistadors butchering *indio* babies, mothers, and warriors on the parapets of a native temple—anchored the display's introductory spaces. These artistically ordinary Leutze works, in turn, were presented in this fashion to contrast their popular reception in their own time, which accepted them as accurate representations of a righteous Western civilization gaining mastery either by peaceful entreaty or by violent assault over pagan American savages, with other much more historically ambivalent readings of these same images from today. Having set the rhetorical stage in this manner, the exhibition unfolded its reinterpretive encounters with "the West" in art works "as America" in the six thematic sections that followed.

The first section, "Prelude to Expansion: Repainting the Past," positioned together a host of explorer-departure, first-contact, and triumphant-return paintings in which all of the typical American grade-school icons of the European age of exploration are posed in luxuriant splendor. Cast by the curators quite accurately as ex post facto legitimations of European exploration in the Americas by nineteenth-century American advocates of new expansion of the American republic into the trans-Mississippian West, these images were reinterpreted by the curators as then-living dead white European males penetrating the unspoiled recesses of a virgin land. The second section, "Picturing Progress in the Era of Westward Expansion," centered on archetypes of American identity: mountain men, brave pioneers, wagon trains, iron horses, Westward Ho!, Manifest Destiny. These values are nicely summarized by John Gast in the imagery of *American Progress* (1872): a book-bearing, star-crowned, flowing-robed, gigantic, blond Amazon floats over the prairies guiding the wagon train, stagecoach, stream train, plowman, goldminer, and express rider westward as she strings telegraph wire behind her and sweeps heathen Indians away before her.

These pictures mostly depicted industrial-era transportation and production technologies sweeping through and over untapped natural expanses to create power and realize progress for "all Americans." Only in the third section, "Inventing the Indian," did the non-European, nonwhite, nonmale other appear at the center of interpretation. These images, in turn, revealed how various rhetorics of representation, ranging from registers of the noble savage to implacable enemy to displaced exile to assimilated redman-cum-whiteman, competed in Western artists' imaginations throughout this period. Yet, ironically, the catalogue's cover art, William Fuller's *Crow Creek Agency, Dakota Territory* (1884), shows the

Indian as he/she was invented in actual practice.[4] That is, an almost Grandma Moses–style primitive tableau casts the Crow as docile inmates in a model Indian agency strategic hamlet built behind white picket fences with quaint new houses, a clapboard school, a village church, and smiling fields all watched over by white guardians intent on getting Indian braves out of their buckskins and into store-bought clothes.

The fourth section, "Settlement and Development: Claiming the West," revisited celebrations of the American domestication of wild frontier as tame landscape. George Caleb Bingham's Missouri paintings were mixed together with renditions of California mining claims, plains state bonanza farms, and Rocky Mountain ranch scenes to illustrate how artists affirmed Western expansion—no matter how costly—in imagery of settlement and development. The fifth section, "The Kiss of Enterprise: The Western Landscape as Symbol and Resource," continued this line of investigation as it displayed how railroad companies, land speculators, and irrigation advocates all schemed together to package the West as a commodity, exploiting its symbolic richness in public relations imagery to draw tourists, sell real estate, and build federal water projects. This section highlighted portraits of California's giant sequoia trees, or Arizona's Grand Canyon, as timber barons and railroad executives commissioned their images for display to the folks back East.

Finally, "Doing the Old America: The Image of the American West, 1880–1920" was the section that focused most directly on the problematic beginnings and endings of what is now regarded as classic Western art, rendered in the styles of Remington or Russell, in the romanticized imagination of Eastern artists. As the real frontier closed, many Eastern American artists scrambled out West to observe its events and personalities, and then went back East to create all of the icons of what are now, ironically, "the art of the Old West" on the rooftops of Hoboken, New Jersey, apartments (like Charles Schreyvogel) or in cozy Connecticut studios (like Frederic Remington). Hence, this section examined the mythos of Indian warriors, mountain men, and pony soldiers as it recombined with the new ideologies of Social Darwinism from the 1890s to the 1920s.

While the curators were a bit heavy-handed with their rhetorics of critique, these representations of how "the Old West" simply was, in fact, another highly successful manufactured product from "the New East" in modern industrial America were extremely challenging in their rhetorical dissection of a very conflicted reality. They were alienating enough to spark a rancorous reaction to their critical rereading of how the Old West was both won and lost in post-1890s ideological struggles. This engagement was crystalized in the photograph—used as a frontispiece to the catalogue and as the only illustration in one public flyer—by an "unidentified photographer," captioned "*Charles Schreyvogel Painting on the Roof of His Apartment Building in Hoboken, New Jersey,* 1903, National Cowboy Hall of Fame Collection, Oklahoma City."[5] In it Schreyvogel, wearing a bowler hat and formal coat, stands at an easel, painting a model posed amidst the chimney stacks and skylights of a tenement house: the model is wearing a cowboy hat, boots, bandanna, and holsters as he kneels and aims a six-shooter at the artist. When this image is juxtaposed against Schreyvogel's frontier realist renditions of cowboys, pony soldiers, and pioneers, one immediately can see how the curators' interpretative agendas were at play in the exhibition. However, what might have been seen as ordinary act of ideological demystification by some obscure art historians in another earlier time became in 1991 an instance of civic religious sacrilege that all national museum venues still have not put behind them.

As a major retrospective examination of paintings, sculptures, graphics, and photographs by some of the greatest artists as well as the lesser-known hacks of the Old West, "The West as America" show was staged, ironically, in the aftermath of the Bush administration's triumphant victory over Iraq and on the eve of the Soviet Union's final collapse. At this unique historical conjuncture, one might have thought that an America flush with such geopolitical successes could have easily tolerated such small ideological countermoves. The exhibition's public program flyer explained the show in very direct (and not at all "radical") terms, namely, that it wished to "critically examine popular misconceptions created by artistic images of westward expansion" as "skillful combinations of myth, symbol, and fact" that, first, merely offered "a highly edited view of the events they appear to document" and basically persuaded "nineteenth-century viewers that appropriating new land was a sign of national progress and individual enterprise."[6] The curators undoubtedly believed that this triumphant world-historical moment for America plainly was a time that could accept such critical reflections.

Unfortunately, the curators guessed wrong. From the get-go, visitors registered many strongly negative reactions. Former Librarian of Con-

gress Daniel Boorstin widely publicized his views of the exhibition, which
he summarized early in its guest book: "A perverse, historically inaccurate, destructive exhibit. No credit to the Smithsonian."[7] As a widely ac-
claimed, although generally deemed middlebrow, historian, Boorstin, by
his rebuke, immediately called into question all of the knowledges, rules,
and subjectivities put on display in terms of perversion/inaccuracy/
destructiveness. That he and many other historians, of course, might
have helped to fabricate the normal/accurate/constructive domains of
knowledge being put to the simple tests of demystification by these exhibits never came up in Boorstin's broadsides. Instead, right-wing sena-
tors, like Ted Stevens (R-Alaska), known for his vehement protests
against a Discovery Channel TV film *Black Tide* about the Exxon Valdez
oil spill—which was being shown at the Smithsonian—for not having
"any balance at all," soon jumped into the melee, raving about the
Smithsonian exposing Americans to so perverted a version of history.[8]
For public exhibitions at a national institution just down the hill from
the nation's capitol, it became clear from anonymous viewer comments
in gallery logs that many among the viewing public supported Boorstin
and Stevens. That is, they expected a clear power play for both America
and Americanism from Smithsonian officials at this highly visible venue.

Senator Stevens, Daniel Boorstin, and many other voices of authority
expressed their shock and outrage over the dissonances in "The West as
America." They naturally assumed that, as a major exhibition at the National Museum of American Art staged by a national government agency,
it should be a show of force, restating and revitalizing the disciplinary
agendas of American nationality. On the cultural plane, their protests
revealed how thoroughly statecraft is often soulcraft as governments try
to mobilize a peculiar sense of governmentality continuously in images,
texts, and performances to reinstate perpetually the power of the state
in common memories.

The Autry Museum of Western Heritage

In many ways, Gene Autry was at the very core of America's reimagina-
tion of the Old West in the movies as well as on radio and TV during
the twentieth century. And he knew it. So Autry founded his museum in
1988 to memorialize what "the West" had become for many Americans,
because he felt that "I owed something. The West has been very kind to
me over the years."[9] Now Autry's museum is an amalgam of fact and

fiction. While it is the home of guns once owned by Annie Oakley and Wyatt Earp, it also holds the costumes worn by Clayton More and Jay Silverheels as TV's Lone Ranger and Tonto.

A native Texan, Autry was discovered playing his guitar in Chelsea, Oklahoma, in 1927 by Will Rogers. Rogers thought Autry should pursue a singing career and think about the movies. By 1931, Autry had made the world's first "gold record," selling a million copies of "That Silver-Haired Daddy of Mine," and became a national radio star for a Sears, Roebuck and Company–owned station in Chicago on its "National Barn Dance" show. His group, The Singing Cowboys, defined the genre of country and western music, and his singing cowboy films were in many ways the epitome of the "B" movie in the 1940s and 1950s. In the late 1980s, when his Western Heritage Museum was opening, Autry and his movie sidekick, Pat Buttram, were back in style. They worked on the Nashville Network, hosting *Melody Ranch Theatre,* which replayed Autry's old Republic and Columbia cowboy movies to a new generation of viewers.[10]

Because of these singing cowboy movies, when many Americans think of "the Old West," they think of Autry's gentle decency rather than the real rough and ready settlers who butchered the buffalo and Native Americans with equal abandon. Autry's "Ten Cowboy Commandments"—including tolerance, honesty, truth, and respect—were not the values that tamed the real Old West, even though many Americans want to believe so because of the times they have spent at many Saturday matinees with Gene Autry, John Wayne, Roy Rogers, or Jimmy Stewart in the reel Old West. Autry's vision of the West was not the West during its actual settlement, but most Americans have wrongly believed it was as far back as the 1920s.

The quiddity of this nationalist heritage in "the West of the imagination," which is what "The West as America" used to tie its narrative together, is captured best at institutions like the Autry Museum of Western Heritage where visitors are encouraged "to follow the story" of the real and the mythical West as told in the "Spirit Galleries" that comprise the museum.[11] While there is a considerable dose of reality at the Autry Museum, the mythical West manufactured by dime novels, cinema, and television from the Civil War to the present is the prime player in these galleries of spirit, which range from the Opportunity, Conquest, Community, and Cowboy Galleries on the two downstairs levels to the Discovery, Romance, and Imagination galleries upstairs. Consequently, real Western artifacts, like Colt 45 six-shooters or cowpuncher saddles, are put on display alongside surreal signs of Western legends, like the get-ups worn by 1950s TV cowboys. Hollywood's Old West now carries the Americanism of the West to most Americans as much, or more, than the authentic histories of Billy the Kid, Wyatt Earp, or General Custer.

This mythic vision of the Old West now is both America's inheritance from the past and birthright for the future. The Autry Museum's two-pronged mission is "to serve as a non-profit cultural and educational institution in acquiring, preserving and interpreting artifacts that document the history of the American West, while at the same time working" to study and collect material related to both the historical West and the fictional West of art, literature, film, and other media.[12] Many museums devote their activities to a straight-up reading of "the history of the American West." However, the distinctive niche, and in many ways the key mission, of the Autry Museum is not really "history" but rather essentially this more unique product of a "heritage" that comes together at the intersection of "the historical West" and "the fictional West." Consequently, an Autry Museum brochure proudly announces the importance of myth in this Western heritage:

> Walt Disney imagineers have designed exciting exhibits and programs to capture the colorful saga of this rugged region.
> Experience the myths. Relive the dramatic history of one of the greatest epics of all times. Return to those "exciting days of yesteryear" when radio, motion pictures, and television featured good guys and bad guys in a struggle to "win the West."[13]

The West was the West, but its real excitements and glories did not pay off until mass audiences began consuming the myths of a Western heritage as the mass culture product of white and black hats during Saturday matinees and after-school TV broadcasts.

All Americans, according to the Autry Museum, should "encounter the legends, experience the legacy, explore the endless possibilities" that are their lot, condition, and status as inheritors of this peculiar national citizenship.[14] The "legacy of the West," then, is a heritable form of consciousness that demands continual cultivation. So "whether it is the art of Albert Bierstadt, Frederic Remington or N. C. Wyeth; the tools, clothing and firearms of people who inhabited the West; or the costumes, scripts, and props of Western film and television," the Autry Museum casts itself as a weaver of mass awareness, bringing together "the threads of different cultures and customs that have contributed to the rich tapestry that is the West today."[15]

With seven permanent galleries of historical exhibits as well as two additional galleries dedicated to special traveling displays, the central organizing theme of the Autry Museum is not history but "heritage." And, heritage is, in turn, essentially "spirit." This semifactual/semifictional concept permits the museum's curators, like Gene Autry himself, to imagineer their vision of the West by interlacing materials from both "the real" and "the fictional" West, like Buffalo Bill, into an entertaining fantasy. And at its Griffith Park location just over the ridge from Hollywood and Universal City, this narrative pose has found an almost perfect venue in which to reinvent America continuously in terms of this "heritage-filled" West.

Art and Political Subjectivity

"Americanness" is a particular persona that requires constant reinvention and reaffirmation by inducing all who occupy American territory to impersonate an approved range of "Americanized" behaviors, values, practices. If the personification of the American nation effectively is resisted by images or texts that would cast cowboys and pioneers as brutal colonizers rather than as benign civilizers, then each impersonation of the American nation might crack a bit, splintering along tiny stress fractures induced by such contradictive rhetorics of interpretation. Forging Americanness, then, is what is at stake in these exercises of authority. For the cultural right, art exhibitions are performances of power, creating states out of the narratives, images, practices endorsed as authoritative in the power plays of the artwork put out on show as a moralistic performance.[16] Questioning "The West as America" also questions America as the West, which raised the spectre of fragmentation, sectionalism, disunity, balkanization on the national horizon. While it may be mostly unfounded, there is a strong fear that unless Americanness is revitalized as something everyone can learn from the cowboys and pioneers of the Old West as a shared heritage, it will disappear altogether in divisive disunity, leaving a Bosnia or Lebanon sorting itself out among the tatters and tears in what was once a strong national fabric allegedly ripped and rent by such "perverted history."

Creating citizens is, to a significant degree, a process of institutionally organized impersonation. Each nation must develop a set of narratives for the political personality that imperfectly embodies the values and practices of its nationhood. Over the course of history, artworks have provided valuable sites for representing many ideals of such individual and collective subjectivity. Putting such systems of acculturation out at public museum sites may push and pull individual members of their audiences to impersonate the values assigned to their images. From "The West as America" pictures, we are supposed to learn "not only what happened," but also how "the westward movement was a complete triumph."[17]

It is an uneven, disjunctive, noncontinuous process, but it appears that artistic representations of Bingham's Daniel Boone, Remington's pony soldiers, Russell's cowpunchers, Bierstadt's pioneers, or Leutze's conquistadors can be mobilized over and over again. At museums, this heritage may help Americans impersonate Americanizing roles and behaviors through viewing their memorialization in squibs of paint or splashes of bronze. Much of this happens so unconsciously and continuously around such displays that these acculturating rituals often are ignored—until, of course, an art exhibition repositions the circuits of civic impersonation in a critical fashion, asking if such a persona should exist or if the regime should continue reproducing such a nation of these personalities, because a reinterpretation now suggests America did not, and still does not, "happen the way pictures suggest."[18]

From the perspective of realist state power, the state always should be able to instate its myths or restate its agendas at cultural venues, like the Smithsonian Institution, if nowhere else, for all persons within its jurisdiction to have the proper codes for interpreting their own impersonations of American citizenship.[19] To reframe a settler civilization as nothing but Eurocentric imperializers at museum sites no longer can be explained away by state authorities as "pomo fever" among the chattering classes; it directly challenges the rites and rituals of American civil religion, which now—like, ironically, the codes of Marxism-Leninism in the former Soviet Union—remain one of the few threads holding together the extremely multicultural, class-stratified, continent-straddling American state, ideologically or culturally. If Americanizing aesthetic images cannot circulate cleanly in the open at permanent federal installations like the National Museum of American Art, then many fear

America as a unified nation-state may well become as lost as those other volatile state systems now melting down around the world—Yugoslavia, Lebanon, Czechoslovakia, the Soviet Union. Aesthetic and historic narratives do shape political subjectivity, individual and collective, in both material and mental ways.[20]

Not accepting "America as the West," as this West was shown shaping America, represented major breaches for the cultural right in the nation's state security, raising the spectre of anti-Americanism disconnecting this regime's circuits for generating its current political subjectivity. Hence, "The West as America" never made it past the Beltway, where it might have contaminated America's heartlands in St. Louis and Denver. The pastiche of myths in that exhibition might appear to be totally unreal, but there are many other museums across the Mississippi, like the Autry Museum, that are also entirely dedicated to its invention and stabilization. And, what is more, they are far more popular and well attended than the "The West as America" exhibition.

First, displays like those at the Autry Museum obviously engage in exercises of heritage circulation to provide more than historic meaning. By associating certain visual images, symbolic codes, or iconic signs together as a cohesive system of meaningful imagining, art shows create symbolic pictorial resources for depicting contemporary social individuality and political community. If you cannot imagine what it is to be an American at the turn of the twentieth century, then look back at these images of America from the turn of the nineteenth century to gain guidance. In a world of geopolitical ambiguity after the Cold War, there is a moral clarity to be found in strong images of Remington's horse soldiers riding wild frontiers in the Old West as well as in John Ford's cinematic replays of their patrols on film. Which pictures are mobilized, how they are displayed, where they are situated, and why they are chosen all constitute a persuasive rhetorical scene for governmentalizing maneuvers, especially at those sites where "the nation tells its story."

Second, these exhibits also cultivate a "Western Heritage" to orient Americans toward their future by way of certain widely approved rubrics. Particular ideological frames, cultural values, or discursive assumptions circulating through governmentalizing discipline can be deployed to dictate authoritatively the shape and substance of the cultural matter put on display. Showing Remington's *Shootout at the Waterhole* with captions that suggest it is an allegory about paranoid white male Eurocentrics surrounded by Third World revolution, which the Smithsonian show did presume to do, is a discursive countermove against the American state's ordinary normalizing impulses. The cultural right's protests about the caption indicate how much museums do count. A powerful curatorial vision, when coupled with a well-scripted performance of elegantly exhibited art, can act as a culture-writing force that rewrites lessons either for or against the incumbent ruling regime. And when individual viewers and exhibition audiences encounter the displays and discourses of any specific art exhibition, a serious episode of true moral conflict over the content of our civic education may well, or not so well, unfold at the show site.

When visiting the exhibition "The West as America," for example, one immediately sensed the counterconventional intentions in its questioning of heritage—revisionist and affirmative, critical and commemorative, resistant and submissive—by the curatorial authorities. Yet their dissonant combination of traditional heroic displays with radical discourses of doubt blocked their designs for rewriting American culture. Instead of producing some sense of guilt, remorse, or even ennui over this bit of "the West" vanquishing the Native American fraction of "the rest," they sparked a stronger sense of indignation or denial over what many saw as a "radical" rewrite of the sacred scripts underpinning America and Americanism.

The insinuation of entertainmentalities into museum space was perhaps gradual, but increasingly it has become overpowering. In the national Holocaust museum, as chapter 3 suggests, the visitor is treated to a simulation of the death camp experience. Indeed, in one sense, the museum is a theme park about genocide as this one idea becomes a narrative vehicle to unwind a chain of little cinematic/dramatic sideshows. In some ways, visiting this museum is like taking a horrendous theme ride through galleries of gore, tunnels of terror, dungeons of death.[21] Each visitor is given an alias upon entry, compounding his or her present identity with a Holocaust persona as the museum effaces personal agency through its death camp routines of people handling. You ride with your alias through its rooms of repellent inhumanity in an uneasy partnership until finally at the end you learn the fate of your Holocaust persona—survivor, victim, status unknown. The pretense is that simulation duplicates "the feel" of it all, but, of course, it cannot deliver the real feel of being transported, gassed, and cremated. It simply manufactures another packaged/guided amusement, reifying the Holocaust into a house of horrors that ends well for visitors if they leave the museum terrorized down to their toes by the gritty spectacle of megadeaths manufactured the old-fashioned way with fascistic brutality married to Teutonic engineering.

Beyond the Holocaust Museum's "successes" with the Final Solution or the "failures" of the Smithsonian Institution at representing the ways of the Old West as entertainmentalities, one could see "Disney's America" theme park (once planned for construction sometime and somewhere in northern Virginia) looming on the horizon. There history would not be perverted or inaccurate, because everything was to have become a mechanically reproduced entertainmentality in the hands of Disney imagineers.[22] The Old West would not be a sad assembly of ratty old pictures. It would have become instead exciting visits to an authentic Indian village, riding a real stagecoach, occupying a genuine cavalry outpost. So too would World War II have become a visit to an Army Air Force aerodrome where flight simulators and virtual-reality generators might "really put you into the action" over Berlin or Tokyo in thousand-plane bomber raids, freeing everyone from contemplating those messy questions about the wisdom, necessity, and morality of starting urban firestorms or using atomic weapons (which chapter 2 examines in more detail). Now this sort of interactive learning experience would go where no museum has gone before. Until all museums follow this path toward highly entertaining infotainment, however, one must deal with issues raised by these ideological battles at the National Museum of American Art over what many citizens believe should be a popular exercise in middlebrow civic education. When it came off like a polemical tract or grad school seminar, many visitors were incensed because they allegedly wanted only to stroll down memory lane to "Melody Ranch Theatre." The big problem for museums is simple: getting visitors to think beyond entertainmentality more often than not induces rage, rather than cultivating reasoned reflection.

Even more ironically, these outside interventions into what are ordinarily neglected realms of curatorial discretion at the National Museum of American Art by the allegedly right-minded guardians of American culture in the U.S. Congress also were sharply at odds with the avowed libertarian or populist loyalties of the neoliberal Republicans ruling there. Of course, one explanation is that these culturally conservative

Republicans now do, in fact, dominate many debates on Capitol Hill precisely because they have exploited the free-floating anxiety and anger associated with America's post–Cold War imperial irrelevance at public events like "The West as America" exhibition. Another explanation, however, is that their actual behavior in these episodes belies a true power agenda behind their professed beliefs of promoting personal self-reliance, individual choice, or civic awareness.

If these articles of faith were, in fact, true to the precepts of the classical liberalism underpinning so much of contemporary American conservatism, then the contemporary right wing should accede to the libertarian wisdom so succinctly stated by John Stuart Mill in *On Liberty*. That is, to test the truth or falsity of any argumentative expression of opinion, it is best to allow it to circulate freely and as broadly as possible. With regard to "The West as America," all opinions about its accuracy or inaccuracy, justness or unjustness, balance or bias will vary widely, and it is a great evil to silence the expression of these opinions. "If the opinion is right," as Mill contends, "they [the viewers/visitors of museums] are deprived of the opportunity of exchanging error for truth; if wrong, they lose, what is almost as great a benefit, the clearer perception and livelier impression of truth, produced by its collision with error."[23] All citizens have judgment granted to them so that they might use it, but the cultural right does presume an infallibility by presuming that citizens will use their judgment erroneously.

In closing "The West as America" prematurely the cultural right told citizens they ought not, and indeed cannot, use their civic judgment at all. The cultural conservatives even presumed that the museum's publics would have used their political judgment erroneously. However, this maneuver compromises the truths on which the cultural right allegedly would rest American political subjectivity. Again, as Mill claims, "there is the greatest difference between presuming an opinion to be true because, with every opportunity for contesting it, it has not been refuted, and assuming its truth for the purpose of not permitting its refutation. Complete liberty of contradicting and disproving our opinion is the very condition which justifies us in assuming its truth for purposes of action; and on no other terms can a being with human faculties have any rational assurance of being right."[24]

Such highly centered notions of real civic agency, however, are not what conservative cultural warriors accept as either true principles or desirable results. They apparently have no commitment to let error meet truth and thereby allow political subjects to exchange error for truth in the collisions of concepts. Instead, they baldly presume truths for the explicit purpose of not permitting their refutation. And, in the process, they seek to occupy the corridors and capillaries of disciplinary power as the highways and byways where political subjects travel from lesser to greater sophistication. Such are the only "information superhighways" that now exist, and the cultural right wants to control the traffic that plies these routes.

Mill's vision of intellectual freedom is violated in quashing this alternative spin on America's history and labeling naysayers as countercultural dissidents. For Mill, "only through a diversity of opinion is there, in the existing state of human intellect, a chance of fair play to all sides of the truth. When there are persons to be found, who form an exception to the apparent unanimity on any subject, even if the world is in the right, it is always probable that the dissentients have something worth hearing to say for themselves, and the truth would lose something by their silence."[25] By dominating the nodes of knowledge, writing the rules of recognition, and shaping the spaces of action used for scripting our political culture, cultural conservatives squelch the intellectual possibilities for promoting popular liberation. They choose instead to seize sites where they can "tell the nation's story" so that the rough contours of injustice, with all its nuance, contradictions, complexity, cross-purposes, or ambiguity in America's Western history, are washed away. In the ruts left behind, they rush to affirm a much more ideological vision of truth, justice, and the American way propounded so well in Hollywood as America's "Western Heritage."[26]

CHAPTER TWO

Nuclear Reactions:
The (Re)Presentation of Hiroshima at the
National Air and Space Museum

This chapter reconsiders the controversy at the National Air and Space Museum in Washington, D.C., that arose in 1995 over the abrupt cancellation of the heavily criticized exhibition "The Crossroads: The End of World War II, the Atomic Bomb, and the Origins of the Cold War." As the proposed title indicates, the show was to have examined the interconnections between the atomic bomb, the bombing of Hiroshima and Nagasaki, and the atomic stalemate of the Cold War by commemorating the fifty years since V-J Day with a display of the partially restored *Enola Gay*. After the rhetorical brawling sparked by "The West as America" show, however, those broader educational goals were dropped in favor of a narrower patriotic fete for the airplane and her crew without any discussion of the atomic bomb or the Cold War.

While this event has been understood as a crass case of political censorship, I want to see it as symptomatic of far larger and more volatile ideological battles in America's culture wars.[1] James Davison Hunter argues that "America is in the midst of a culture war that has and will continue to have reverberations not only within public policy but within the lives of ordinary Americans everywhere," and this cultural conflict can be understood as "political and social hostility rooted in different systems of moral understanding."[2] Although he strangely ignores museums, Hunter argues that "*it is in the context of institutional structures that cultural conflict becomes crystallized, because cultural conflict is ultimately about the struggle for domination.*"[3] And domination always is well worth struggling to attain within any institutional structure inasmuch as it means getting power. Cultural forms of power are the most potent, because they carry a vital prerogative: "the power to define reality... nothing less is at stake than a sense of justice and fair play, an assurance that life is as it should be, indeed, nothing less is at stake than a way of life."[4] Most battles in these culture wars center on defining "a way of life" with sufficient moral authority to assure everyone that "life is as it should be." These undercurrents pulled strongly on the body politic in the 2000 presidential election as Vice President Al Gore's cerebral understandings of the country's contemporary challenges were tested in the voting booth against Texas Governor George W. Bush's gut checks of America's more traditional heritage. Today in the United States many fights are triggered by museum exhibitions, as the nasty polemics about "political correctness" in "The West as America" show at the National Museum of America Art discussed in chapter 1 illustrates.[5]

Occurring in the fiftieth anniversary year of the end of World War II, the patriotic uproar over the exhibit's alleged "political incorrectness" caused great consternation on both sides of the Pacific, but this chapter looks beyond and behind the international affair to examine how the Hiroshima bombing first was to be put on display, and then was moved off center stage, in the exhibition at the Air and Space Museum. Eager to counterattack any resistance to its conservative and nationalistic (re)imagination of America's exceptional moral mission and uncontestable global power after the USSR's defeat in the Cold War, cultural conservatives seized onto the meaning of historical artifacts and events, like the *Enola Gay*, the Little Boy A-bomb, or Hiroshima, to reaffirm them as instances of "strategic necessity," "good decision making," or "world-class engineering."

Even though these artifacts' dark magic as signs of nuclear credibility for the Cold War deterrence system of mutually assured thermonuclear destruction is no longer essential, any other commemorative assessments, which might attempt to recall their Cold War–era significance, are censored as politically incorrect. After World War II, America's nuclear monopoly was meant to keep the USSR in line. Stalin breached the monopoly in 1949, and Brezhnev brought the USSR up to nuclear parity with United States by the early 1970s. The balance of terror lasted nearly three generations until the Soviet Union simply collapsed in 1991. Fifty years after Pearl Harbor, then, America's superpower once again became essentially a monopoly. While a few might question the nature of such superpower, many others stigmatize such questioning as left-wing "political correctness." Therefore, the cultural right as well as the seventy-somethings of the World War II generation would coalign to use the *Enola Gay* as a sign of celebration, victory, and deliverance from totalitarianism. As Speaker of the House Newt Gingrich declared, "political correctness may be O.K. in some faculty lounge, but the Smithsonian is a treasure that belongs to the American people and it should not become a plaything for left-wing ideologies."[6]

Recognizing this generational division is quite important. The Manhattan Project, B-29s, Hiroshima, and World War II Axis surrenders are one constellation of particular geopolitical icons, but they have a very specific historical meaning for most people over sixty. Moreover, a peculiar state formation—American superpower in World War II's Grand Alliance of United Nations as well as the victorious Cold War protagonist over the now vanquished USSR—has had a vested interest in associating these symbols in particular ideological contexts that attained stable canonical forms in many social/political/moral/economic/cultural networks from 1945 to 1995. Because these ideological frameworks anchored political debate and social alliances for nearly fifty years, publicly funded national museums, like the National Air and Space Museum, have always played a significant role in the "history-making process" by associating heroic human beings, whether they were ordinary Americans at work in Manhattan Project labs, GIs at war in the U.S. Army Air Force, or Japanese victims in Hiroshima, with nonhuman objects, like B-29 aircraft or atomic bombs, in spectacular performances of American power during the Cold War.[7]

By memorializing various important linkages between war, technical innovation, peace, and organizational development in the technoscience practices of flight, the Air and Space Museum has always served explicitly on many levels as a high-visibility memorial to the fight that was World War II. It implicitly also has been a celebration of America's continuing nuclear strengths, providing a point of pride in the struggle against communism. After defeating fascism in the 1940s and communism in the 1990s, most Americans, as then–Speaker of the House Newt Gingrich claimed, are "sick and tired of being told by some cultural elite that they ought to be ashamed of their country."[8]

So the surviving flyboys of World War II imagined that the *Enola Gay* should serve, like the airplanes at the Pima Air and Space Museum dis-

cussed in chapter 9, as a unique memorial to that war and America's triumphant superpower in 1945 *and* 1995: a purpose that the museum's
curators openly acknowledged as legitimate.[9] Yet, in an effort to give
some textured historical balance to a fiftieth-anniversary celebration of
that power's costs and benefits, the curators wanted to append some
memoranda of liabilities (the Cold War, nuclear terror, atomic tests, nuclear fuel cycle dangers, Japanese bomb victims, etc.) to the memorial,
which clearly expressed another set of cultural associations with the
Enola Gay for many people under the age of fifty. From these efforts to
be objective, a firestorm erupted, mostly over the nature of these ideological associations and political subjectivity in America after the Cold War.

Factuality and fictiveness can become the objects of pitched rhetorical battles as history gets remade by museum displays, particularly if, as
was the case with the *Enola Gay*, many of the original "history makers"
are still around to help refine and/or define what is fact and what is fiction. The display of artifacts, the discourse of historical authenticity, and
the disposition of individual agency all must come together in history
museums to show how "this presentness" followed from "that pastness."
The 1990s "as a present" were made possible by events in the 1940s "as a
past," but who should be, or will be, allowed now to remember then,
and for whom, and in what fashion? These interpretative issues are unstable isotopes, and a critical mass of ideological contradictions insepa-
rably chained to American superpower rapidly initiated many nuclear
reactions to how the *Enola Gay* might be displayed at the Air and Space
Museum. To discover the permissible political possibilities of "who, whom"
in these equations of intergenerational translation and ideological purification, one can reread the politics of complex cultural contradictions
behind their aesthetic and rhetorical implementation in museum displays. Therefore, any museum's displays of meaningful divisions between
the past and the present have a distinctly politicized character as founding writs of our reality. Indeed, relations of power and powerlessness in
the world at large script such sociol ontologies unfolding at the core of
museum exhibits.

Collision at "The Crossroads"

The ferocious political combat over America's past at the National Air
and Space Museum can be chalked up, in part, to the prestige of the
venue itself. As a major institution receiving public monies to display

cultural truths in the nation's capital city, this museum might be expected to appear "objective" or "nonpartisan," because it is at these places that America, in some sense, tells its stories to itself in the broadest possible terms.[10] Hence, in an August 1994 *Washington Post* op-ed piece, The National Air and Space Museum's director, Martin Harwit, argued: "This is our responsibility, as a national museum in a democracy predicated on an informed citizenry. We have found no way to exhibit the *Enola Gay* and satisfy everyone. But a comprehensive and thoughtful discussion can help us learn from history. And this is what we aim to offer our visitors."[11] Yet it was precisely such rhetorical assumptions about objectivity or partisanship that the authors of "The Crossroads" script ended up contesting. If the terms of "how" we learn from history and "what" history we actually learn conflict, then the museum performance often must justify why it varies from what visitors expect.

As it was constructed by national media and the Smithsonian Institution from "The Crossroads" script, "The Last Act" exhibition, which was what the show came to be labeled after the media controversy, had fairly complex origins, because it was designed with the negative reactions to "The West as America" show at the National Museum of American Art during 1991 very much in mind.[12] To commemorate the fiftieth anniversary of the atomic bombings of Japan by the United States in 1945, the Smithsonian Institution's National Air and Space Museum drew up plans in 1993 and 1994 to stage a major display around a thorough renovation of the *Enola Gay,* which was the B-29 Superfortress that dropped the Little Boy U-238 fission bomb on Hiroshima. It sought to defuse public criticism by circulating the show's script among all interested groups as a strategy to vet the exhibit; indeed, it already had disassociated the *Enola Gay* from another exhibit on strategic bombing planned during the late 1980s.[13]

Harwit's sense of the *Enola Gay* exhibit, however, proved prophetic as he recalled the earliest discussions on the exhibition at the Smithsonian: "There were two points everyone agreed on. One, this is a historically significant aircraft. Two, no matter what the museum did, we'd screw it up."[14] Consequently, the Smithsonian sought to allay public criticism by circulating the script among any interested group to vet the exhibit.[15] Yet when the authors shipped their proposed script out to historians, military experts, and World War II servicemen, intense protests began almost immediately. Most importantly, the Air Force Association (an organization for retired and active personnel of the U.S. Air Force) and the American Legion (a national veteran's association) quickly mounted a massive lobbying offensive against the exhibition in the media and Congress to pressure the Smithsonian into excising its allegedly "revisionist" representations of the atomic bombings of Hiroshima and Nagasaki from the 1945 commemoration.[16]

As originally conceived, the exhibition went well beyond already ideologically stabilized renditions of the Manhattan Project's technological heroics to ask why the bombs were dropped, who had been harmed when they exploded, and what has been the influence of nuclear weaponry in the post-1945 world.[17] As the newly inaugurated Secretary of the Smithsonian, I. Michael Heyman, claimed at his investiture in September 1994, this approach was legitimate. A former chancellor of the University of California, he asserted, "The Smithsonian could have avoided controversy by ignoring the anniversary, simply displaying the *Enola Gay* without comment, setting forth only the justification for the use of atomic weapons without either reporting the contrary arguments or indicating the impact of the bombs on the ground. My view is that the Smithsonian has a broader role than simply displaying items in the so-called nation's attic or eschewing important topics because of the political difficulties created by an exhibition."[18]

Consequently, the original script for "The Crossroads" exhibit was to have examined much of the post-1945 infighting over whether Washington should have dropped the bombs, the cultural significance of seeing all those burnt bodies of women and children from the blast zones in Japan, and the discursive elaboration of the nuclear mythos from the Cold War era that first arose out of the mushroom cloud over Hiroshima.[19] These historically valid associations, however, were impure ideological translations, which threatened existing forms of political detachment from nuclear war. Veteran's groups claimed these displays were both "too soft" on Japanese aggression in World War II and "too hard" on American servicemen who sacrificed their lives to defeat Imperial Japan. Responding to such protests, the Smithsonian removed material that some historians considered critical for understanding what happened when and why. Other historians then denounced the revised script as a "historical cleansing" that substituted patriotic propaganda for careful commentary. After nine major rewrites, and in the face of threatened reductions in funding, the Smithsonian simply threw in the towel during January 1995.[20]

Rather than staging a major display about Hiroshima and atomic weapons, the National Air and Space Museum did exactly what Heyman promised it would not do a few months earlier. That is, it merely brought out pieces of the B-29 airplane itself, displaying a large section of the *Enola Gay* fuselage with bland news release copy about Hiroshima along with a celebratory short film about this B-29 and its crew to mark this major anniversary in world, American, and Japanese history. Even this was seen as blasphemous by many. The surviving members of the 509th Composite Group, which was the unit formed in September 1944 to deliver America's atomic bombs, had been angry for years that the *Enola Gay* was not already fully restored. Its pilot, Brigadier General Paul W. Tibbets Jr., described this display "without wings, engines and propellers, landing gear and tail assembly" as a "package of insults" that accentuates "the aura of evil in which the airplane is being cast."[21]

The *Enola Gay* has had a checkered history after being handpicked by then Lieutenant Colonel Tibbets from the Martin Aircraft factory line in Omaha, Nebraska, in May 1945. On 6 August 1945, Tibbets flew this B-29 over Hiroshima, while his crew delivered the first atomic bomb on any city in war. During the summer of 1946 the *Enola Gay* was retired from active service. It was put into storage at Davis-Monthan Air Force Base in Tucson, Arizona, until restored to operational condition and flown in 1948 to Chicago, where it was deeded into the Smithsonian's inventory. It sat out in the open on a parking apron at Andrews Air Force Base in Maryland from 1953 until 1960, when it was disassembled and moved to Silver Hill, Maryland. In 1984 a thorough mechanical renovation was begun on the *Enola Gay*, but after a million dollars and nearly eleven years of work, one engine and the forward section of the fuselage were all that was ready for display in June 1995.[22] This somewhat ambivalent treatment of the airplane over the past five decades perhaps reflected the division within the American public over its ultimate historical importance and cultural meaning. Is it the penultimate artifact of American victory in World War II or the first dark signifier of the Cold War's atomic stalemate? For those born after 1945, many of whom, ironically, could be born only because of Hiroshima, since their fathers might otherwise have been cut down on the beaches while invading Japan, the *Enola*

Gay represented not deliverance from war but delivery to a world of mutually assured thermonuclear destruction. The *Enola Gay* is—like so many other sites in the 1990s—a flashback to the 1960s rather than the 1940s, reflecting an ongoing generational struggle for power and identity.

As Air and Space Museum Director Martin Harwit suggested, "the commemoration the Museum has planned is designed largely for the benefit of those generations of Americans too young to remember how the war ended. It is they who will have the most to gain from the lessons to be learned."[23] Particular political subjects, like any American too young to remember the 1940s or even the 1960s, would have much to gain or lose as political agents from the lessons to be museum-learned, not book-learned/school-learned/film-learned, from the curators of "The Crossroads." In many ways, the exhibition was simply designed to showcase a collage of diverse perspectives on the atomic bombings, leaving it up to the viewer/visitor to conclude what the key messages were in its complex arrays of information.

Radical differences in historical perspective, such as those ignited by "The Last Act" controversy, typically are not taken as honest disagreements over either the raw facts or those various sets of individual and group assumptions that often let the same facts speak differently to assorted sets of listeners. As one negative analysis noted, the American veterans claimed the exhibition "turned history upside down, casting Japan as a victim rather than the aggressor, and implying American servicemen were little more than war criminals. Moreover, *Enola Gay* was presented as an impure hybrid, symbolizing nuclear terror, rather than as a machine that brought a rapid end to an agonizing war. The veterans said the display failed to reflect the sentiments and realities that existed in 1945, but instead promoted the antinuclear leanings of the museum's curators 50 years later."[24] As the *Washington Post* concluded, "what's taking place is a tug-of-war for the perceptions of future generations between those whose political sensibilities remain anchored in the anti-government, anti-war sentiments of the Vietnam era and those whose perspectives include allowances for other times and all other circumstances."[25] Once again, it was "the 1960s generation" refusing to grow up or make sensitive allowances for other times and circumstances. As Major General Chuck Sweeney—the only man to fly on both the Hiroshima and Nagasaki missions—observed about the planned exhibit, "I don't need some '60s-type professor poisoning the minds of our kids about how terrible America was."[26] Ironically, it was an attempt to make allowances for other times and circumstances, including those of the Japanese victims and non-Japanese onlookers, that was in play in "The Last Act" exhibition.

Instead of "The Last Act" being the product of forty-something American New Left longmarchers through the institutions, refusing to countenance the times and circumstances of seventy-something ex-GIs, it actually was planned carefully by two foreign immigrants to America. Martin Harwit, the Air and Space Museum director, was born in Prague in 1931, raised in Istanbul, and educated at Oberlin and MIT after coming to the United States in 1946. His appraisal of nuclear weapons was cultivated at the Pacific atoll H-bomb test sites in the 1950s, when he served as a physicist for the U.S. Army to assess thermonuclear weapon effects. As the Smithsonian's project manager, Tom Crouch, noted, the *Enola Gay* exhibit "was really Harwit's baby," because "he had seen himself what nuclear weapons can do and felt strongly about their danger."[27] Harwit's other key aide, Michael Neufeld, is a Canadian citizen born in 1951. Educated at the University of Calgary in the 1970s (which the *Washington Post* took special pains to note is located in Canada, or that country where young Americans fled "to escape the Vietnam War"), he is a historian, specializing in German aerospace technologies of the Nazi era.

Even so, Harwit and Neufeld's script shipwrecked on the reefs of the Smithsonian's higher managerial and outside advisory boards at the very beginning of its voyage through a public review process. In July 1993, Smithsonian Secretary Adams protested mightily against the preliminary plans, asserting there was a lack of "what will be perceived by some as balance" in what "should be an exhibit commemorating the end of World War II . . . I continue to be uneasy that later sections of the planning document treat fully the horrors of the bombing. . . . but do not present in adequate depth . . . the horrors experienced by the Americans during the island invasions culminating with Okinawa."[28] However, it was former congressman and Smithsonian regent Barber Conable who put the sharpest point on the disagreement's general outlines at this juncture. An ex-marine who had been slated to hit the beach in Japan until the Hiroshima bomb fell on Honshu and the Nagasaki explosion visited Kyushu, he saw the curators' allowances for views from other (non-American) times and circumstances in these terms: "I think it would be a big mistake to take that approach . . . Do you want . . . an exhibition intended to make veterans feel good, or do you want an exhibition that will lead our visitors to think about the consequences of the atomic bombing of Japan? Frankly, I don't think we can do both."[29]

Here is the conflict *in nuce*. The curators wanted visitors to think about the consequences of bombing Japan with atomic weapons and their links to the Cold War, but in 1995 (during the fiftieth anniversary of the end of World War II) museum directors and regents also wanted veterans to feel good. The parameters for shaping political subjectivity through memory were at odds with the impulse to use this commemorative moment either to induce guilty introspection or to entertain strong national pride. As Conable sagely warned, the vantage points of retired American servicemen who had been close to contemplating Japanese beachheads from an LCI under heavy fire in March 1946 cannot mix with those of one-time Japanese bomb victims who had been floundering in rain gutters near ground zero at Hiroshima to cool their radiation burns in August 1945. In this environment, the veterans prevailed, particularly once the surviving *Enola Gay* crew members weighed in. Now eighty years old, but still "hale and hearty," General Tibbets asserted that Harwit and Neufeld's interpretations were little more than "a package of insults" in which "*Enola Gay* has been miscast, and a group of valiant Americans have had their role in history treated shamefully." Another World War II B-29 crewman noted, "There is no need to glorify it, but there's no need to denigrate it, either."[30]

As the *Wall Street Journal* put it, the Smithsonian Institution is "the American museum whose business it is to tell the nation's story," and in the case of "The Last Act" exhibition (as well as the earlier "The West as America" show) there is a sense that the Smithsonian "now is in the hands of academics unable to view American history as anything other than a woeful catalogue of crimes and aggressions against the helpless peoples of the earth."[31] John Correll, editor in chief of *Air Force Magazine,* saw no place for conflicted interpretations or ambivalent views in the nation's appraisal of Hiroshima. In his magazine, he argued that the decision to drop the two bombs was "a legitimate military action taken to end the war and save lives"; hence, no one should be exposed to "countercultural morality pageants put on by academic activists."[32] The distinct possibility that questioning the decision could be part of the nation's story or that the story is, at least, contradictory, contestable, or conflicted seemed utterly out of the question. Yet what is in dispute here?

Assertions in "The Crossroads" script, such as the following, are what the American Legion protested. Are they distorted or decontextualized? "For most Americans, this... [World War II] was a war of vengeance. For most Japanese, it was a war to defend their unique culture against Western imperialism."[33] For most Americans, World War II was a brutal war of vengeance to deliver retribution for Pearl Harbor, Bataan, and Correigedor. John Wayne, Humphrey Bogart, and Ronald Reagan attest to this truth over and over again every week, in old war movies on American Movie Classics or Turner Network Television. And from the Tokugawa shogunate's designation of Nagasaki as Japan's only open port in 1639 to Fat Man's descent from another B-29, *Bockscar,* over Nagasaki in 1945, Japan's rulers did see themselves defending their unique culture against Western imperialism, first by closing the country to outsiders, and later (thanks to Commodore Matthew Perry's entreaties at Edo in 1854) by emulating Western-style imperialist methods against non-Western (China, Korea, Russia) foes and sites and then, later, Western (British, French, Dutch, American colonies) foes and sites. Japan under imperial war governments was not a helpless Third World victim, but plainly the West also had been an aggressor.[34] Two wrongs do not make a right, but two different rights seemed to have ended with a wrong.

In a less anti-intellectual time or in a more intellectual culture, such complexities in Japanese and American memories of World War II might be appreciated, even though they might not make us "feel good." Because American GIs in the years 1941–45 were almost totally ignorant about Japan and its history, and because they and their children learned little during the Cold War, these facts were seen as "revisionist, unbalanced and offensive," as Senator Nancy Kassenbaum (R-Kansas) dictated in her condemnatory Senate resolution against "The Last Act" exhibition.[35] Given this fact, it is no surprise, as chapter 4 indicates, that Tokyo now invests in blockbuster cultural exchanges to explain Japan's history to America's public. And because Japanese subjects were essentially ignorant about how America had been attacked by the Imperial war machine from 1941 to 1945, they could not comprehend the apparent operational necessity for staging atomic bombing strikes as a contextually warranted strategy, a blow of righteous retribution concocted by balanced democratic decision makers. Still, in sacrificing the possibilities of seeing how such contradictions always coexist uneasily in the specific context of struggle, in order to stage another sort of truly revisionist, unbalanced, offensive "feel good" commemoration of World War II at the Smithsonian, another vital opportunity for cultivating the faculties of such historical/moral reasoning was lost.

The line taken by the American Legion ultimately set the tempo for the whole affair inasmuch as William M. Detweiler, the Legion's national commander, concluded that the National Air and Space Museum was badly damaged by "its own mismanagement and zeal for revisionist history."[36] After going through a line-by-line rewrite of the exhibit's 500-page script, spending nearly $300,000 to revise the display, and managing a firestorm of protest that led to 82 members of Congress demanding the removal of the Air and Space Museum's Director, Martin Harwit, and the exhibition's curator, Michael Neufeld, the Smithsonian Institution's Secretary, I. Michael Heyman, canceled the planned exhibition on 30 January 1995. Heyman thought it premature to dismiss Harwit in the midst of such a passionate public protest, but promised to "look with great care at the management of [the] Air and Space [Museum] in an organized way."[37] Sensing how volatile these museumological escapades of rhetorical reexamination were becoming, both houses of Congress planned separate hearings on the *Enola Gay* exhibition. Newly appointed Smithsonian regent Senator Thad Cochran (R-Mississippi) promised to recommend to the Senate Rules Committee, now chaired, strangely enough, by Senator Ted Stevens of Alaska, that the Senate would consider "how the Smithsonian will be managed in the future and what standards will be developed for interpretive exhibits."[38]

Acts of direct legislation from the halls of Congress, then, promised to recenter the actions of indirect legislation propounded by the Smithsonian Institution in its exhibition halls. Congress, of course, rarely does anything quickly or right, but in this case it moved with great dispatch far to the right by promising to investigate the ties behind art, history, and subjectivity. In the meantime, Smithsonian Secretary Heyman promised to stage the sort of exhibition that he thought Congress would be comfortable having all Americans visit. That is, "the new exhibition should be a much simpler one, essentially a display, permitting the *Enola Gay* and its crew to speak for themselves . . . with labels that don't get into the wisdom, necessity and morality of using atomic weapons."[39] Finally, in complete frustration, Harwit resigned in May 1995, leaving the museum's now heavily bowdlerized exhibition to celebrate the *Enola Gay* simply as an airplane.[40]

Revealing the First Draft

Even though Heyman canceled Harwit and Neufeld's exhibition, parts and pieces of "The Last Act" were displayed in Washington during the summer of the fiftieth-anniversary of the end of World War II. They appeared, however, at two different venues. At the Air and Space Museum, a massive propeller and engine, the vertical tail fin, and two-thirds of the *Enola Gay* fuselage, which displayed the cockpit, bombardier's station, and bomb bay, were put on display for an indefinite run in late June.[41] The maximum daily capacity was 3,000 visitors, admitted by a timed-ticket system to the display, which revolved around a sixteen-minute film featuring the crew and their memories of the mission. Beyond the basic "who, what, where, when, why" of the aircraft, its crew, and the Hiroshima bombing, the exhibition's wall captions said very little other than acknowledging the obvious: "Something more than an airplane," the *Enola Gay* now fifty years later "seems almost larger than life; as much an icon, now, as an airplace. After all this time, it still evokes intense emotions from gratitude to grief, its polished surface reflecting the myriad feelings and meanings and memories we bring before it."

Aptly reflecting the divisions in the nation over the exhibition, American University hosted a second, very low-profile display of artifacts and images from Hiroshima and Nagasaki that Harwit had planned to integrate into the Air and Space Museum show. Titled "Constructing a Peaceful World: Beyond Hiroshima and Nagasaki," this show ran from 9 July through 27 July 1995 at the University's Butler Pavilion.[42] Nearly 20 percent of this exhibit's materials were to have completed the *Enola Gay* display, ranging from photographs of the blast damage at ground zero to a charred school lunchbox filled with the ashes of peas and rice left behind as its owner was burned to death by the blast. Facts, figures, and faces that are ignored at the Air and Space Museum were, however, named at the American University exhibit.

Indeed, this was its most telling difference from the Air and Space Museum show. The Hiroshima lunchbox's owner is named: Shigeru Orimen, a middle-school student. And the fact that it was his mother who found his unidentifiable body and the lunchbox also is recorded. Like the pieces and parts of the *Enola Gay,* these efforts to put another face on Hiroshima's inhabitants also tell a story from 6 August 1945 about other hybridizing associations of humans and machines. Unlike glorious war stories from the *Enola Gay*'s crew, these exhibits, as the American University administrator overseeing the show noted, presented "something people just don't want to think about."[43] And while attendance was capped at 3,000 a day for the *Enola Gay* display, the paucity of visitors to the American University exhibition suggested a much more difficult subject matter; attendance there hit only 80 to 100 a day over its three-week run.

Here is where Harwit's and Neufeld's project violated all of the rules for the museum's discursive power play. In posing a moral conflict at the center of the Manhattan Project, and in exposing political contradictions in a liberal democratic state choosing to conduct nuclear warfare against civilian targets in a fascist empire, the original *Enola Gay* script remembered World War II in Strangelovian Cold War terms, associated Tibbets's 509th Composite Group with thousands of charred corpses in Hiroshima instead of millions of cheering citizens on V-J day, connected FDR's atomic bomb project with Hitler's atomic bomb project, and unified the *Enola Gay* with the start of a thermonuclearized cold war with the USSR instead of the end of conventionalized hot war with the Axis. The Cold War linkages between good humans (America's heroic B-29 flyers) and bad nonhumans (Japan's defeated militarists) shifted their ideological polarities to and fro, collectivizing good nonhumans (A-bomb artifacts) with bad humans (Hiroshima's and Nagasaki's dead women and children).

These more reflexive associations were taken as impure mistranslations, particularly when those aviators, who are now old veterans, sought a memorial to their acts rather than ambivalent post–Cold War introspection. Rather than simply presenting historic objects as authentic relics of the glorious past, which would respect the detachment of the visitors from the material as well as the separation of museum representations from external realities, "The Last Act" narrative openly crossed the road of apparent objectivity with its abstract universal point of view to follow its own concretely subjective path of antinuclear remembrance. The canonical collectivization of the *Enola Gay* with V-J Day parades, postwar prosperity, and American superpower was recoded in highly contradictive terms, confusing the *Enola Gay* with blast effects at Hiroshima's hypocenter, postwar radiation deaths, fifty years of nuclear proliferation.

Furthermore, fifty years after the defeat of Nazi Germany and five years after the collapse of the USSR's empire in Eastern Europe, it was no longer as clear whether the bombings were worth the cost.

In the mid-1990s, America's military superpower often seemed almost irrelevant. Accordingly, the need felt by World War II veterans to memorialize America's once-vaunted military prowess taps into deeper fears about collective identity and purpose for the United States in the future. Many seventy-something members of the World War II generation wanted a second vindication for Hiroshima and Nagasaki inasmuch as these two atomic targets were the most tangible proof of America's nuclear credibility during the Cold War.[44] This American desire to cleave to the spirit of 1945 was seconded, ironically, in Japan. After failing to express much regret over World War II for fifty years, the Japanese Diet issued a tepid declaration in June 1995, expressing "remorse" for "the unbearable pain" Japan had brought to people abroad. Unfortunately, the word chosen to express "remorse," *hansei*, also means "reflection," so that the remorse signaled was the kind meant when, for example, a pupil at school misses a homework assignment.[45] While then–Prime Minister Tomiichi Murayama and Emperor Akihito later bolstered their nation's sense of apparent contrition with more effusive apologies, it is clear that many Japanese do not see World War II in guilt-ridden terms. Consequently, a kind of balance binds Japan and America fifty years later. On the one hand, those few Japanese military men who were tried and executed by General MacArthur's war crimes tribunal now are worshiped as deities at one of Tokyo's major religious shrines where government leaders pay their respects every year during war commemoration rites. On the other hand, the surviving members of the 509th Composite Group and the U.S. Air Force resolutely maintain that Americans should not feel sorry for the atomic bombings of Japan, because, as Richard Hallion, the chief historian for the Air Force, claims, these nuclear attacks were America's answer to "15 years of aggression, atrocities and brutality"[46] by Imperial Japan.

From the perspective of realist state power, the government should be able to instate its myths or restate its agendas at cultural venues, like the Smithsonian Institution, if nowhere else, for all persons living within its jurisdiction to access the proper codes for interpreting their own impersonations of American citizenship. Not celebrating Hiroshima at the end of World War II, because the atomic bombings shown in "The Last

Act" were pictured as America's truly most lasting action, represented a major breach in the nation's state security to many citizens. Raising the spectre of anti-Americanism and antinuclearism in how some viewed a museum exhibition became a means of reaffirming this regime's circuits for generating political subjectivity. Just as "The West as America" in 1991 never made it out West to contaminate America's heartlands in St. Louis and Denver, "The Last Act" was never performed, even in Washington, D.C., as it had been planned.[47] As it happened, "the West" of brave cowboys and hardy pioneers civilizing Indian country "as America" gained reauthorization from the cultural right's campaigns in 1991, allowing the *Enola Gay's* dismembered fuselage in 1995 to stand starkly still as a totem of American superpower: the key signifier of the first and second-to-last delivery of a strategic nuclear weapon in wartime, which continues to be a sign to dangerous others across "The Indian Country" in today's Third or Fourth Worlds that America possesses a violent will to sustain today's fragile nuclear peace.

The standard account of America's superpower defined Americans as humans and Japanese as nonhumans in clear, consistent myths that resurface in old World War II movies and Japan-bashing rhetoric every day. In the Cold War canon, the properties of Imperial Japan were those of a predatory feudal empire whose relations with America were sinister, untrustworthy, and antidemocratic. All of Imperial Japan's subjects rightly were grouped together as worthy targets of American air power, and the capabilities of Imperial Japanese objects working for those sinister subjects were ones of suicide, genocide, ethnocide. Harwit and Neufeld's apparently "objective" reinterpretation of these canonical readings amounted to a series of radical amendments to the popular constitution of American superpower, which would have reread existing translations to propose some other impure possibilities. Furthermore, these pedagogical maneuvers also consciously moved against the objective detachment of museums to shake the subjective attachments of their visitors.[48] Thus, to begin the week leading into the fiftieth anniversary of the end of World War II, former U.S. Secretary of the Navy James Webb did a cover story interview in *Parade* magazine (the most widely distributed U.S. Sunday newspaper supplement) with Major General Chuck Sweeney. Their discussion entirely brushed over the Japanese A-bombing victims, concluding with Sweeney's succinct final assessment of the *Enola Gay* and *Bockscar* missions: "We saved thousands of lives, we shortened the war, and we obviated an invasion."[49]

Different generations with opposing identities exist along this divide. Is *Enola Gay* the penultimate artifact of American victory in World War II or the first dark signifier of the Cold War's atomic stalemate? Paul Fussell, who served in France as a GI during 1945 and had been put on notice for reassignment to the Pacific, summed up generational differences in his controversial 1988 book, *Thank God for the Atomic Bomb, and Other Essays*. Criticizing younger critics—like the political philosopher Michael Walzer or the revisionist historian Michael Sherry—of Truman's A-bomb decision, Fussell observed that Walzer was a ten-year-old kid and Sherry was not even ten months old in August 1945. For Fussell, "the farther from the scene of horror, the easier the talk"[50] about its morality or immorality.[51]

History and Political Subjectivity

To a very real degree, the *Enola Gay* not only brought Imperial Japan to its knees; indeed, it also started the campaigns of atomic defense that kept the Soviet Union at bay until it collapsed from its own internal contradictions. Harwit and Neufeld tried to show this historical reality, but they felt that it was impossible to do so without addressing the dark side of the Cold War. In fact, the show's curators saw their exhibition fulfilling James Smithson's original intentions for the Smithsonian, namely, serving "for the increase and diffusion of knowledge."[52] In the aftermath of the 1994 elections, however, a new conservative Republican leadership in the Congress successfully cast Harwit and Neufeld as having "an ideological, narrow-minded, special interest—of dispensing opinion rather than fact."[53]

The narratives guiding "The Last Act" exhibition fractured the objectivity of modern museum operations, because Harwit and Neufeld's text pointed out how, unlike Chernobyl in the 1980s, Hiroshima in 1945 is *not* everywhere. Instead of being out there in some stabilized material reality to be remembered, separate from us and today by being firmly fixed in the past (World War II) and elsewhere (Imperial Japan), the *Enola Gay* exhibition attached Hiroshima directly to bubbling anxieties from the present or uneasily repressed fears experienced here and now. And it did so in terms whose significance conveyed how this atomic bombing created a global nuclear contract whose underlying premise remains simple: nuclear war is only twenty minutes of any ICBM's flight away. The *Enola Gay* ended the war for GIs in the Pacific theater of operations—the fact that most seventy-somethings want to be memorialized. Yet it also transformed today's global theater of transnational Pacific relations into an unending skit of strategic deterrence stuck in a daily re-creation of that first B-29 atomic mission with each operational flight of SAC's B-52, B-2, and B-1B bombers today—the fiction of credible nuclear threat that others would recognize as topping the memoranda of liabilities still with us from the Manhattan Project.

Cultural conservatives prefer that visitors to the *Enola Gay* exhibition at the Air and Space Museum reconfirm their predictable patriotic orthodoxy. And the "history wars" in the 1990s, like the culture wars, were being fought over the terms of political subjectivity to determine what is patriotic or who defines orthodoxy. Even with highly entertaining "infotainment" at any museum, however, one must deal with the issues raised by these ideological struggles at the Smithsonian. The big problem for museums is simple: getting visitors to think beyond the diverting occupations of entertainmentality more often than not induces rage rather than cultivating reasoned reflection. The unwillingness to see Shigeru Orimen's lunchbox alongside General Tibbets's airplane in the same building in 1995 sadly illustrates this fact.

CHAPTER THREE

Memorializing Mass Murder: The United States Holocaust Memorial Museum

The United States Holocaust Memorial Museum is an exceptional, but also contradictory, enterprise. First, it is a museum and memorial in North America for what was essentially a European event. And, second, during a decade marked by spirited public outcry against widely perceived undercurrents of politicization in many major museum exhibitions across the United States, the generally positive reception of the Holocaust museum's displays stood out as a clear contradiction.

Perhaps this is because the museum is one sort of monument to political correctness. Who, after all, could speak out against solemnly memorializing Hitler's victims? Perhaps it is because the museum also poses as a short course in the civic ideals of American democracy. Who, at the same time, would protest against such educational aspirations after America's triumph in the Cold War? Perhaps it is because the structure concretely represents Israel's close geopolitical ties with the United States. Who could openly criticize this special relationship, when all is said and done, without being suspected of being anti-Israeli? Somewhat surprisingly, then, the historical exposition of genocide at the Holocaust museum has been an overwhelming success. The would-be visitor learns that it draws so many patrons each day that a commercial ticket system (such as Ticketron) is needed, in part, to ration access, and every actual visitor, as he or she prepares to leave, can read through thick comment books testifying to the serious emotional impact the museum has had on many previous patrons.

In this chapter I reconsider the aesthetics and politics of exhibiting genocide at the United States Holocaust Memorial Museum in Washington, D.C., as well as the Museum of Tolerance in Los Angeles, to account for these exceptions and contradictions. This is not easy, but one central point must be made clear from the outset. I see this museum as crucially important inasmuch as it stands forthrightly against all of the far-right or neofascist attempts to deny that the Holocaust even happened in any of the thoroughly documented, historically grounded forms during the rule of Adolf Hitler and the National Socialist party in Germany. In resisting the spread of this insidious denialism beyond the hard edge of far-right radical movements, the United States Holocaust Memorial Museum fulfills a highly significant educational purpose.

An exhibition as complex and disturbing as this one, however, can be read in many ways for several different purposes. The museum's displays do document exhaustively the origins and operations of the Holocaust, making its horrors very vivid to visitors of new generations far too young to remember anything about World War II. In this regard, it is far better to have a Holocaust memorial museum in Washington, D.C., than not to have one at all. Keeping memories of this event alive is a vitally important undertaking, even though the Holocaust as an event became an iconic entity only beginning in the 1950s. Nonetheless, it is this very vividness that clouds the Holocaust museum's displays. Because almost all members of the Holocaust museum's audiences come to it from the mediascapes of contemporary informational culture, its educational role has forced it into the registers of entertainment. And it must be said that many of the entertainment-oriented moves trivialize what is depicted at both the Holocaust museum and the Museum of Tolerance. The unspeakable is said, the unimaginable is seen, and imcomprehensible is simplified in ways that are far too "entertaining."

Using entertainment as a rhetorical device for memorializing the victims of Hitler's time wrongly transforms many of that era's brutal realities into mass media idols—some evil, some good. As a multimedia experiential simulation, the Holocaust here becomes a key subplot in World War II—victims replay the formulaic scripts of a thousand television shows and feature films. For some, the mobilization of entertainment-industry techniques to serve as agents of education may make the Holocaust seem more real; yet, for many, these devices may make the Holocaust more unreal as its unfathomable evils are recast as stock characters, plot staples, or moral clichés in the diverting simulations of this museum's shows. Perhaps the Holocaust museum is now so popular because it also is, ironically and strangely, entertaining? This question must be considered carefully here.

Like art exhibitions, history museums formalize our norms of how to see without being seen by ratifying well-practiced forms of vision or refocusing little-used modes of imagination. Using its representations of acts and artifacts, a museum rewrites conventional understandings that are made manifest or left latent in the audience's encounters with its narratives as each visitor starts learning how one must act in these spaces or why one should deal with its artifacts.[1] As one set of disciplinary conduits for imposing the normalization poised to impel persons to more easily impersonate the normative ideals of the political regime, history museums might be approached as exercises in governmentality by which disciplinary discourses, the order of things, or specific intellectuals all can affect the behavior and consciousness of museum visitors to advance various governmental agendas.[2] Today, however, alongside the unrelenting display of mass media culture, these ethnographic intentions in systems of museum-mediated governmentality increasingly must compound themselves, as chapters 1 and 2 have argued, with entertainment practices.[3] By occupying this zone of history so thoroughly, the governmentality accords of the Holocaust museum are poised to hold its visitors together on several key rhetorical points as well as to underscore the evils of the Holocaust as unique for those who believe them to be so.

The Holocaust Museum: Origins and Operations

The victimology of the Holocaust at the United States Holocaust Memorial Museum reflects both European historical realities and American political pressures. For the historical realities, the victimological profile is explicitly stabilized. "The Holocaust," as the museum defines it, "was the state-sponsored, systematic persecution and annihilation of European Jewry by the Nazis and their collaborators between 1933 and 1945." As the museum suggests, "while Jews were the primary victims, Roma (Gypsies), and the handicapped were also targeted for destruction for racial reasons. Millions more, including Poles, homosexuals, Jehovah's Witnesses, Soviet prisoners of war, and political dissidents also suffered grievous oppression under Nazi tyranny."[4] These admissions of Nazi

Germany's victimizing nearly eleven million people of various types are quite significant, but the rhetorical focus of this display falls directly on the six million Jewish victims and the special persecution of all Jews by the Nazi regime.[5] Indeed, this definition is used, first, to keep the Holocaust among Jews, separate and apart from all other "genocide-like" historical events, and second, to hold its followers together in an almost cultic devotion to its supreme horrors. The exhibits in this Holocaust museum are organized to stress the plight of Jews under Nazi persecution as well as to reemphasize the necessity for Israel's sovereign autonomy as a nation-state after World War II. Indeed, the very outline of the exhibition itself, beginning with the Jews in Diaspora, leading into the Holocaust, and concluding with the creation of Israel, underscores this stance. These twists also help explain how the museum was planned, authorized, and funded from 1978 to 1993.

The Holocaust museum project began during the Carter administration. Worried about his standing with the Democratic party's Jewish supporters and concerned about American Jews' protests against his decision to sell advanced F-15 warplanes to Saudi Arabia, Carter invited Elie Wiesel to chair a national commission on the Holocaust during 1978. The connection of the museum to America's relationship with Israel, therefore, is quite plain from the beginning. Much of its comparatively easy development might be attributed to this factor. That commission's report to Carter in 1979, which identified the desirability of building a museum to memorialize the Holocaust and its victims, became a basis for the institution's initial programs. A unanimous vote by Congress in 1980 affirmed the commission's plan for the museum by allocating a plot of federal land on the Mall in Washington, D.C., as the museum site. Under development during the Reagan and Bush years, the museum was dedicated by Bill Clinton (another southern Democratic president anxious about his levels of Jewish support and foreign policy prowess) on 22 April 1993.

Because the United States Holocaust Memorial Museum was chartered by Congress in 1980, its institutional economy has been deeply rooted in the American fiscal crisis of the 1970s and 1980s, which has required it, in turn, to operate through "a unique public-private partnership."[6] That is, it is "a federal institution" sitting on federal land, but it was built thanks to "the generous contributions of more than 150,000 Americans."[7] And these member contributions also "provide essential funds for the Museum's programs and operations."[8] Almost all of the money, in turn, was raised within the Jewish community. This community continues to donate, because the Holocaust museum is a tangible sign of the American-Israeli alliance as well as a visible pledge by Washington "never again" to tolerate any deadly threat to the Jewish people here or abroad.

Built entirely with private donations, the museum's architecturally striking building was free to articulate its rhetorics in bricks and mortar. Begun during 1987 and completed in 1993, it was designed by James I. Freed of Pei Cobb Freed and Partners. The rectangular structure arrays all of its display spaces around a central atrium called the Hall of Witness, making the structure an exercise in architectural mimesis. The absence of the Holocaust's victims in post-1945 history is meant to be made present by this void, which, in turn, is riven by a stark dividing line running through the floor as a sign of division/break/rupture. The complex banks of exhibition space, tying together all of its exhibit areas, rise on its sides inside of display pods that are strung along a continuous corridor, winding counterclockwise. Another large hexagonal pod, containing the Hall of Remembrance and Meyerhoff Theater, is attached on the small western side, while a semicircular façade, holding all public reception areas, opens on the short eastern side. Its architectural tropes also refer to the Holocaust itself. The four small towers on the north side cite the death camps' watchtowers. The repetition of triangles in most spaces recalls the system of triangular cloth patches used to classify different prisoners (i.e., Jew, communist, homosexual, handicapped) in the concentration camps. The distorted shapes of the museum's spaces— oddly proportioned stairways, mismatched windows and doors, strangely scaled arches—also reinforce concretely a sense of the deep rips rent into European society by the Nazi dictatorship.

Clearly, these messages, as they are embedded in the design, have contributed to the success of the Holocaust museum. Its planners modestly hoped to draw at least a million and a half visitors annually to the facility, believing that their attendance figures might be comparatively low given the horrendous nature of what they intended to display. Yet the museum has been packed to capacity almost every day since its opening, and the first year's attendance levels far exceeded expectations by reaching nearly two million from April to December. In fact, its design has made the museum into one of the most popular sites for visitors to Washington, D.C., despite its out-of-the-way location.

Genocide on Display

The Holocaust museum is designed in part as a solemn memorial, in part as a historical display space, and in part as an experiential simulation of the Holocaust itself. Ironically, because of the generalized sense of physical insecurity in Washington, D.C., today, these efforts to simulate the anonymous violence of the Holocaust system begin at the door, where all visitors are forced to submit to a bag search and body scan at airport-style metal detection systems to insure that no one enters these spaces armed and dangerous. The museum's security services are there at the door, intimidating visitors to submit to their institutional rules inside these heavily policed spaces. Compliant acceptance of the system in their discipline is key. One might tarry for a moment at the museum gift shop or slip into the atrium for a brief rest, but to get on their tour visitors must line up quickly in overburdened queues to begin their processing. Access is timed by a hard-to-get ticket: a simulated deportation order that directs you when and where to show up. Failing to comply denies access that day.

This disturbing bit of theater getting into the queue leads visitors past a bland counter stacked with "identification cards." All visitors are directed to take one for themselves, categorized by gender and age. One already is becoming a bureaucratically processed human packet, and now everyone acquires an individual persona, or "the story of a real person who lived during the Holocaust," that personalizes this monstrous event for visitors as they clutch their simulated official *Passes* from their own Holocaust victims. On each floor during the tour, one must turn a page in this document. Journeying through time by going through space, visitors turn over the pages of this *Pass* to advance with their Holocaust persona, experiencing how they conjointly fare in their passage through the museum's display spaces and the Holocaust years. Gradually the queue crowds into one of the elevators, executed in steel plate and raw metal girders, which lifts its overstuffed cargo of Holocaust victims/Holocaust museum visitors up to the fourth floor, while a video monitor plays old newsreels of the American liberation of the concentration camps in

Europe during 1945. The museumic narrative cum simulation begins to unfold.

On the fourth floor, one is pushed into narrow, crowded corridors that open the museum's reconstruction of the Holocaust in three main chapters: the first is a multimedia analysis of "The Nazi Assault, 1933–1939." The narrative begins with a huge photo blowup on the immediate wall of American soldiers gazing in disbelief at a pile of calcinated corpses at the Ohrdruf concentration camp, and a quotation from General Dwight D. Eisenhower after his visit there, directing that American forces gather as much firsthand evidence as possible in order to be able to prove that their accounts from 1945 about the death camps were "true." In his own letter to General George C. Marshall reporting on this visit to Ohrdruf, Eisenhower underscores this point: "I made the visit deliberately, in order to be in position to give first-hand evidence of these things, if ever, in the future, there develops a tendency to charge these allegations merely to propaganda." Obviously, these words on the wall from a former American president and the supreme Allied military commander in the European theater attest to the neofascist far right that what one will see should also be seen as "truthful testimony." To the denialists on the far right, then, this exhibition uses great American military leaders to assert that it is not propaganda. While its factuality is uncontestable, the meanings of its facticity become increasingly problematic as audio-visual overload constantly intrudes on rational truthful testimony, making it difficult to focus reflectively or reflexively as one progresses through the exhibit. The players in this Holocaust theater already are conjured in the viewers' minds; the museum simply provides the settings and costumes. At this turn, a black steel gridwork looms around the displays hung with prisoners' uniforms from the Reich's death camps—a material sign of how Nazism as a uniformed, one-party dictatorship even forced the victims of its Holocaust into a system of tightly regulated dress.[9]

After detailing some background information about the history of the Jews in Europe, the displays illustrate the dynamics of Hitler's takeover in 1933. With photos and film clips of SA men arresting communists, state police harassing people on the street, the Reichstag fire, crowds adoring Hitler at party rallies, and boycotts blocking Jewish shops, the narrative stresses how Hitler used nominally constitutional means to impose an unconstitutional dictatorship during the spring months of

1933. Moving to arrest trade unionists, detain communists, harass Social Democrats, and then suppress free speech, purge the civil service, and re-staff the judiciary, Hitler opened the first concentration camps and began the persecution of his regime's declared enemies: Jews, communists, so-cialists, Freemasons, Christians, Gypsies, and anarchists. Later, homo-sexuals, the handicapped, Jehovah's Witnesses, and dissident Protestants were added to the list. Again, newsreel footage recounts the times: the book burnings, Nuremberg rallies, *Kristallnacht,* SA terrorism, Jewish refugees, scientific racism, Aryan purity laws, the Nazi party-state.

The narrative carefully illustrates how the consolidation of control within Germany soon led to expansion abroad, first without violence in the Rhineland, Austria, and Czechoslovakia, and then later by blitzkrieg in Poland, Belgium, France, Norway, Denmark, and the Netherlands. Enemies of the Nazi state who were eliminated first at home, in turn, begin to be hunted down in the newly conquered lands as well. The Third Reich's mobilization of new technologies in blitzkrieg were paral-leled by its mobilization of information-processing machines, like the IBM Hollerith punch card machines shown in the exhibit, to gather and analyze information on the millions of Jews declared unfit for Ger-man citizenship by the Nuremberg Race Laws of 1935. The small groups of refugees who made it to freedom in the United States, England, Latin America, or China are touted by the displays, particularly the intellec-tuals and artists who emigrated to America. However, the restrictions on resettlement in Palestine after 1939 as well as the ill-fated voyage of the S.S. *St. Louis* in May 1939 also are highlighted to underscore the tremendous moral indifference of much of world community during the 1930s. From 1939 to 1941, the Nazi conquest of Europe set the stage for the Holocaust. And, ironically, the mobilization of the German psy-chiatric community in the T-4 program in 1939–1940 prefigured the larger technological design of the Holocaust. Doctors were deputized to access and then process for "euthanasia" most of Germany's physically disabled, mentally retarded, or emotionally disturbed populations at six killing centers by starvation, lethal injections, and gassings. To complete this cycle of destruction, several crematoria also were constructed to dispose of the bodies.[10]

Here the narrative is suspended as the visitor files down to the third floor over a glassed-in bridge. On its clear walls, the names of hundreds of "lost communities," or Jewish villages destroyed in the Holocaust, are etched in commemoration. The path also leads through a section detailing the indifferent U.S. response to Hitler and the Holocaust before 1939, and displaying stark black-and-white photos by Roman Vishniac of Jewish settlements in Poland, Ukraine, and Russia before the Nazi invasion. Finally, and most powerfully, a huge room is hung with photos of people of all ages over several decades from Ejszyszki, a small shtetl of 3,500 people in Lithuania. Showing life in the community from 1890 to 1941, it gives a photographic look into a single village that was wiped out from 21 to 26 September 1941 after being overrun by the German invasion of the Soviet Union. During these days, everyone was marched out of the village by German troops and Lithuanian auxiliaries, first the men and boys, and then later women, the old, and very young children, to be shot along open pits that became the village's mass grave.

The displays of the third floor, then, examine the second chapter in the exhibit: "The Final Solution" propounded by the Nazi regime from 1940 to 1945. Images of horrors beyond belief, particularly from the terror in Poland in 1939–1940, already have assaulted the visitor in the initial galleries, but this section goes through the systematic proliferation of an evil that remains beyond imagination. Exhibits in these spaces are working continually to concretize the depths and dimensions of the horror by alluding to ordinary artifacts and everyday routines: the Lódź ghetto hospital door, toys from Thereisenstadt, the Cracow synagogue windows, bricks from the Warsaw ghetto wall. A re-created rail siding with an authentic period-piece freight car demonstrate a typical place of deportation as well as the spaces endured by transportees. The camp reception routines with SS men deciding who lives and who dies also are depicted before a replica of the Auschwitz camp's entry arch with *Arbeit Macht Frei* crudely spelled out in steel. These crowded spaces lead to areas with replicas of prisoner barracks, displaying the rough beds, food bowls, and camp routines of Auschwitz II-Birkenau. Finally, a small monochrome scale model of the death system reenacts in three-dimensional form the processing of new transportees through each stage of their destruction: receiving, culling, undressing, gassing, processing, cremating. A separate area, "Voices from Auschwitz," features recordings of survivors, recounting their experiences at Auschwitz, and then the corridors lead away past some large bays. There thousands of shoes are piled high and bland photos show bizarre mounds of human hair. Both references capture the victimization of millions in these traces from hundreds of individual bodies. And most coldly, a Majdanek table—where dental gold and platinum were pulled from corpses for shipment to and reprocessing at the *Reichsbank*—casts another light on the political economy of the camps. Finally, the path again leads through the village of Ejszyszki, along another level of photographs of the residents, recounting its obliteration by Lithuanian police collaborators.

On the second floor, the displays cover the third chapter in the show: the collapse of the Third Reich and the war's aftermath in "The Last Chapter." Here, the exhibit relates the defeat of Germany on the battlefield as well as at home. Recounting the rescue of Jews all across Europe as well as the protection of whole national populations (Italy, Denmark, and Bulgaria), it also examines anti-Nazi resistance in Germany, Poland, Czechoslovakia, Slovakia, France, and Jewish ghettos elsewhere. Quickly, the corridors lead into spaces showing the days of liberation when Soviet, British, French, and American forces finally arrived to free the death camp survivors. The impact of the Holocaust on children in ghettos and the camps, in foreign emigration, and after liberation also is given special attention, particularly in terms of how their Jewish, national, or even gender identities were hidden in hopes of guaranteeing their survival.

Other sections treat the plight of displaced populations after the war, the formation of Israel, and the war crimes trials in Germany, Slovakia, Romania, France, Hungary, and Poland. Arguably, the creation of Israel becomes the culmination of the Holocaust in the Holocaust museum's narratives, especially inasmuch as America's promotion of Israel's autonomy and guarantee of its security since 1947 are made quite plain. Another rack of camp uniforms, like the one at the opening, marks the closing of the Nazi death camps. A final audiovisual space, the Theater of Survivor memories, plays personal recollections of the Holocaust era from ordinary people who survived. Another space repeats in detail the American response to the Holocaust, centering on the first news of it, the war and the Jews, rescue, the U.S. Jewish response, and encountering the camps. Finally, words of warning written next to the federal government's American eagle symbol sum up the agenda of the museum: "For the dead *and* the living, we must bear witness." And, having turned the pages of one's *Pass* for his or her Holocaust persona, the visitor must now bear witness to that person's fate, discovering whether this soul met death or continued living in the aftermath of the camps.

Leaving the display, the visitor is free either to return to the immense atrium around which the displays are wrapped or to learn more about the Holocaust in the interactive multimedia Wexner Learning Center. If both of these alternatives are unattractive, the hexagonal Hall of Remembrance on the museum's west side provides a marble and limestone space for silent meditation on the facts and faces that the Holocaust narrative has presented on the upper three floors. In many ways, this space is the most traditional inasmuch as it works as the direct antithesis of the multimedia used elsewhere for museum exhibits: open, not closed; light, not dark; uncrowded, not claustrophobic; minimalist, not overdone; contemplative, not theatrical. Unlike the disconcerting red brick, *feldgrau* steel, and bare glass in the museum itself, its marble and limestone surfaces are inviting, even comforting. Its own eternal flame burns in commemoration, and words from Deuteronomy 4:9 are etched into black marble: "Only guard yourself and guard your soul carefully, lest you forget the things your eyes saw, and lest these things depart your heart all the days of your life, and you shall make them known to your children and to your children's children."

Rethinking Holocaust Rhetorics at the Museum

As an exhibition, this "American" Holocaust memorial museum in Washington, D.C., works so well because much of it, ironically, was anticipated in a totally opposite "European" form five decades earlier in Nazi Germany. As part of its execution of the Final Solution, the machineries of the SS and Gestapo systematically collected artifacts and recorded images during the 1940s as part of the destruction of European Jewry. After the triumph of the Nazi regime, a museum was to have been established in Prague, taking full advantage of these artifacts and images, to celebrate the eradication of the allegedly subhuman populations. Some of these caches of artifacts, images, and possessions accumulated by the Nazis were the source of materials for the American curators of the Holocaust Museum.

These sources of the museum's material indicate many of the difficulties involved today in planning museum exhibits. The Holocaust museum has an almost impossible task to perform as "a museum," which its borrowings from the Nazi hoard of Holocaust artifacts illustrates. How can an evil of such ineffable scope and incomprehensible dimensions be represented by the conventional rhetorics of museum practice? These events are so extreme that they can seem unreal; this very unreality is what the denialists exploit in contemporary propaganda in defense of fascism. Legible traces of victimhood, even the vast piles of shoes, hair brushes, suitcases, or shorn hair—all once possessed by real people reduced by state terrorism to the status of mere victims—do not register the depths of its terrors. The grainy black-and-white newsreel footage of naked Jews being shot on their knees by bored *Einsatzgruppen* troopers in rural Russia is now both so familiar and so surreal. For decades, it has been run and rerun as stock historical reference for news stories, educational documentaries, TV miniseries, World War II films, or coffee table history books. The newsreel images are "proof," but are they overexposed? For many today, they do not have the shocking impact that one might imagine, especially for museum visitors seeing them in such unrelenting repetition.

Such signs, then, can be interpreted in different ways. For some, their crudity may equal authenticity. In today's media culture, however, which pumps videotape nightly in real-time, full-color, stereo-sound coverage of murder victims at the local fast food restaurant into millions of suburban homes, banal documentary stills of barracks life in Auschwitz may not sizzle or shock. Such images may even unwittingly seem to be crude propaganda. Instead of serving as truly definitive evidence, their obscene repetition may make them appear more like faked home movies of UFO sightings or dubious amateur photos of Bigfoot in the Oregon woods to audiences on contemporary global mediascapes. Jaded by witnessing hundreds of televisual murders (either real or dramatized) a week, suspicious of moral projects pretending to sort right from wrong easily in the gray haze of televisual reality, misled with rhetorics of horror in which Nazis now are merely one of Hollywood's gang of screen villains, today's museum visitor can be difficult to educate with such sustained entertainmentlike performances.

The Museum of Tolerance

This inventive use of the latest audiovisual technologies at the United States National Holocaust Memorial Museum, however, is arguably far outclassed by the curators at the Museum of Tolerance in Los Angeles. Located in the Cheviot Hills neighborhood of West L.A. near Century

City and the Twentieth-Century Fox film studios, the Museum of Tolerance is "a high-tech experiential museum featuring interactive exhibits illustrating the history of racism and prejudice, including the civil rights movement in America and the events of the Holocaust."[11] With a grant from the state of California, donations from major corporations, and contributions from many Los Angelenos, the museum's planners constructed a display space divided into two major sections. As Rabbi Marvin Hier, founder and dean of the Simon Wiesenthal Center (of which the museum is a part), directed, the first goal is "to combat widespread intolerance and hatred to ensure a harmonious world for future generations. The Tolerancenter focuses on human behavior as it relates to the American experience," while the much larger Beit Hashoah, or "House of the Holocaust," reminds future generations of the disastrous consequences of intolerance run amok, using the Nazi Holocaust as the ultimate example of "man's inhumanity to man."[12]

Mobilizing the local talent of Hollywood media producers, the Tolerancenter features thirty-five hands-on exhibits that highlight contemporary American conflicts over race, gender, religion, ethnicity, and class. Entrance into the display space comes after one passes by a corridor of images, "We the People," in which the visitor's shadow passes across huge photo blowups of marching bands, a football game, children at play. Meeting two doors—one marked in purple "Prejudiced," the other in green "Unprejudiced"—the visitor must choose, but is blocked by design from entry through the "Unprejudiced" door. Having received the message that the potential for violent prejudice exists in everyone, the visitor soon encounters a Naim June Paik–like TV sculpture with "the Manipulator" on all nine screens, who softsoaps the visitor with sugary praise coupled with dark scowls. His voice recurs throughout the maze of this space, probing everyone's assumptions and conscience as they view the other exhibits.

On the whole, the Tolerancenter is fascinating, but also mostly fantastic in its referents. Somewhat counterintuitively, it mobilizes stereotypes and mythic discourses to check most Americans' tendencies to engage in stereotyping and perpetuate discursive myths in their intolerant behavior. While the sixty-foot-long American history "Time Line Wall" nicely juxtaposes an illustrative band of "Historic Milestones" in American history with two contrapuntal bands of other illustrations labeled "Intolerance Persists" and "In Pursuit of Tolerance," its serious factual interplay juggles against the "Revolving Drums." This assemblage distills decades of American history in film-stock sprocket-banded mixes of disembodied imagery, including cartoon figures, famous athletes, popular automobiles, iconic food packages, and pop singers, all spinning together to signal how the culture industry prepackages our thinking. Whited-out manikins with TV-set heads, labeled Joe Cool, Mr. Normal, and Miss Uptight, use prerecorded video to show how the mass media, including prerecorded video, allegedly shape their consciousness and conscience. Yet using such culture-industry devices to bracket, indict, or question the culture industry allows viewers to use the same personal escape hatch that they use every day, namely, that those images of prejudice shown or recorded in replay here might be bad, but I, the visitor, am not like that.

The exhibit's clever side displays like "Me . . . A Bigot?," "What We Say, What We Think," "Dangerous Words," "Words Break More Than Bones," "Cartoon Wall," or even "Ain't You Got a Right?" tend to theatricalize intolerance to the point that their mimetic instruction can be evaded. A naively simple premise, the standard injection theory of popular media reception, drives the entire exhibit. It openly assumes that what is on the airwaves/screen/billboard/printed page/listserv/street picket is what viewers absorb. Consequently, the potential for misrecognition, misinterpretation, or mistakeness in mass media is ignored in favor of highlighting a higher will to rational truth. Individuals, we are told, can choose not to succumb to intolerance, but so too it would seem they can choose not to accept enlightenment. The open question about "the awesome power of words," which is "tempered by reason," and whether it can lead directly to modern masses embracing FDR and Mao Tse-tung, Gandhi and Mussolini, Nelson Mandela and Hitler, is begged by the belief that only evil emotions will lead people to embrace the latter evil figures just as fair rational choice leads citizens to accept the former good ones.[13]

Despite these curatorial failings, this exhibit does try far more systematically than the United States Holocaust Memorial Museum to weave the events of the Holocaust into the larger fabric of genocide around the world. A ten-minute film, *It Is Called Genocide*, focuses on the Armenian genocide in the Ottoman Empire, Pol Pot's reign of terror in

Cambodia, and the massacre of native peoples in Latin America today. In turn, a study in "Demogogues" takes up Pope Urban II's call for the Crusades in 1095, Ayatollah Khomeini's war on Iraq in 1980, and the Spanish Reconquista's pogroms against the Moors and Jews that ended in their exile, conversion, or execution after 1492. These historical events are examined alongside a cross-section of contemporary neofascists and historical totalitarian rulers. Yet, once again, the attribution of such events purely to demogogues, who artfully exploit mass fears and frustrations among receptive audiences by using personal magnetism to attack scapegoat populations, simplifies all of history's genocidal episodes to fit the same psychic profile given to Hitler and the Nazis in Germany from 1918 through 1945.

Thus violence is traced back to fanatical political movements devoted to charismatic leaders instead of acts of individual aggression or communal frictions. Even though the Museum of Tolerance far outclasses the Holocaust museum in the scope and depth of its comparative analyses, the Tolerancenter at the end of the day disappoints by returning to this problematic and not terribly sophisticated reading of how intolerance grows in advanced industrial society. Partly a persistent artifact of the totalitarian school of Holocaust history, partly a smug presumption of power by the mass media designers who constructed these narratives, and partly a prelude to the bigger story in the Holocaust section, the high-tech experiential spin of the Tolerancenter permits one a vicarious thrill in violence and fear, like Mr. Toad's Wild Ride at Disneyland, that can be forgotten or misremembered as soon as the doors fly open to the next section. Premised on the possibility that "It Can Happen Here," the Tolerancenter pitches a line of tolerance to an intolerant people convinced that "It Can't Happen Here." Except for an intriguing study of the 1993 Los Angeles riots in the aftermath of the Rodney King beating, the Museum of Tolerance also dodges the opportunity to examine how the original inhabitants of Cheviot Hills were annihilated by Anglo and Hispanic settlers or how Hispanic, Asian, and African American people have been recurrently abused by the liberal democracies (dominated by white Americans) known as the city of Los Angeles, the state of California, and the United States of America since the 1840s.

The Holocaust section of the Museum of Tolerance is presented to the visitor through the metaphor of a time machine. A narrator invites everyone to "imagine you are going back in time—to Berlin, a great city, right in the heart of Europe," and then asks that everyone take a photo Passport Card, or a smart card, that depicts a Holocaust victim. The card is needed to get through different sections of the exhibit, and a final account of the person's fate is printed out for the visitor at the exhibition's conclusion. With these theatrical assumptions, the museum patron is put into typical "street scenes" and a "cafe" to recreate the aura of 1920s Germany.

These odd tableaux, however, are set off by even more bizarre rhetorical devices: the "Designer's Studio" and "Researcher's Office." Archly recognizing how spectacular these simulations of Nazi Germany appear, these self-reflexive representations of narrative-in-production anchor the showmanship with an aura of scholastic weight. In a very strange echo of stereotyping for such an antistereotype operation, the visitor meets an authoritative trio of figures—a Historian, a Designer, and a Researcher. They are introduced as pale white specters of the Facts, the Pictures, and the Interpretations that are vended to visitors as the Holocaust section. As Hollywood typecast characters, the Historian is a sixty-something, bald, white professional-type in tweed coat and tie; the Designer is a forty-something white guy who still has his hair but sports a bow tie and artistic sweater; while the Researcher is a thirty-something white woman in pants who has a man's tie and a professional short haircut. Recounting how they choose the facts, find the images, and stage the skit that the visitor now is visiting, these narrators/directors/producers also have their accounts positioned in a professional's office full of computers, books, maps, and slide files. Their grayness suggests scholastic authenticity, but at the same time mocks the pursuits of intellect and imagination as the dronelike labor of gray people in dowdy clothes and crummy offices.

Having situated visitors in this milieu, the narrative moves into a bizarre projection room with six life-size screens about the rise of Nazism, with archival film footage and animated maps of the German conquest of Europe. The film looks at the *Kristallnacht, Anschlüss* with Austria, and the blitzkrieg of 1939–1941. Here the obviously incredible allure of fascism's spectacular powers comes into stark juxtaposition with the deviant imagery the Nazis used to depict Jews and other outsiders as subhuman. The exhibition then takes on one of the key episodes of the Holocaust: the Wannsee Conference of 1942. Using a fly-on-the-wall perspective, this exhibit replays the transcript of the meeting as one looks at empty chairs around a paper-strewn table in the Wannsee villa at a moment when everyone perhaps had left for the morning coffee break. The consensus of the meeting concerns methods of annihilation: agreeing to use shooting, poison gas, mobile carbon monoxide trucks, and stationary carbon monoxide killing chambers to eliminate Jews.

The next exhibits look at how Jews—along with Gypsies, Poles, Slavs, communists, socialists, the handicapped, and many intellectuals—were all rounded up and executed. Side exhibits on the Warsaw Ghetto and Jewish Resistance as well as a vast railway map with all of the camps across Europe bring home the enormity of the Holocaust's horror as well as flashes of human courage in opposing it. Passing through a replica of Auschwitz's *Arbeit Macht Frei* gates into the tunnels used by the SS to cull the two of every ten the Reich kept alive to work in the camps, one finally enters the Hall of Testimony, which reproduces a gas chamber from one of six big death camps. Here eight video monitors replay testimonies of survivors as well as the reactions of horrified Germans about what happened in chambers like this one. Leaving the Hall of Testimony, one enters a final space with a Wall of the Righteous (recounting forty-nine representative accounts of the eight thousand good souls recognized by Israel's Yad Vashem as those who aided the Holocaust's victims under Nazi rule) and a wrap-up briefing on "Who Was Responsible." Finally, the visitor can get a printout on the fate of the person depicted by his or her Photo Passport Card and can view a film on the culture of Jewish communities destroyed in the Holocaust, "Echoes That Remain."

While all of these displays are quite commendable, their glitz often is weightless. On the second floor of the museum, the visitor is invited to consult the Multimedia Learning Center, where thirty-two computer learning stations permit researchers to access 5,700 separate files on World War II, the Holocaust, the Jews, the Nazis, and other topics related to anti-Semitism.[14] There also is an array of Holocaust artifacts displays, including correspondence by Anne Frank, a bunk from the Majdanek death camp, and Nazi accouterments. These low-tech displays on the Nazi Party and Nazi Terror, however, house one of the museum's most riveting exhibits: a standard issue G-98 Mauser rifle. It is positioned next to a grainy photo blowup of a Nazi trooper with such a rifle drawing a bead at virtual point-blank range on a woman with a child. Her back turned to the rifleman, clutching a toddler to her breast, the woman is caught by this photographer, who clicks the image just before the trigger is pulled, killing both the woman and child. At the bottom of the photo, below the weapon, a single expended rifle cartridge lies just as it would on the ground in the next seconds following the photoframe, smoking in the aftermath of this execution. A single shot, a double death: inhuman killing efficiency racking up two more casualties on the way to six million Jewish victims. Of all the many high-tech experiential moments in this theater of cruelty, none approaches the impact of this one simple, static exhibit.

The United States Holocaust Memorial Museum

In too many respects, the Museum of Tolerance in Los Angeles and the United States Holocaust Memorial Museum in Washington only echo the cultural economies of Disneyland in California or the Universal Studios theme park in Florida. After being prepared for nearly fifty years by hundreds of World War II movies and thousands of TV hours about the Allied struggle against the Axis, has the consuming public been prepped for a visit to a Holocaust theme park today? At Disneyland the American audiences for *Davy Crockett* or *Snow White* can visit Frontierland or Fantasyland to experience, as a built environment, the imaginary spaces to which they first were exposed by Disney film products. Likewise, today's viewing publics can closely reenact in live mechanical simulations various scenes from their favorite movies—*E.T.*, *Back to the Future*, or *Star Trek*—hitherto experienced only in cinematic form.

The treatment accorded to the Holocaust at the United States Holocaust Memorial Museum eerily parallels these "experimental" entertainments. What most visitors have known only as a photographic/televisual/cinematic product is repackaged in the museum's people-handling system, narrative voice, and informational representations as an experiential theme ride, carrying the visitor through a simulation of the Holocaust death machine as if he or she were amidst the masses of its victims. Unlike the Disneyland or Universal Studios theme parks, however, this experience is profoundly unsatisfying. Reliving the Holocaust as a movie does not reawaken feelings of delight. Subjecting these overcharged visual images to simulation treatment can leave one feeling very empty—morally or politically—at the end. The entertainment does succeed at holding together the Holocaust cult by rehearsing all of its horrors as well as keeping its special status among sympathetic viewers anxious to preserve the uniqueness of the Holocaust among all other genocidal events in history. These payoffs of entertainmentality easily can seal off the moral outrage needed to rededicate mass publics to realizing the ultimate lesson of the Holocaust: "Never Again." Of course, its displays are polyvocal and open-ended. A few viewers may uncover a logic of resistance, an opening for moral outrage, or some wave of outrage to help them to map images of the European Holocaust onto today's "genocidal acts" in war-torn regions. Still, most of those thousands who visit the museum every day can return home or to their hotels, flip on CNN, and passively gaze at mounds of corpses piling up in Bosnia, Rwanda, or Chechnya with little more political resolution than if they had returned from a blockbuster movie at the mall.

Like the death camps themselves, the Holocaust museum can seem like an elaborate edifice dedicated to repeating mechanically reproduced processes: arrival, culling, transportation, preparation, dispatch, disposal. The fascist qualities of all the automatic means integrated into any ordinary materials-processing technologies, which are always heedless of the ends to which they are put, are rarely identified in modern life, even though this phenomenon is one of the technical bases on which the whole Holocaust museum, as well as the Holocaust itself, rests. In fact, the museum's "Disneyfication" of the death camps ignores how deeply and easily the death camp can nest inside of the routines of Disneyfication.[15] So much of modern industrial living is about millions of people experiencing their ordinary everyday life within the process-eventuation apparatuses of railroad travel, truck traffic, population centers, chemical treatments, meat processing, refuse collection, or waste disposal. Henry Ford allegedly got the idea for his Model T automobile assembly plant after seeing the "disassembly processes" of modern meatpacking plants at work. The same political economy that inventively assembled V-1s, Tiger tanks, or ME-262s at some sites simply reversed these logics in human disassembly plants at other sites. Seeing the potential for recombining these constellations of technology in new actuation arrays for producing modern industrial death, as occurs every day at any meat plant, was a flash of evil genius. But the same bureaucratic consciousness that makes it work every day still prevents many from recognizing how everyone lives every day amidst the same slumbering systems of extermination. As Hannah Arendt observes, the evil banality of fascism lurks in any complex system mindlessly dedicated to putting efficient means to enacting prescribed ends.[16] Dehumanization begins inside these machineries, as one accepts any and all of the anonymous mechanical outcomes that befall human beings as somehow being "normal," which also is where fascist dehumanization often ends. Megamachineries begin denying that all life is sacred; they openly assume that all life is profane, but some lives will be less profane than others. Therefore, many can be sacrificed to maintain the illusion that some indeed are sacred.

The museum, then, expertly details how the Nazi regime, at least during the later phases of its more organized efforts to attain a final solution, turned the Holocaust into an elaborate perversion of its capitalist economy's industrial livestock management and modern meatpacking technologies. Mass movements of living people, like mass movements of animal livestock, were organized as the feedstock for an intricate value-adding process wherein a political value was added in this system by extracting them from Nazified space, executing them at crudely engineered death camps, and taking any useful resources from them before, during, and after the system caused their deaths. The process, like many industrial enterprises, was incredibly wasteful and run at a loss, but it did produce a socially accepted product—mass extermination of racially designated "dangerous" people—kept in constant demand by the Nazi state.

Millions of people were pulled out of their homes, transported by road and rail to concentration camps, and divided into two groups defined in terms of either their fitness or unfitness for forced labor. Those fit for labor were assigned to arduous work in support of the wartime economy until they died or became unfit. Everyone unfit to work was sent to death camps. There they were stripped of all their belongings, which were sorted and recycled for further use. Eyeglasses, hearing aids, gold teeth, canes and crutches as well as money and jewelry were expropriated. In some camps, hair, skin, and even tallow were harvested for limited industrial uses. Food and fertilizer applications, so commonly exploited with animal livestock, were ignored, and the millions of bodies produced by the death camps were cremated or buried nearby. The main value-added from the perspective of the regime was the eradication of politically defined "pests" to safeguard the ideological, biological, and racial purity of a people it saw as endangered by Gypsies, homosexuals, communists, Jews, and the disabled. Even though the Holocaust museum is performing a major cultural service by documenting these events to refute Holocaust denialism, the horror of it all is oddly made even more horrendous by transforming its workings into mechanically reproduced spectacles in the rhetorics of museum entertainment.

Holocaust Normalization

The Holocaust museum also reworks the old adage that history always is written by the victors, not the losers, of great battles. This is a history recounted from the perspective of victorious Americans, who liberated the survivors of the Holocaust in 1945, after defeating Nazi Germany with the aid of France, Great Britain, China, and the Soviet Union in World War II's Grand Alliance. Yet Israel also is here, anchoring the conclusion of the narrative. With the Israeli epilogue, in which the Holocaust justifies and explains the need to create the state of Israel, the American Holocaust museum acquires a unique historical perspective. It is an "American" museum, but it presents a history of non-American victims, not all of them, but most of them, and especially the most numerous of them, European Jews, who are now so important to many Israeli and American Jews. These double turns in narrative voice, then, enmesh the museum in many ideological networks, charging them with remarkable cultural friction.

After all of history's many holocausts, why this museum for this holocaust at this time, in this place, and to what end? On one level, one already knows: President Carter began it to mollify American Jews and Israel; subsequent presidents and Congress followed in his footsteps for the same reasons. Americans can see that it also is a lesson about why America or NATO must defend Israel's interests against future assaults. Yet, on another level, if it is to serve as a warning beacon, signaling that humanity must "never again" accept such madness, then it already is a miserable failure. Certainly this is not a reason for not continuing with it, but it is a sign that the museum may never be much more than an entertainmentality engine. The entire machinery of modern life is deeply embedded in so many holocaust-generating potentials that no aesthetic packaging of any moral precautions can check it. Moreover, memorializing the events of one holocaust by moving millions to memorize its horrors to keep its special qualities among them perhaps can only mystify the machinations of new brutalities.

Even though "the Nazi label" has been easily hung by Washington on anyone the United States opposes, from Ho Chi Minh to Saddam Hussein to Slobodan Milosevic, no American enemies since 1945 have been hunted down as thoroughly as those of Nazi Germany. The violence of the Cold War and now post–Cold War eras show that the carrying capacity of any one person's conscience is, even when the enemy is tagged as "a Hitler" or "a Nazi," a limited resource. In an era besotted with so many chances for victimological memorialization, it can be quickly exhausted. This Holocaust museum might even contribute to preventing "holocaust detection" inasmuch as its entertainment logics heavily stylize how a genocide might be recognized. By dressing it up in the *art moderne* costumes of Nazism, genocide happens only when a highly modernized state makes heavy capital investments in high technologies: vast death camps, special trains, macabre gas chambers, jackbooted guards, and wild sociopathic *Übermenschismus*. Hence, entertainmentality works by occupying history rhetorically to hold these meanings among those who hold together by keeping this faith.

If contemporary brutalities do not conform to the exacting criteria of this classic checklist, then "holocaust status" cannot, and, of course, will not, be verified. The millions slaughtered since 1945 in low-budget, accessible-technology nightmares around the world rarely appear at approved academic victimology centers. When they are sighted, many of them—look at Guatemala, Sudan, Angola, Myanmar, Kurdistan, Mozambique, Tibet, or East Timor—can be classified as unverifiable or noncertifiable genocide sittings. Washington's policy makers now can cover their holocaust bets with a visit to the local museum, and downplay the horrors of any new Cambodia, Rwanda, Ethiopia, Iraq, Bosnia, or Argentina, even as they occur, as mere "state murders" or "gross violations of human rights." After starting out strong in his 1992 campaign, even President Clinton admitted to seeing only some "genocidal acts" in Bosnia, not a full-fledged "holocaust." While he vigorously condemned Serbia's ethnic cleansing of Kosovo in 1999, he also stopped short of using full-blown holocaust rhetoric about the mass graves detected by spy satellites throughout the conflict. Entertainmentalities now keep us all together on how to recognize a holocaust when we see one; you can verify it for yourself at the Holocaust museum.

Despite all of the breast-beating about remembrance, the Holocaust museum, in too many ways, may simply be ennobling neglect. State-sponsored systematic persecutions of many peoples from the get-go of disorganized ethnic cleansing to the finish-point of complete annihilation have held the headlines of our recent history from 1980, at the time of the Holocaust museum's charter under President Carter, to 1995, under the administration of the museum's dedicator, President Clinton. Indeed, Clinton's own comments now greeting visitors straightaway at the museum's entrance already are hauntingly false: "This museum will touch the life of everyone who enters and leave everyone forever changed—a place of deep sadness and a sanctuary of bright hope; an ally of education against arrogance, an investment in a secure future against whatever insanity lurks ahead. If this museum can mobilize morality, then those who have perished will thereby gain a measure of immortality." Speaking these words in his 1993 dedication remarks, Clinton sat stony-faced as Elie Wiesel, the first chairman of the Holocaust Memorial Council that built the museum, denounced the ethnic cleansing of Yugoslavia. Addressing President Clinton, Wiesel declared, "I cannot tell you something [about conditions in Yugoslavia] ... we must do something to stop the blood shed in that county."[17] The museum did not succeed as a secure investment against insanities that lurked ahead in Bosnia, Rwanda, Chechnya, and Iraq during 1994, and it did little to stop the madness in Kosovo in 1998–1999. In fact, if its curators are to be believed when they say it is more than "a memorial to the Jewish genocide. It stands as a testament, and perhaps a challenge to the central ... responsibility of individuals in a free society, and of a nation dedicated to democratic values, when human freedoms are placed at grievous risk,"[18] then the moral challenge of this museum is being ignored.

The Failure of Entertainmentality

As a memorial for the victims of the Nazi regime, the Holocaust museum is powerful; yet it also is lacking. The entertainmentalities of its displays diffuse its memorial intent with their distracting diversions. Even its Hall of Remembrance deflects much of the gravity that should be accorded to memorializing the Holocaust; it feels more like a yet-to-be-developed satellite atrium in a suburban mall than a solemn memorial space. For a Holocaust memorial with real gravitas, one might turn to something like the low-technology, nonmultimedia Neue Wache in Berlin. Housed in a structure designed by Karl Friedrich Schinkel and built from 1816 to 1818, it served as a memorial to Germany's war dead after 1931 for the Weimar Republic and Nazi regime, then as a memorial for all the victims of fascism and militarism for the German Democratic

Republic, and now it is the Federal Republic's memorial for all victims of totalitarianism and war. An "eternal flame" lit by the GDR for an unknown soldier and resistance fighter was snuffed out after reunification. In its place there now is a life-size casting of Käthe Kollwitz's powerful sculpture *Mother with Dead Son.*

The somber stone floor, a circular opening above the sculpture to the sky, stone patches in the bleak gray stone walls' hundreds of bomb and bullet holes, and iron gates create a memorializing space by refunctioning a Prussian state property, which sparks far more emotion with its classical forms and contemporary repositionings than many of the Holocaust museum's spaces. Part of this might be the site: positioned a bit south of the *Kristallnacht* synagogue and slightly north of what once was the Opernplatz, where the Nazis staged their infamous book burnings of May 1933, the Neue Wache, once the guardhouse for the Hohenzollerns' palace watch, sits between the once Nazified Alexander von Humboldt University and an old Prussian state armory, the Zeughaus. Most of its power, however, derives from the simplicity of the building, the emptiness of the regimes that once abused it, and its engaging memorial to the dead without any pretext of entertaining its visitors.

The multimediatization of the Third Reich at the United States Holocaust Memorial Museum with engaging displays full of old newsreel footage, period pieces, and Nazi memorabilia proves unconvincing. They give far too much away. They do not show how people could fall under the sway of Hitler. They do not demonstrate the dangerous excitements of fascism. They also require too little from the visitor, who can get swept into the pulse and pace of the show, awed by the artifacts, wowed by the statistics. They do not indicate how necessary it was to think and fight back, right then and there, like many German communists and socialists tried to do. They do not illustrate how hard it was to resist the Nazi movement and state, whether one was Jewish or Protestant, communist or conservative, gay or straight. Instead the Holocaust Museum totally accepts Hollywood's versions of *Der Führerprinzip* as its narrative theme: Hitler was a great leader, spellbound people did his bidding, and a great evil grew out of Germany's entranced masses following his bad leadership.

Real human complexities—the individual acts of resistance as well as personal decisions to accept fascism—are not given much weight at the Holocaust Museum except in the last sections. These panels are devoted to reconsidering the Final Solution when it was well on its way toward generating its dark tally of megadeaths with industrial efficiency. Even the "Topography of Terror" exhibition in Berlin, first mounted during the years of the old East German communist regime, does a somewhat better job in this respect by singling out individual Nazi leaders to illustrate how their personal careerist fortunes rose or fell with the development of National Socialism.[19] In this documentation of the Gestapo and SS use of buildings on the Prinz-Albrecht-Terrain off of Wilhelmstrasse and Prinz-Albrechtstrasse in central Berlin as the Reich's internal security headquarters, one can see stark black-and-white photos of Gestapo and SS men living and working together to advance themselves and the Reich by murdering innocents. The photos here are astounding: SS officers blandly smile as they pull the triggers of their automatics stuck in the back of a Jewish farmer's head or smugly stare out of their own official photo fully conscious of the power this photograph gave them when affixed to their Nazi party *Pass*. By using the ruined buildings on this site with recent excavations of the penal cells built in their basements, the exhibit fits together photographs of both the oppressors and the oppressed to position their coevolving individual life histories within the Holocaust inside these ruined spaces. This simple, low-technology personalization of the Holocaust works powerfully; it shows how the Holocaust unfolded by empowering and disempowering certain individuals, who were then members of the officially defined categories of friend or foe, either to kill or be killed after some ordinary bureaucratic formalities. Such direct concrete examples of how the Holocaust worked make it much more comprehensible than the B-movie scripts from cinematic war stories used to construct the Third Reich at the Holocaust Museum.

The United States Holocaust Memorial Museum is a superb entertainment vehicle whose apparent success as a simulation ironically can undercut its more important institutional intentions: propagating educational lessons or sparking moments of personal remembrance. Because its horror is fixed so firmly in one time and place—Germany after 1918 through 1945 as the Weimar Republic rises, falters, and collapses in a mad fascist takeover—the Holocaust is now typecast by this museumic performance. Its own excesses transform its fluid shapes into the rigid roles played by Hitler, stormtroopers, Gestapo agents, Goebbels, Jews, gas chambers, Himmler, crematoria, concentration camps, Göring.

This story is not false, but it also has a strange rhetorical spin, echoing many of the Israeli state's foundational myths as well as the American superpower's writs of authority as they have been understood in the United States.

Consequently, "the Holocaust" is not merely banal evil snuffing out individual lives one by one, but rather it must be shown as a perverse Hollywood epic in which evil extravagance systemically consumes entire nations in orgies of horrific death. A new global theater of identity and difference with its own scales of hyperreal authenticity now can be held together by the museum, making its depictions of one past event the benchmark of our horror for any present or future catastrophe. If today's terrors cannot match this museumic taxonomy's rigorous requirements, they may not even be acknowledged as such. Bad as they are, today's acts of political violence are *only* more ordinary varieties of death such as one might expect to witness in ethnic strife, nationalist turmoil, internal war, religious conflict, or even nation building. The juries of history can, and certainly do, ignore these killings as instances of "a Holocaust." Here, the entertainmentality functions of the Holocaust museum successfully bring us together and keep us apart by holding the Holocaust special and above other acts of genocide.

In some ways, the entertaining lessons of the United States Holocaust Memorial Museum implicitly operate as a vehicle for genocide denial rather than "holocaust recognition" for many of the disunited quasi-states of the present. To preserve the full power of the Nazi original, its meanings must be hoarded, and its identity saved from any profligate application of its significance elsewhere. The United States Holocaust Memorial Museum is a shrine for the Holocaust cult that took hold among many contemporary American Jews in the 1950s. As Michael Goldberg observes, this effect may not have been planned, but it is, nevertheless, quite welcome for both American and Israeli Jews.[20] Keeping the Holocaust somehow "special" keeps its potent symbolic powers among the faithful, allowing them to be steered toward new cultural, political, or social ends by contemporary Jewish leaders. Allowing its lessons to be mapped out elsewhere indiscriminately would weaken its symbolic energies and create commonalities in Europe today, or in Africa, Asia, or Latin American tomorrow, that surviving Holocaust victims might not wish to acknowledge. So, ironically now fifty years later, as genocidal acts continue unabated elsewhere, despite museumic genuflections such as this to their containment, few people will admit to seeing new holocausts abroad. And the Holocaust museum's entertainments simply support these preoccupations.

Whether it is land mines in Angola or Afghanistan, AK-47s in Cambodia or Sudan, poison gas in Iraq or Iran, or bayonets in Bosnia or Kosovo, these state-sponsored killings are not judged as being anywhere near as bad as history's Nazi-proportioned productions. A morality of numbers kicks in—only thousands are dying, not millions. A standard of systematicity takes over—only disorganized bands are killing, not disciplined regiments.[21] An ethic of efficiency is invoked—only some are suffering a bit, not everyone is victimized totally. These rules, however, only comfort Holocaust survivors. They give little solace to today's equally dead victims.

Like so many other collisions of events, persons, or ideas with the techniques of the culture industry, the Holocaust at the Holocaust museum is an unstable/multivalent/polyvocal product. Nonetheless, it is a distressing package. Difficult, historically conflicted material is transformed deftly into dramatic simplicities by turning the conflicts into racial hatred—a formula, of course, that now flies in America.[22] Such moves are true enough to not be false, but yet so incomplete that they do not constitute satisfying explanations. Racial hatreds endure in many places without exploding into organized genocide; such dramatic simplicities miss how much contradictory complicity with fascism there was throughout the "shocked" liberal democratic world up to the actual outbreak of war in 1939. Fearing something they imagined as worse, pundits and politicians in the West sold visions of Hitler as a bulwark against Marxism, a first-line defense against the Soviet Union, a guardian for chaotic Weimar Germany, a guide to economic recovery for *Mitteleuropa*, or a proponent for traditional law and order. All of these interpretations were widely touted by businesspeople and diplomats outside Germany as gays, socialists, communists, Christians, Gypsies, Jews, and others were being sent to the camps. Class hatred, self-hatred, nationalistic hatred, ideological hatred, religious hatred all coursed in and out of the Holocaust constantly in ways that reducing all of them to the racial hatred of all Jews by Aryan Nazis simply cannot explain.

The same logics of representation, validation, and conversion used to mass-market entertainmentality to suburban consumers at a Disneyland or Universal City Studios tour are misused here. Simulate space, constitute a total environment, give people a theatricalized role to emulate what happened, dress up the site in authentic costume, and then let "the experience" happen. At the Holocaust museum, one enters a hidden past, closed quarter, or lost province excised from Disneyland—it is a Nightmareland, not Fantasyland; Downerland, not Adventureland; Yesterdayland, not Tomorrowland—wrapped up in streamlined perfection. Main Street, U.S.A., folds back on itself in the building's claustrophobic simulation of a concentration camp, while the visitor experiences Nazi Germany on a small Disneyfied scale as *Ghettostrasse, Hitlerzeit.* The entertaining dramatization of the Holocaust as simulation succeeds all too well, a sense of awe/repulsion/wonder often is generated, keeping the uniqueness of the Holocaust among its followers and holding together those who have had fascism explained to them this way for decades. It is much less clear, at the same time, how much sober reflection or critical judgment is engaged in once the visitor leaves the building. The Holocaust museum may awaken a new moral vigilance, but it also seems just as likely to leave the highly entertained visitor with an uneasy faith that this sort of horror can never happen again even as so many other terrors seem never to end.

CHAPTER FOUR

Signs of Empire/Empires of Sign: Daimyo Culture in the District of Columbia

Politics is an art, and art today, as chapters 1 and 5 illustrate, has a great deal to do with politics. The mobilization of national cultural heritage properties or fine art to serve as diplomatic tools in the uneasy relations of major world powers was a practice that worked well during the Cold War, and it continues today in the competition of great economic powers. A quick examination of the art exhibitions in Washington, D.C., easily confirms this observation. There one finds the culture ministries of various American allies and adversaries being touted in the local press for funding this exhibit of early modern European silversmithing or that display of ancient Oriental art. At such exhibits, mass publics and diplomatic experts both are afforded a chance to weigh the merits of overseas entanglements against the set-piece dramas of museum displays.

In this theater, the association of national interests with cultural acts and artifacts allows international rivalries to be explored by museum-going publics amidst the cultural riches of the various foreign societies. Whether it is aesthetic diplomacy, cultural imperialism, or handicraft propaganda, museum exhibitions clearly can be interpreted as significant international/intergovernmental/intercultural events (as chapter 2 made quite plain in its account of the *Enola Gay* exhibition). I explore the ins and outs of associating culture and politics in this chapter by considering two blockbuster shows of Japanese art a decade apart in the capital of the United States of America: the first during 1988–1989, titled "Japan: The Shaping of Daimyo Culture 1185–1868," and the second staged in 1998–1999, "Edo: Art in Japan 1615–1868." The political dimensions in these events may be more suggestive than definitive, but the texts and subtexts need further exploration.

After a visit to Japan in the 1960s, Roland Barthes called this nation an "empire of signs."[1] In the slightest wisps of everyday Japanese life, he found rich cultural messages. Such claims provide one trail into these similar, but also quite different, exhibitions of Japanese art at the same downtown Washington museum—a prestigious venue that remains in many ways an enduring sign of empire. By nationalizing the tenor and trope of many nations' art and culture for Americans in its galleries, the National Gallery of Art continuously drafts, evaluates, and ratifies definitive bills of aesthetic particulars about the nature of foreign cultures. America's popular images of Japan as the home of swashbuckling samurai, alluring geishas, and meditating monks is drawn broadly from Edo Japan and rooted deeply in Daimyo culture. Revisiting late medieval and early modern Japan, then, on Constitution Avenue in Washington, D.C., is a very suggestive sign of empire for many Americans: at one time it could perhaps be seen as one of empire receding, while at other times it might be taken as one of empire expanding.

Many international alliances link back to ineffable elective affinities between peoples, nations, and leaders. Art is one venue where I see such cultural affinities being tested, and new world orders electively won. At the same time, the *Washington Post* Sunday arts section of 15 November 1998 was casting Edo-period Japan as "A Japan of Intricate Contrasts," the National Gallery of Art served as an authoritative site for finding and fixing a few contrasting intricacies in the "true alliance" of Japan's and America's mutually coimperalizing relations. Displays of Japanese art in Washington are a definite sign of empire even as curators and audiences struggle to define the quiddity of this empire of signs. A decade earlier, the Sunday "Show" section of the 30 October 1988 *Washington Post* underscored these dynamics in its editorializing exclamations about the Daimyo culture exhibit and its rare valuable contents: "This is cultural diplomacy at a high level: Because of the importance attached to the relationship between their country and ours, the holders of the great public and private collections throughout Japan were persuaded to relinquish many of their most valued icons for the exhibition . . . which will be seen only in Washington."[2]

This chapter is not a sustained study of official cultural diplomacy, because these gallery-bound international relations transpire in an unofficial realm where the elective affinities between ideas, images, and interests in museums, media, and markets can reign. The pictures are not clear, my readings are not final, and the meanings are not indisputable. Nonetheless, my review of these art displays at particular times and places in the unfolding of international relations reveals suggestive signs of other powers and knowledges at work in the affairs of state. Museums, then, are much more than dusty old collections for any society's days of future passed. They are instead highly political agencies, which become engaged in authoritatively allocating scarce cultural values by helping to define who means what to whom, where, when, and how. By compiling signs in expressive arrays of meaning and meaninglessness, museums operate as ontologues, or definitive foundational sources of what is real, which they then rewind through their displays as what is also rational. Here I merely explicate how some of these ontologues are written, what the ontologues display, and whose interests the ontologues articulate in the rhetoric of their relics and the spectacle of their specimens.

"The Shaping of Daimyo Culture," 1988–1989

Opening a week prior to the 1988 presidential election, and closing on the inaugural weekend following the swearing-in of America's forty-first president, who once flew a torpedo-bomber against the Imperial Japanese Navy, the Daimyo culture exhibition raised new doubts about the once unquestioned arrangements of that *Pax Americana* founded on VJ Day 1945. "The Shaping of Daimyo Culture" exhibition was organized by the National Gallery in close collaboration with Japan's Agency for Cultural Affairs and the Japan Foundation with the financial backing of the R. J. Reynolds Tobacco Company, the Yomiuri Shimbun, and the Nomura Securities Company. For many reasons, the inescapable mystery of Daimyo Japanese culture evokes a sense of almost extraterrestrial mystery in the United States. In a society whose silent majorities long ago forgot who fought whom in World War II or why, on what continents or in what oceans major foreign powers lie, and which even now cannot easily locate Kosovo, the Persian Gulf, or Korean peninsula on the map, an intricately layered and infinitely sophisticated history of medieval Japan was presented coldly *de novo* with great detail. While the presentation's sweep was overpowering, and its impact left audiences with some sense of feudal Japan's style and decor, few deep insights into Daimyo Japan's actual political, economic, and social dynamics were presented at the exhibition. Even so, the coincidences swirling around this show compounded themselves in strange serendipities.

In 1980, Japan still was running a distant second or third in global rankings against the United States in most measures of economic and technological power. After a decade of Reaganism, however, the outcomes of ill-considered fiscal, monetary, and trade policies were rapidly rearranging the relative rankings and absolute positions of Japan and the United States as global powers.[3] No longer a net capital or technology exporter, the United States in the 1980s saw Japan surpass it in one area after another—automobile output, high-tech innovation, consumer electronics, manufacturing efficiency, and robotized production. Throughout the Reagan era, the Tokyo stock market gradually came to rival New York's Wall Street in its size and importance. The yen challenged the dollar as the major global currency. Japanese investors bought billions of dollars' worth of American firms, land, and securities. Gradually, but not imperceptibly, the world's financial, technological, and economic center of gravity seemed to be slipping out of the Atlantic, into the Pacific basin, and toward Japan. What once was believed to be only a colorful and relatively backward corner of the globe emerged in the 1980s as the new core region of the world capitalist system.[4]

Fifteen years, twenty years, or thirty years earlier, the Daimyo culture exhibition would not have been presented in the manner it appeared. If it had been staged at all, such a show undoubtedly would have been shown in a less prestigious space and on a much smaller scale. Like the art of South Korea, Thailand, the Philippines, or Mexico today, it would have had a tinge of faraway places that still were not yet fully modernized—much like Japan was when Hirohito first ascended to the throne in 1927. Obviously, however, it was neither staged earlier nor elsewhere. Instead, it made its appearance in 1988–1989 in the premier art space of the nation, which gave Japan's extensive economic power a highly visible cultural presence to flex its political clout. In 1987 the magnificent new Arthur M. Sackler Gallery of Oriental Art opened in Washington. Yet this facility is stuck away on the less grandiose Independence Avenue side of the Mall, hidden behind the old original Smithsonian Institution "Castle." It also, like the West's deep consciousness of its Asian roots, is placed mainly deep underground. While such an unauspicious architectural space may be suitable for generic displays of tribalistic "Asian" and primitive "African" art, it clearly does not have the presence or prestige of the East Building of the National Gallery on Constitution Avenue at the base of Capitol Hill.

One might have expected this Daimyo culture show to have been the Sackler Gallery's first big blockbuster exhibition. However, we no longer live in ordinary times with obscure professionals exercising mere curatorial discretion in deciding where a major Japanese exhibition might appear. The East Building alone carried an appropriate weight for a show such as this on the art and culture of Japan in the Daimyo era. In a fascinating reversal of the logic demonstrated by the display of Daimyo Japan, the 1990 exhibition of Yokohama wood block prints *was* mounted deep underground at the Sackler Gallery. During a time when the Japanese equivalents of Commodore Perry and the treaty port of Yokohama were operating out of every Toyota dealership, Hitachi franchise, and Sony factory based in America's heartland, it perhaps did make some sense to recall the opening of Japan and the end of the shogunate in the Sackler's subterranean caverns of Orientalist exoticism.[5]

On one hand, very little was said openly in this exhibition of feudal Japanese culture about contemporary Japan's rising power and growing prominence. On the other hand, however, the entire show spoke endlessly about it in its silences. By showing what Japan no longer is, and what it never will be again, Japan's power gained its greatest voice by stressing images of its past. The spectre of America's uncertain future also was raised uncomfortably by these images of another nation's almost indecipherable past. Having much of its capital and energy in modernizing the nations of the Pacific Rim, America confronts the insurrection of hitherto subjugated cultures imposing their demands for respect and attention in Washington with blockbuster aesthetic offensives somewhere on the Mall. The art treasures of the Daimyo were only the first wave, soon followed by displays from South Korea, Thailand, Singapore, Taiwan, or China as they either become important economic powers in their own right or continued to be invaluable vassals in Japan's empire of signs.

Given the climate of Japanese American relations in the 1980s, the significance of this tremendous art blockbuster was quite clear. Public-opinion polls in February 1989 showed that more than 60 percent of all Americans believed Japanese imports into the United States should be restricted; 45 percent said Japanese nationals must not be permitted to buy property in the United States; 80 percent wanted limits on Japanese corporate takeovers; and more than 60 percent thought Japanese firms outcompete American business by using unfair trade practices.[6] The historical era emphasized by the show, then, was not insignificant. Its multilayered representation of feudal Japan highlighted basically quaint and nonthreatening pictures of a preindustrial, premodern, and pre-Westernized society that once had chosen consciously not to be state of the art by global economic, military, or technological standards. Rather than portraying the contemporary arts of a society that has equaled and/or surpassed virtually all of the once hegemonic Western powers in the world capitalist system in a little over a century, this show gave one a lingering look at the larger cultural context behind the passing glimpses of feudal Japan hitherto provided to most Westerners only in art house showings of samurai swordplay movies.

The 1988–1989 exhibition unfolded carefully as a comprehensive cross-section of Daimyo Japan, encompassing most of its entire material and symbolic culture. Tracing the emergence of the Daimyo feudal lords back to the Kamakura period (1185–1333), when the first of the shogunates that would rule Japan until 1868 was established, the presentation unfolded historically through many of the stylistic shifts and cultural changes of the Muromachi (1333–1573), Momoyama (1573–1615), and Edo (1615–1868) periods of Daimyo Japan. In keeping with the ideals of the era, the show's curators took special pains to balance equally the ways of *bu* (arts of the sword) and *bun* (arts of peace) in the display. To present *bu*, many artistic examples of samurai swords, sword guards, battle armor, ceremonial armor, and warrior imagery were scattered throughout the display rooms. And to illustrate *bun*, very elaborate examples of calligraphy, ink painting, poetry, and court rituals were shown in their many variations from the Kamakura to the Tokugawa shogunates. The religious dimension, in particular, was given quite close consideration. Numerous images of Buddhas, Shinto divinities, and Zen priests were marshaled to signify the ambiguous but powerful spirituality of Daimyo Japan.

Augmenting these artifacts of war and peace, the exhibition also gave detailed attention to the decorative arts, architecture, screen painting, and costumes of the Daimyo era. The mastery of medieval Japanese ceramics, lacquerware, silk weaving, and screen art all received their appropriate recognition. Most importantly in this regard, the Japanese government included three of the nation's most valued national treasures to round out the showing of Daimyo art. The paintings of Minamoto Yoritomo (1147–1199), Kanesawa Sadamasa (1302–1333), and Hojo Sanetoki (1224–1276), which hung prominently in the first rooms of the exhibition, had never left Japan before. Their inclusion, of course, was the critical sign of Japan's own perceived closeness to the United States as well as its ultimate aesthetic entreaty for greater respect in Washington as an ally and vital cultural force.

Nonetheless, the extent of Japan's new economic and technological dominance in the 1980s seeped out of every crack and crevice of this exhibition right down to its material modes of aesthetic production. Basically, in the manner of any colonized Third World country, the United States provided the physical site, cheap labor, and mass audience to stage the exhibition. Virtually everything else, save, of course, a few raw materials, came "Made in Japan." Beyond the art treasures and cultural artifacts themselves, the documentary films, air transportation, printed guides, financial backing, and elaborate catalogue were essentially all Japanese, leaving American gallery-goers to silently bob through the displays, nodding in bemusement and listening to the guest curator's, Yoshiaki Shimizu, recorded acoustiguide tour on Japanese minicassette players.

Finally, the exhibition also included brief treatments of Nō theater, the Zen aesthetic of Japanese gardens, and the art of the tea ceremony. Full-scale replicas of a Nō stage and the Ennan teahouse with a suggestion of its grounds and garden brought these aspects of Daimyo culture into three-dimensional verisimilitude. During the exhibition's run, live tea ceremonies were staged daily, and Nō theater performances were held every other day, both as vivid testimonies of performance art to lend even greater lived reality to the vital significance of this household rite and such dramatic traditions in aesthetic, spiritual, psychological, and social terms.

The subtexts were crystal-clear: a complex medieval aesthetic was reduced and recast into positive modern ethnography only to be sold as a brightly wrapped bit of bridge-building cultural insurance. The arcane ritual and obscure symbology of tea ceremonies or Nō dramas, the exhibit suggested, are the "real" core of Japanese life and values, not buying real estate, financing movie studio takeovers, or transplanting automobile factories in the United States. Thus, Japan "the economic superpower" is shown as merely a thin veneer, which has been laid over the solid core of traditional Nippon only recently, hiding "the real Japan" that still can be (or must be) ritualistic, backward, and mystical in the eyes of American audiences.

Living in a world where everyday life increasingly was being colonized by the corporate products of Toyota, Sony, Nissan, Mitsui, Honda, Toshiba, and Mitsubishi, it was apparently comforting to Americans in 1988–1989 to see the authentic signs of this "other Japan," replete with tokens from Nō theater, samurai armorers, Shinto priests, bamboo teahouses, and Buddhist temples. The Japanese recognize this reality, and they plainly seek to manage it as artfully as possible as one more province of their empire of signs. As a result, the entire run of the Daimyo show was touted weekly in the pages of the *Washington Post* with a full-page, first-section photo ad anchored by a painting of a fourteenth-century samurai warrior. This image comfortably anchored a "safe" mental picture of Japan that most Americans want to carry with them forever—colorful, exotic, anachronistic, backward, quaint, feudalistic.[7]

Public opinion polls conducted in the United States during February 1989 on the eve of Emperor Hirohito's funeral showed that 54 percent of Americans named Japan as the "strongest economic power in the world today."[8] Similarly, 40 percent felt Tokyo was a much greater threat to the United States than Moscow. While some Americans regarded Japan as a looming danger, 70 percent were still positively impressed by Japan, and 60 percent continued to see it as a very reliable American ally.[9] This approval, then, poses the question: did these aesthetic displays of Daimyo civilization represent the further solidification of a transpacific zone of Japanese-American coprosperity or did they mark another tortured gasp of a dying alliance trying to postpone its final collapse through grandiose dog-and-pony shows like this? Here art consciously was mobilized as an ideological tool to communicate many messages on different levels to many audiences. On one level, this exhibit clearly could have been one of the first, biggest, and strongest signs of a coming Japanese cultural imperialism that seemed poised in 1988 to follow the tides of Japan's entrenched financial and technological imperialism. The exhibition was fully funded by a consortium of major Japanese banks and industrial conglomerates whose clout opened the spaces of the ever-conservative and uninnovative National Gallery of Art to an essentially historical, if not anthropological, display of medieval "national treasures and art objects" from Daimyo Japanese culture. These comforting exotic images of a Japan now long gone would make it much easier to divert some attention from this approaching juggernaut. The lingering anti-Japanese spirit that the *Enola Gay* controversy sparked subsequently in 1994–1995 suggests that this effort was not entirely successful.

On another level, the exhibit also came when, contrary to rhetoric about bringing America back from dark days of military defeat and failed diplomacy in the 1970s, the United States under President Reagan was watching over, and largely approved of, this unprecedented expansion of Japanese power in the 1980s. Without Japanese investment, American macroeconomic policies would have collapsed. Without Japanese consumer goods, many American consumers would have gone wanting. Without Japanese industrial expansion in the United States, America's employment and productivity would have dropped. Without high-technology Japanese components, even America's front-line, first-generation, high-tech weapons systems would have been useless. Despite the recalcitrance of these realities, Reagan also recognized that Japan and the United States must work in both directions on a two-way street. Without American markets, Japan's economy would go into a tailspin. Without American military power, Japan's access to global resources and markets could collapse completely. And without American economic prosperity, Japan's producers and consumers would lose their first prospects for continuing economic growth. Although many Japanese saw their national economy as more innovative than America's, they also recognized that their individual enjoyment of its wealth falls far short of American standards of living.

Japan's growing power in 1989 was so pervasive that it even could induce sitting American presidents to lend their official aura or sell their personal dignity to dress up a home-islands extravaganza. When Emperor Hirohito finally died of cancer on 7 January 1989, President-elect Bush agreed almost immediately to represent the United States at Hirohito's elaborate state Shinto funeral. After the animosity that marred the early years of Hirohito's *Showa*, or Enlightened Peace, era with war, the quite recently inaugurated President Bush gladly attended the February 1989 funeral rites to start off Emperor Akihito's *Heisei*, or Achievement of Universal Peace, era on a much more positive note as well as to provide a final seal of approval of Japan's full reintegration into the world community. Bush's visit was meant to be a key sign of Washington's regard for its Tokyo ties, and Tokyo enthusiastically touted these signs with exactly this spin on their significance.

Likewise, in October 1989 former President Reagan delivered two speeches and served as master of ceremonies at the "Premium Imperiale of the Arts" in Japan for the Fujisankei Communications Group. Fronted by Charles Wick of the United States Information Agency during one of his last official visits abroad in October 1988, the deal for this appearance by the former president was signed, sealed, and delivered in February 1989 for about $2 million. Having been at one time a big-business shill for General Electric, Reagan was not new to such a well-paid gig. Again, in this trace, one could read shifting patterns of influence, prestige, and authority as the rising sun bought the Gipper without any shame on the part of either party. The Japanese could have found another podium presence, and Ronald Reagan did not "need" the money, even though this $2 million for one week's service exceeded by five times his public pay for two terms as president. For one more moment in the global limelight, this bringer of "Morning Again in America" caught the rising wave of Japan, Inc., and let himself be imported, like American lumber, copper ore, wheat, or crude oil, as yet another commodity for Japanese consumption.

"Edo: Art in Japan," 1998–1999

Exhibits like the Daimyo culture show in 1988–1989 are freeze-dried helpings of set-piece cultural understanding. Packaged and presented by their sponsors to provide the "right" picture in art and culture, they aim to further cement crucially important transnational political bonds. Everything Japan was, had become, and is today was up for appraisal in the glass cases and display rooms holding the Daimyo artifacts. And with Emperor Akihito's new era blazing new directions for Japanese power, the stage was set for considerable cultural transformation. The Daimyo exhibition staked out some of the new fault lines of shifting world hegemony in the signs of arcane medieval art and culture. Yet, in many ways, the big changes have not come to pass.

Up to 1992, an aura of the new world hegemony clung closely to Tokyo, even though Japan's stock market and economy already were sputtering in the early 1990s. The collapse during 1993 of the Liberal Democratic

Party's uninterrupted single-party rule in the National Diet ended one era of predictable prosperity and social stability.[10] What seemed like an unstoppable economic powerhouse in the 1980s has turned out in the 1990s to be one of the world's biggest bastions of crony capitalism plagued by bad bank loans, excess industrial capacity, irrational market arrangements, and shrinking national output. Threatened by strong pressures to manage exports from Washington, strategic missile tests staged by North Korea's increasingly bizarre leadership, and collapsing trade ties with its close East Asian partners, Japan during the late 1990s and early twenty-first century no longer seems poised to take away Washington's leadership in the Pacific Basin, much less in the world at large.[11] And with the worsening trade imbalances of the Asian crisis forcing many Japanese firms to undercut American producers simply to survive, Japan again is characterized as dumping cheap exports in the United States. As job loss in America continues in the wake of economic dislocations caused by the larger Asian financial crisis, the nature of Japan's culture and society again acquires a new diplomatic importance.

From the Kanobori kites looming over the entrance of "Edo: Art in Japan 1615–1868" to the cybersimulated tour at the NTT (Nippon Telegraph and Telephone) pods booted into "Virtual Edo" with their simulated city tour of Edo under the shogunate, it is quite clear that the mercantile triumphalism of a "Japan That Can Say No" in 1988–1989 slipped away to a place that is long ago and far away from the much more melancholic and traditionalistic 1998–1999 exhibit. The 1988–1989 show on Daimyo Japan plainly played out the armor and sword motif for the samurai mode of management in a very big way; so big, in fact, that Japan seemed ready to rightfully claim world hegemony in 1989 as the United States and USSR battled themselves into mutual exhaustion. The 1998–1999 show, however, deeply discounted the Bushido ethic of the Daimyo. Instead it highlighted, first, how empty and theatrical the samurai life became under the shogunate, while, second, it accentuated the alluring exotic aesthetic qualities of Edo. This interpretative shift also underscores how deeply the collapse of the bubble economy in the 1990s undercut the salaryman as samurai motif of the 1980s. Of course, the foci of "Work" and "Samurai" are not absent in this exhibition, but the less threatening themes of "Style," "Religion," "Travel and Landscape," and "Entertainment" were the real heart of the exhibition. Instead of inspiring awe and respect for its industrial might, "Edo: Art in Japan" cast the nation once ruled as the Tokugawa's realm as a fabulous assemblage of world heritage sites well worth visiting on any extended holiday.

"Edo: Art in Japan 1615–1868" was the first major exhibition of art from the Edo era itself staged anywhere in the world, including Japan.[12] The show featured more than three hundred works of art, ranging from textile arts, laquerware, and porcelains to woodblock prints, samurai armor, and painted screens. The first suite of works from the November 1998 opening was changed in mid-January 1999 with a fresh rotation of material that replaced about 80 percent of the display.[13] Refreshing the display was much more than showmanship, because of the fragility, rarity, and value of many objects, but it suggested an openness to Washington and a willingness to please from Tokyo. Indeed, the curator was able to procure forty-seven works that Japan regards as national treasures, important cultural properties, or important art objects. Many of the screens, scrolls, and kimonos cannot endure much exposure to light, and a few were simply too rare to remain on display through the final days of the exhibition. Sakai Hoitsu's screen "Spring and Autumn Maples," for example, has never gone on public display in Japan or overseas, and the six panels of the Hikone Screen, which curator Robert T. Singer regards as the "Mona Lisa" of Japanese painting, never had left Japan previously.[14]

Organized around narrative thematics instead of aesthetic schools, media, or periods, the two levels of the Edo exhibition filled several gallery and mezzanine spaces in the National Gallery's East Building. This show was the largest single display of Japanese art in the 1990s anywhere in the world. And, as curator Robert Singer observed, "The concepts behind the show make it an immense show. It was much harder to organize because of space, but it is more interesting to the viewer."[15] In addition to the colorful opening gala with festival dancers, jugglers, and the O-Edo Sukeroku Taiko drummers, a series of lectures by Singer and other Japanese art experts, who wrote pieces for the exhibit's catalogue, were staged in the days leading up to the mid-January rotation of the show's displays. Emphasizing how many national treasures and important cultural properties were included in this show, Hiroaki Fuji, president of the Japan Foundation, cast this new show, ten years after the Daimyo spectacular, as another important opportunity "for the people of the United States to become more familiar with Japanese culture and thereby deepen the friendship between our countries."[16] According to the exhibit's guest curator, no Japanese museum had ever attempted to stage a single show about Edo because of its rich vast complexity. "But it is a worthwhile project," Singer suggested, "for the West, where the image of Japan consists primarily of Edo art-woodblock prints, and paintings of sumo wrestlers, kabuki actors, women of the pleasure quarters, and famous sites in the landscape; porcelain, both blue and white, and brilliantly colored; and gold lacquer of extraordinary craftsmanship."[17] Because this was the Japan that Commodore Perry and his black ships opened to the world in 1853, Japan's image as a second-tier subordinate often is reenergized with Edo art. Still, this prevailing image could not persist unless Westerners and Japanese continued to coproduce their shared symbolic sense of Japanese culture out of this definitive era's aesthetic stock.

Blockbuster exhibitions like "Edo: Art in Japan 1615–1868" definitely display deep differences in cultural practices and values. At the same time, however, this one suggestively showed where different peoples share many cultural practices and values across the divides of time and space. While Japan remains proud of its uniqueness, the geopolitical context of 1988–1989 and the geoeconomic situation of 1998–1999 motivated many, including Japan's ambassador to the United States, to underscore how much they wanted the medieval Daimyo and early modern Tokugawa cultures of Japan "to deepen the degree of understanding among Americans of Japanese culture."[18]

Despite some doubts, many Americans in 1999 continued to believe in the necessity of close ties between Japan and the United States. Even though the Soviet Union no longer exists, continuing uncertainties in the new Russian state coupled with North Korea's unpredictability and China's growing assertiveness continue to give the historic U.S.-Japan alliance ongoing importance. While the executive leadership of the American and Japanese governments continue to tussle over trade arrangements and fiscal affairs, public opinion polls in 1996 and 1997 showed large numbers of American citizens supporting mutual defense treaties with Japan to maintain the military influence of the United States throughout the Asia-Pacific regions.[19] Just like the old imperial order in the Momoyama period before it, the salad days enjoyed by late Cold War Japan have slipped away into history. A "Japan that can say no" to its senior partner in the Pacific basin in 1989 became a "Japan that can't say no" to crony capitalism, old-style machine politics, and salaryman careerism by 1999.[20] Once again, the Edo period with the tough Tokugawa clan as Japan's lord protectors is spotlighted for answers. While it is not the best option, a measured traditionalism in the post–Cold War Japan vies for preeminence against the mean transnationalism of global markets. In this semiotic struggle, Edo can serve many purposes.

The crossroads that opened to Edo from 1853 to 1868 are not unlike the new conjunction of forces being experienced in Japan after the collapse of Liberal Democratic Party dominance in the 1990s. What had worked so well for so long under the shogunate created a bustling bourgeois economy and society. Internally, this system could no longer be contained by the old internal samurai ruling classes, but externally it also could not claim an effective dominant place on the world stage. While a system of dictatorial rule had made Edo possible, it was impossible for Japan to continue thriving in its strict national isolation and comparative structural stasis. Only new ideas and fresh implements from without in the 1860s seemed likely to provide promising paths out of this impasse. Parallels like these are never exact, but putting Edo Japan once again on display only a decade later in Washington, at the same venue as the Daimyo show of 1988–1989, pulls strongly on such cords of contrast and comparison.

Japan's relative prosperity in 1989 slipped away in the stock market crash and lingering recession of the 1990s.[21] The Liberal Democratic Party machine of the Cold War era has proven incapable of aggressively or effectively restructuring Japan's economy, civil society, or state to respond to the challenges of a Pacific century once again led by Washington rather than Tokyo. The subtle superiorities of Japanese craftsmanship in many manufacturing industries are increasingly irrelevant in the computerized, robotized, postnational mode of modular production that works out of many countries but no longer truly counts any one nation as a unique point of origin for its circuits of valorization. The new message brought by black boxes from Microsoft, Cisco Systems, or Intel, like the first sign of Admiral Perry's black ships in 1853, is that the hermetic perfection of Japan Inc., developed during the Cold War, perhaps has become baroquely irrelevant in ways that today are not unlike Edo society under the shogunate. In this hour of doubt, America might once again stand ready to guide Japan toward its future; Tokyo's and

Washington's mutual interests in the 1990s are as they were in the days of Edo. Most importantly, Japan should assume the role of a more submissive partner for the United States, because it fell behind world-class levels of economic performance in the 1990s, even though it does not lag as far as it did in the 1850s. This pattern of submission continues into the twenty-first century despite continuing tensions caused by events as varied as the *Ehime Maru* disaster off Hawaii and repeated incidents of crimes committed by American military personnel in Okinawa. After all, as *Businessweek* magazine declared in February 1999, Y2K would bring not "a Pacific century," but the return to an Atlantic century as Japan remains in political and economic eclipse.[22]

Conclusion: Culture as Coalignment

Cultural exhibits are not executive pronouncements of new diplomatic doctrines. They are instead some of the detailed tactics of productive power by which people are guided toward their understandings of how they should, or should not, coexist with other people and things in the prevailing regimes of governmentality. The reduction of Edo art to aesthetic curiosities, which are shown to inspire Vincent Van Gogh's paintings, underpin classic Westerns with samurai subtexts from the films of Akira Kurosawa, and shape porcelain manufacture through Enlightenment *chinosierie* collections, was a secure sign of American empire in 1999, because so many feared in 1989 that the empire of signs would propagate its Bushido ethic in every corner of ordinary American life during the coming decade.

While Japan may well be an empire of signs, the need to put Japan on display in the District of Columbia is a sign of another empire: an essentially American one that operates transnationally through commerce as well as coercion. Although its hegemony is always being contested, its preeminence in 1998–1999 was even more firmly fixed than it was in 1988–1989 when many still saw the USSR as something of a military rival and were thinking that Japan might challenge it as a true technological, economic, and cultural successor. So we see the politics of display at the 1988–1989 Daimyo culture show of Tokyo aggressively questioning Washington's dominant place in the world. Yet, as geopolitical events unfolded in the Communist bloc and Middle East in the years 1989–1991, and as geoeconomic trends progressed from 1989 to 1999, the display of politics in the 1998–1999 Edo art show perhaps underscored a reluctant renewal of uneasy geopolitical submission by Japan to the United States.

Because so many people continue to learn about the art, culture, and history of most other nations from museums, these sites must be considered more carefully. Museums create, circulate, and control authoritative displays that are then taken as definitive renderings of other people's history, culture, and art.[23] How value/valuelessness, identity/difference, and mastery/submission are represented in displays should not be dismissed as some small insignificance.

As centers of scholarly research, museums train both museum-visiting publics and museum-managing professionals to accept particular representational practices as the stuff of reality. Museums develop a shared sense of spatial and temporal order whose political particularity emerges and then endures, in part, because this sense is imparted at specific authoritative sites to maintain the privileges accorded to some peculiar historical chronology, cultural typology, or aesthetic methodology. As products and producers of national modernization for the state, museums can help fabricate a mass consciousness of the nation's geopolitical context and technoscientific power. From repositories of artifacts and artworks, museum-going resocializes people to test or confirm their presuppositions against artful exhibitions of material objects and spiritual subjects. At these two exhibits, however, there was very little to stretch the preexisting prejudices of America's experts or mass publics about Japan.

Museums must not be viewed as isolated enterprises. They are frontline fortifications in an unending war of position whose aesthetic/symbolic/historic expositions constantly reposition channels of power and conduits of knowledge to produce very particular types of subjects from their learning communities. Collective understandings of nationhood, national alliances, and nationalism do not fall fully formed from the sky; they must be mixed, worked, and cured again and again by capable craftspersons and willing audiences at events like these about Daimyo culture and Edo Japan. Museums should be read as ontologues whose passages and presentations reveal an important dimension of international relations that few other indicators provide. The year-by-year processes of U.S.-Japan relations have never been warm, but events like these two art shows can ease painful pressures caused by uncomfortably close ties. Blockbuster museum exhibitions are neither the root cause of everything nor the casual rustle of nothing in foreign affairs. Staging them, however, is clearly much more than a passing insignificance, and this study simply has followed some of the small streams of significance in them back to the ideological headwaters of America's contemporary global empire.

CHAPTER FIVE

Inventing the Southwest:
The Fred Harvey Company and
Native American Art

Nothing in the realm of culture and society exists naturally. Cultural form and substance need to be invented. Once invented, they must be continually cultivated, as chapters 1 and 2 show with regard to history or chapters 3 and 4 indicate with respect to culture, in ongoing efforts to refine those rhetorics of representation. In this enterprise, museums frequently assume a leading role in cultural economy as authoritative sites where such systems of meaning, value, and identity are, first, invented and, second, contested after their presentation by other social forces seeking to appropriate the cultural forms and materiel that museums accumulate and mobilize for their own economic or political purposes. This dynamic can be seen at work many places, but I believe the multicultural complexities of the American Southwest provide many unusual instances of these interpretative struggles. An exhibition in 1995 at the Heard Museum in Phoenix, Arizona, titled "Inventing the Southwest: The Fred Harvey Company and Native American Art," provides a vivid case study of how one museum's founders and operations have collaborated with local social forces to invent the form and substance of Arizona's cultural economy.[1]

Like most human institutions, the Heard Museum is packed full of contradictions and inconsistencies. On one level, the Heard Museum is a valuable and vital ethnological resource for the entire nation. It was one of the first museums in America devoted exclusively to what are now classified as "Native American" culture and art. Its collections are a significant cultural repository for works from many Southwestern Native American cultures, and it has done a great deal to support individual Native American artists and craftspersons for several generations.

Yet, on another level, it also is a quite localistic, and even parochial, institution, which has operated in various ways since 1929 as a high-visibility cultural screen to help invent a mystique of "the American Southwest" that Phoenix has, in turn, exploited continuously as an economic development tool. The travel guidebook *Fodor's Arizona '95*, for example, beckoned tourists with a very positive blurb on the Heard Museum, asserting that it has become "the nation's leading museum of Native American art and culture."[2] Moreover, the Heard offers not just a stultifying, highbrow museum experience; instead, it has something for everyone: "modern Native American arts, interactive art-making exhibits for the children, and live demonstrations by artisans are always at hand."[3] Similarly, *Frommer's Arizona '95* informed would-be visitors to the state: "considered one of the finest museums in the country that deals exclusively with Native American cultures, the Heard Museum should be among your first stops in Arizona."[4] Indeed, *Frommer's* continues to spotlight the Heard Museum as one of the top attractions in Phoenix—a must-see site even if one has only one day in the city. With nearly seven million passengers passing through Phoenix's Sky Harbor airport annually, and millions more driving through Arizona over its interstate highways, this sort of cultural guidance about the Heard Museum pays off every day for Phoenix and Arizona in heavy tourist traffic.

And, on a third level, while this museum certainly has aided some Native American artisans, it also has promoted theatricalized rhetorics in representing the Southwest's Native American cultures, which mostly serve the material interests of Anglo-American landowners, building contractors, or commercial developers, even though these rhetorics elaborate cultural codes that are mystifying, inadequate, and problematic. As *Valley Guide Quarterly* suggests, the Heard's "internationally famous collection of artifacts and art from Southwest Native American tribes" as well as its "numerous festivals, performances, and workshops" are a major attractor of new visitors and residents to the Valley of Sun.[5] Phoenix is "a place where," as one Valley megadeveloper claims, "you can retreat to casual Southwest living at its finest. Come experience the expansive parks, lush trails and world class golf, and see life from a different view. Homes from the $130s to over $500,000."[6]

The Heard Museum

"Inventing the Southwest: The Fred Harvey Company and Native American Art" examines how the partnership of the Santa Fe Railway and the Fred Harvey Company, with its hotels, restaurants, and shops, first mobilized these routines of representation as they created "the Southwest" and "Native American art" out of the daily routines of a mass-tourism industry. By showing how travel to the Grand Canyon, New Mexico, or southern California by train led to packaging the Southwest as a leisure-time destination, as well as defining many destinations in the Southwest with leisure characteristics once travelers arrived, the exhibition chronicles how the cultural economy of Southwestern tours developed over the years from 1896 through the mid-1960s when rail travel mostly died out. Yet, by providing the venue for this display, the Heard Museum oddly erases any trace of itself from the elaborate historical records documenting these events as if it had not been, or is not, somehow integrally involved within them.

Like many museums, the Heard Museum evolved out of a small curiosity cabinet in the home of a rich patron. In this case, however, the small curiosity cabinet in the house of Dwight B. and Maie Bartlett Heard became so immense that it engulfed their family dwelling and eventually grew large enough to merit its own museum building.[7] Dwight B. Heard moved to Chicago from his native New England in the 1890s and began working for a major hardware supplier, Hibbard, Spencer, and Bartlett (the original precursor of the present-day True Value hardware chain). He soon became a protégé of Adolphus Bartlett and wed his daughter, Maie Bartlett, in 1893 in an elaborate high-society wedding. A lung ailment forced him to seek a dryer, warmer climate, and the Heards moved to Phoenix in 1895. Not much more than a small farming community of 4,000 in the Salt River Valley, Phoenix had just been made Arizona's territorial capital in 1889.[8] The Heards founded the Bartlett-Heard Land and Cattle Company soon after their arrival, and began raising cattle, alfalfa, citrus, and cotton on the land around their first house, "Buena Ranche." Hard work, adequate capitalization, and being in the right place at the right time helped their company grow quickly into one of the largest landowners in the area. Indeed, Dwight Heard was a critical force behind the development of the Salt River Valley Water Users Association and the building of Roosevelt Dam in the Tonto Basin—the first

major federally supported western water project from the 1902 Recla-
mation Act. As the head of the Arizona Cotton Growers' Association, he
moved the state into global markets as a major cotton-growing center.
With his considerable financial assets and personal acquaintance with
national political figures like Theodore Roosevelt, Dwight Heard also became quite active in local Republican party and Arizona state politics.[9]

As transplants from Chicago, Dwight and Maie Heard traveled extensively on the railroads, especially the Santa Fe Railroad, to get to and
from Arizona during trips back east. Somewhat serendipitously in 1896,
the Santa Fe Railroad chose to promote tourist travel to the Grand Canyon
and to clean up its corporate image with elaborate advertising campaigns
devoted to popularizing "the heritage of America, the wilderness, and
the Indians."[10] Commissioning painters and photographers to travel
through the Southwest to produce asserting images of its beauties for
mass reproduction as corporate advertising, the Santa Fe also appropri-
ated the American Indian as one of its key symbols. The Santa Fe Railroad's Indian symbol purposely was designed so that it "possessed an
aura of glamour. An intangibility. An ineffable essence. The idea was to
present a radiant image of Indian life. The Santa Fe Indian represented
a prototype of preindustrial society. Simplicity. Freedom. Nobility. This
was the life and culture that inhabited the Santa Fe's 'friendly' oasis of
the desert Southwest."[11]

Ironically, this advertising campaign "worked" inasmuch as millions
of Americans soon were caught up in the region's mystique, including
apparently the Heards, as they traveled along the Santa Fe railways from
the 1890s to the 1920s. Making this observation is not to say the Heard
Museum is a mouthpiece for one railroad company. Instead it marks an
intriguing elective affinity: two newly arrived settlers from Chicago in
Phoenix start to appreciate the cultural heritage of Arizona's Native
Americans in terms not unlike those mechanically reproduced in the
tourism discourses of Santa Fe Railroad advertising. And, in turn, they
begin to fill their home with Indian arts and crafts purchased in Fred
Harvey shops during their train trips with the Santa Fe Railroad.

During 1903, as part of their vocation for real estate development,
the Heards launched the development of an exclusive subdivision, "Los
Olivos," on 160 acres along Central Avenue north of McDowell Road in
what is now central Phoenix. Their new house, "Casa Blanca," on Monte
Vista Road, anchored the development, which soon became one of the

most desired neighborhoods for Phoenix's social elite. Casa Blanca became as well known among this same elite as a display center for arts
and crafts objects collected by the Heards from Arizona's Native American peoples as well as cultures in Latin America, Africa, and the Pacific.
The Heards assembled such an extensive collection of Southwestern Indian baskets, jewelry, pottery, textiles, and other artifacts in their new
home that they soon were overwhelmed by this hoard of art objects.
Their daughter-in-law, Winifred Heard, encouraged them during the
1920s to consolidate the family collections in a formal museum. The
Heards began constructing a Spanish Colonial Revival–style building
that was completed in 1928. As the display cabinets and other fixtures
were being installed, however, Dwight Heard died unexpectedly on 14
March 1929. His wife and son carried on with the project, securing formal incorporation for the Heard Museum on 18 June 1929.

Maie Heard truly was the force behind the museum's founding and
early operations. Much of what the Heards collected was chosen by
Mrs. Heard; and, in the museum's first years, "visitors to the museum
would first ring the door bell at Casa Blanca. Mrs. Heard would answer
and take the visitors over to the museum, unlock the gate and give them
a tour."[12] In addition to her extensive philanthropic work for many organizations in Phoenix, Maie Heard continued expanding the institution's collections until she died on 14 March 1951.[13] Later the Heards'
son acknowledged how much the Heard Museum had become a significant cultural resource for the entire city of Phoenix by reorganizing it as
an independent nonprofit institution, administered by volunteers and a
board of trustees drawn from the Phoenix area.

The Heard Museum still occupies its original building, although it
has been expanded and modernized considerably since 1929. With a
sizeable plot of land from their Casa Blanca estate deeded to it by the
Heards, the museum just opened another 43,000-square-foot addition
on these grounds to enlarge its library, archives, gift shop, and display
areas as well as to add new classrooms, a four-hundred-seat auditorium,
and a food-service area. By 1951, when Maie Heard died, the Heard Museum had more than 3,000 objects in its collection, but this already re-
spectable inventory has increased more than ten times through 1998 as
new galleries and storage areas were opened in 1999 to hold 32,000 objects. Visitors today enter the museum's heavily stylized building through
a long courtyard complete with desert trees, an elaborate fountain, black

wrought-iron fittings, and spindle-barred windows, which all orchestrate an air of fantastic exoticism for the facility. The fact that permanent colonial Spanish settlement never took hold in the Phoenix area is, of course, irrelevant. Like the romanticization of Spanish California in San Diego's and San Francisco's twin 1915 Pacific expositions, the facility's Spanish-style features "look" like they belong there; hence, in the classic Arizona land development logics pioneered, in part, by the Heards, they must be there to anchor the myth. The Heard Museum's prime directive can be found on the museum building's dedication plaque in the original courtyard. Dwight and Maie Heard saw the mission of their museum as being quite simple: "to preserve the cultural heritage of those who have so enriched our lives." Ironically, this somewhat bland dictum clearly has had more than one meaning in the institution's history.

Representing the Southwest

While the Heard Museum stops short of exploring its own complicated role in reproducing ideological codes in Arizona since the 1920s, the "Inventing the Southwest" show at the museum does begin to examine a few of the earliest sources of "the Southwest" as a thoroughly stylized fantasy suitable for sale as a tourist commodity. Most importantly, it reconsiders how the Santa Fe Railway and the Fred Harvey Company sought to offer "travelers a swift, safe, comfortable journey West—with a touch of adventure" by mobilizing potential travelers with Indian imagery wrapped within "sophisticated marketing techniques to advertise the exotic and romantic Southwest."[14] Organized at the Heard with financial support from the National Endowment for the Humanities, the Santa Fe Railway, the Lila Wallace–Reader's Digest Fund, and the Flinn Foundation, this show reveals how the contact of Native American peoples with modern corporate enterprise generated a series of industrial capitalist myths. To substantiate these myths, the Native American cultures' personal property and household implements—jewelry, blankets, pottery, baskets, and spiritual icons—became commodified as "curios" or "souvenirs." To affirm these myths, Santa Fe and Fred Harvey transported, housed, fed, entertained, and guided thousands of leisure travelers a week from the cities of industrial America out into the open expanses of California, Arizona, New Mexico, Colorado, and Kansas.

From the main office in Kansas City, the Fred Harvey Company's Indian Department created a huge demand for Indian artifacts by siting small museums for artists' demonstrations and sales rooms in its hotels, many of which were designed by the Fred Harvey Company's architect, Mary Colter.[15] First, Fred Harvey Company "anthropologists," like Herman Schweizer and J. F. Huckel, bought thousands of artifacts in bulk, and then encouraged Indian producers to make new ones to satisfy the insatiable demand they were creating for such goods among tourists, private collectors, and museums.[16] Soon Indian artifacts, once made for home use or tribal rituals, were reimagined for store sales or corporate retail outlets. Handwoven textiles once worn as clothing became Navajo blankets; household pottery was made smaller, lighter, more refined; massive silver jewelry once used to display wealth became more delicate, less heavy, more ornate; baskets were made more decoratively and much smaller—all of these changes responded to what tourists fancied, could carry, would put on their fireplace mantels back home. Riding on the crest of the Arts and Crafts Movement in Europe and North America, turn-of-the-century Native Americans collaborated wholeheartedly in the commodification of their cultures just as the last of them were being successfully pacified by the U.S. Cavalry and Bureau of Indian Affairs. As Huckel asserted, "Fred Harvey has done more for all the Indian tribes in the Southwest than thousands of people who have written books, people in Congress, humanitarian committees, etc., because we have created a market for their goods."[17] Nonetheless, it is a market mostly for goods as tourist outlets defined them to suit their buyers' desires.

At the Alvarado Hotel in Albuquerque, the Hopi House at the Grand Canyon, La Fonda Hotel in Santa Fe, and El Ortiz Hotel in Lamy, New Mexico, the Fred Harvey Company adapted display conventions from the World's Fair at St. Louis in 1904. At these sites, it could exhibit simulations of Native American dwellings, build demonstration stages for cultural reenactments, and organize display spaces for artifacts all integrated into sales rooms in which the Southwestern myth was sold as part and parcel of dance performances, rug-weaving displays, and Indian jewelry vending. They worked so well that the Santa Fe Railway financed extensive presentations by the Fred Harvey Company of Native American peoples and crafts at both the 1915 San Diego Panama-California Exposition and San Francisco Panama-Pacific International Exposition. From La Fonda and El Ortiz, tourists would depart on "Indian Detours" through rural New Mexico in automobile caravans. Guided by young, college-educated Anglo women in ten-gallon hats, Navajo jewelry, and velvet blouses, travelers visited Indian pueblos, Hispanic villages, and prehistoric ruins before returning to their Harvey House hotels and Harvey Girl restaurants on the rail lines. Dwight and Maie Heard were first exposed to collecting Indian artwork at these Fred Harvey outlets, and in reproducing the same representational approaches at their museum, they paid tribute to the Harvey projects' rhetorical power as cultural performances.

The core of the Heard Museum's fixed displays today, for example, is a "museum exhibition," "Native Peoples of the Southwest: The Permanent Collection of the Heard Museum," which is, as the gallery guide indicates, an exhibition of "Southwestern Native American artifacts: kachina dolls, pottery, baskets and jewelry."[18] In one sense, all of these objects are ethnological artifacts, but in another sense they also are one of the key subsets of all valuable cultural signs that the Anglo-American community of Arizona—beginning with Fred Harvey, Herman Schweizer, J. F. Huckel, and the Heards—has valorized as prestigious "art objects" in its formal discourses and local markets. The exhibition of the artifacts, however, contextualizes these reserves of cultural currency and their native producers "environmentally" in three ecological zones to illustrate the respective Native American cultures' adaptations to their natural environments: the Sonoran Desert, the Uplands of the Mogollon Rim Country, and the Colorado River Plateau. In turn, the displays attempt to illustrate how these artifacts fit into the everyday economies of the people who produced them.

Although this natural/historical narrative credibly locates these Indian cultures in terms of Arizona's geographical space, the narration in the display fixes its gaze upon the Native American peoples in very indistinct temporal historic terms borrowed essentially from the leisure industry anthropologists of Fred Harvey Company and the Santa Fe Railroad. For the most part, the view is highly ahistorical, focusing on Native American cultures before or beyond their contact with European invaders in order to freeze their cultural economies in the forms of an ideal type. Yet these pre-encounter views of Native Americans are supplemented by photographs of contemporary individuals—wearing traditional costumes, making traditional foods, building traditional dwellings, or constructing traditional art objects.[19] The tone is celebratory, but at the same time these genres of interpretation are an ensemble of moves that permanently collect the peoples of the Southwest in the discursive net of "native-ness," which sustains ironically the themes and tropes from a Fred Harvey imaginary of the Santa Fe Indian. To generate the iconic grounding of an idealized present of Arizona's growth and prosperity, there needed to be this idealized past/otherness of permanence and security. Today's Native Americans are reimagined, then, as they have been continuously since Remington's and Russell's conventionalization of these representational codes during the 1890s, as unsullied reflections of noble savages living and working in harmony with nature— a maneuver also deeply embedded within the Santa Fe Railroad's representation of its *art moderne* locomotives as "Super Chiefs" in its corporate logos.

Native American Art Now

In addition to these longstanding efforts at sustaining the mythos of the Southwest by freezing most of its Indian cultures in ahistorical time and space, the Heard Museum's involvement with many Native American cultures more recently has moved away from the Fred Harvey/Santa Fe Indian ensemble: defining Native American culture through "fine art." While a remarkably ethnocentric system for defining cultural production mistakenly keeps most Native American artwork on the "decorative arts" or "crafts" side of many aesthetic categories, like rugs or kachina dolls, other works that fit easily into the "fine arts" slot have been produced by Native Americans for decades.[20] Following the lead once set by the Philbrook Art Center in Tulsa, Oklahoma, as a venue for American Indian painting and sculpture, the Heard Museum has started using some of its other spaces quite differently. Most significantly, it has organized an important biennial Native American fine arts invitational exhibition to encourage and document works from the Native American Fine Arts Movement, which has mixed the styles and methods of mainstream Anglo-American art practices with images and themes from Native American arts to continue introducing "the art community and the general public to artists with great potential."[21]

Beyond these recent efforts to serve as an institutional sponsor for some Native Americans' production of fine art pieces, the Heard Museum continues to operate quite conservatively as the local patron of those indigenous peoples who have so enriched the lives of everyone living in Phoenix. Most directly, its displays of Native American cultures and art anchor the cultural categories needed by non–Native Americans for understanding Indian ways in a fashion that benefits them rather than Native Americans. Its representational idioms, despite recent countermoves by some Native American employees, essentially still visualize Native American peoples as exotic beings, producing all of those crafts that serve as identity-generators for the city of Phoenix with its Southwestern lifestyle as well as journey-markers for all those outside visitors eager to return home with some tangible sign of their Southwest visitations. By framing culture in terms of such decorative art objects, the museum also serves to valorize the collection, accumulation, circulation of ethnic objets d'art that might otherwise be ignored.

These moves, in turn, stabilize the otherness of Native Americans, fixing them mostly as curio makers, rooted to the forms and figures of a time before their initial contact with Hispanic or Anglo cultures. The contemporary culture of many Native Americans, which is tied increasingly in Arizona to running huge casinos and resorts, working off the reservation for railroads and mines, or subsisting in small back-country settlements on some government dole, is virtually ignored except, of course, in the angst-ridden themes of occasional "high art" objects shown in the Fine Arts Invitationals.[22] Yet these products often are not remarkable; most of them are either "fine art" extensions of traditional Indian tropes or "fine art" emulations of foreign art practices of Anglo-American artists, who went to the same university art schools.[23] Thus the Heard Museum mainly sticks with tried-and-true representational forms begun long ago by the Santa Fe Railroad and Fred Harvey Company.

For example, the museum's fascination with the Hohokam (the people that inhabited the Salt and Gila River basins for centuries until their culture collapsed around 1400 A.D. just prior to European settlement of the Americas), reinventing them as pre-Columbian irrigation engineers, desert agriculturalists, or city builders, helps to naturalize the fast capitalist projects of rapid growth in modern Arizona, especially those first undertaken by Dwight and Maie Heard. A clear environmental determinism driven by water use is projected as an ecological imperative for whoever occupies the Valley of the Sun. What the Heards and others have done in Phoenix since the 1890s merely continues a timeless natural necessity that would hold true for any human being choosing to live on these lands. The Hohokam provide an indigenous old way both to legitimize and to mystify the transformation of Maricopa County and the state of Arizona by private capital and public power. Without water, as Dwight Heard realized, Phoenix could not grow. Thanks to his politicking inside and outside the state, Phoenix grew, with the help of federal water projects, from a village of 4,000 in 1895 into a huge metroplex with nearly 2.3 million people, covering more than one thousand square miles in 1995.[24] The land development industry of post–World War II Arizona, then, truly draws much of its energy from the enriching cultural heritage of the Native American peoples in Arizona. As the Heard Museum documents, their "primitive economy" anticipates the present-day era, only at a lower level of technological capability, although their sophisticated arts and crafts can still beautify contemporary Arizona with images and objects of tremendous mystery. Their languages create auras of utopian exoticism in place names and space titles. And their enduring presence as decorative artisans still enlivens everyday life with spectacles of alien being to the delight of residents and travelers alike.

Native American arts and crafts have been commodities since the Anglo and Hispanic cultures first made contact with Arizona's native tribes—a truth that "Inventing the Southwest" both exposes and recharges in its many displays. Still, this institution's operational shift from a private family hoard into a public museum site also has greatly helped to rationalize and popularize the commodification of these arts. Not only are they beautiful, not only are they made of precious materials, not only are they works of rare skill as any white trader at a reservation trading post might claim, but they also are worthy of acquisition by a museum that continually produces new disquisitions in its own formal exhibitions about the skill, value, and beauty they evince. In this vein, the Heard Museum also sponsors the Guild Indian Fair and Market on the first weekend in March. Featuring a prestigious juried show of Native American art and craftwork, the show brings local residents and out-of-state visitors together to see Native American cultural displays as well as to assist all of those would-be Dwight and Maie Heards in making new acquisitions for their collections today.

This complementarity between the museum and marketing continues into the twenty-first century. At el Pedregal in far north Scottsdale, which bills itself as the "Festival Marketplace at The Boulders: A Shopping Experience of Galleries, Boutiques, Apparel, Artisan Crafted Gifts, Restaurants and Cafes...," the trustees and curators of the Heard Museum opened the doors of "the new Heard Museum Extension" as its permanent second site on 13 January 1996.[25] Affluent snowbirds from "back east," vacationing at the ritzy Boulders Resort, now need not motor all the way downtown into Phoenix's increasingly seedy and mostly high-rise Central Avenue corridor. Imagining that one can become immersed in the romantic aura of the Southwestern desert is virtually impossible now at the Heard Museum as the high-rise corporate headquarters of major national corporations tower over what was once Dwight and Maie Heard's rancho on Monte Vista Road.

Like many of the Fred Harvey Company's Harvey House hotels, the "Desert Shopping Destination" at el Pedregal is a timber and stucco fantasia. It artfully blends elements of a quasi-Moroccan frontier fort with a semi-Taos pueblo in "Southwest style" purples, pinks, and blues set amidst the boulder-strewn foothills of Carefree and Scottsdale, Arizona.[26] Here thirty miles north of Phoenix's inner city, the el Pedregal shopping mall reproduces Fred Harvey's original designs for locating a "museum" inside of a business establishment by allowing the prestigious Heard operation to extend itself as the Heard Museum North at this high-end shopping venue. What the exhibitions at the Heard Museum North legitimize as valuable artwork can, in turn, be purchased at this desert shopping destination's many galleries and boutiques so tastefully tucked away on the various levels of this simulated Southwestern adobe pueblo. Should those outlets seem too tawdry, then "at the Heard Museum North is a shop featuring only the finest in authentic Native American art—hand-made baskets and pottery, beautifully woven textiles, exquisite jewelry, kachina dolls and a selection of fine art."[27] And, like the Heards at the museum's downtown Phoenix site, the Heard Museum North is backed by another bloc of real estate developers from the Scottsdale and Carefree areas surrounding the el Pedregal complex, including the Boulders Resort, Del Webb Company, Giant Industries, Inc., and Mr. and Mrs. Russ Lyon Jr., as founding benefactors.

By showing how other social forces, like the Fred Harvey Company or the Santa Fe Railroad, worked to "invent the Southwest," the Heard Museum ironically evades its own implication in these processes of cultural reproduction by suggesting that it was other commercial agents and industrial interests who created and sustained these myths long ago. This fact is painfully obvious every day at the Heard Museum's shop and bookstore where—in the tradition of a Harvey House hotel's "museum" in the 1920s—almost as much floorspace (and even more theater) is assigned to the sale of Native American artifacts as is to displaying them as educational experiences inside the museum itself. What you see in the Heard Museum, you can buy in the museum shop. This organic connection is openly celebrated by *Frommer's Arizona '95*, which observes that the Heard Museum "sells the finest selection of Southwest Native American arts and crafts in the valley—both traditional and modern—at its gift shop."[28] And for those neophytes needing some instruction in the basics of Native American art, Frommer's assures visitors that "the museum is the ideal place for learning about whatever medium or art form interests you and to see Native American artists and artisans at work almost everyday."[29]

Unlike American or European art museums where the operational divide between artwork and art reproduction is clear, then, the Heard Museum sells artworks at all price points in its shop spaces, works that often are essentially identical to those it displays in its exhibit spaces. Of course, ordinary bric-a-brac, ranging from coffee mugs, T-shirts, and key rings to maps of Phoenix, cookbooks, and cowboy hats also are available here, but the key displays vend jewelry, rugs, baskets, pottery, and paintings as lovely as any found inside the museum to tourists and locals now rightly informed about how to make wise investments in Native American arts after a Heard Museum visit. At the Heard Museum North, the display space is not much larger in size than the shop spaces, leading visitors in the gallery to ask, "Is this stuff for sale?" and patrons in the shop to ask, "Is this stuff only on display?"

Southwestern (Re)Inventions

To whom, then, and for whom is the Heard Museum representing Native peoples in exhibitions like "Inventing the Southwest"? The words of the museum's prime directive again may give some guidance. It does preserve a cultural heritage received from those Native Americans who have so enriched new migrants, like the Heards and thousands of other Anglo-Americans, by motivating millions to travel to Arizona. Millions of non-native people have been moving to Arizona for more than a century, and many of them came first to behold the mysterious cultures of Native American peoples. Hence, it is to these outsiders that the Heard Museum is, in part, representing these Indian tribes, and, in part, for those who have mobilized and profited from these mass migrations of people. The beauty of Native American cultures drew and kept people in Arizona, and the Heards among many others were enriched significantly from drawing, housing, and provisioning those who stayed in the Valley of the Sun. Once there, European Americans, Asian Americans, Hispanic Americans, African Americans did not go native; instead, they bought lots of land, thousands of homes, and tons of agricultural produce from local developers/agriculturalists/ranchers, like the Heards. And they also began buying into the national advertising images of Native American peoples first launched by the Santa Fe Indian and then repackaged along with jewelry, pots, and rugs at local curio shops, only to be ratified later by the institutionalized approval of the Heard Museum.

In many ways, the "Inventing the Southwest" exhibition about the Santa Fe Railroad and Fred Harvey Company celebrates each of these phases in the evolution of the Southwestern mystique from the 1890s through the 1960s, when the last of the Harvey House hotels were closed. The Heard Museum memorializes the influence of the Fred Harvey Company by pointing to a diverse array of cultural legacies at work today in theme parks, Indian markets, and municipally sponsored art festivals (where Anglo-American artists now also can produce "authentic Indian jewelry" and African American painters might romanticize the ahistoric era of Native American culture). Yet, the Heard Museum dodges any exhaustive examination of its own extensive role in continuing, and even enhancing, the past ideological practices of the Santa Fe Railway and Fred Harvey Company in present-day performances through the museum's exhibits.

On one level, the Heard Museum continues the Harvey formula in an era of automobile- and jet-based individual travel, one in which *Fodor's* or *Frommer's* suggests where tourists must visit, rather than tourists having to stay in one spot near a railway line by an alliance of Fred Harvey and Santa Fe.[30] On another level, whereas Indian artisans once judged the quality of their work by the quantity that sold in Indian markets, today one finds the permanent displays and invitational shows staged by museums, like the Heard Museum in particular, providing professional juries to vet the quality of Indian artisanship. Of course, the measure of the market still counts, but the prices that artisans can command rises significantly with formal museum exposure and recognition. So, on a third level, the Heard Museum revalorizes the Southwest as an exotic/romantic/mysterious site by revisiting the Harvey House era in such nostalgic terms. For many, Phoenix itself is an el Pedregal tourist mall on a metropolitan scale—a "desert-shopping destination" with galleries, boutiques, restaurants, and hotels featuring golf courses, swimming pools, craftworked gifts, and exotic art. Paralleling how Native American cultures go "from ritual to retail" with their artifacts, the Heard Museum makes the link "from museum to market" that valorizes artworks as assets inasmuch as they can appear as exemplary artifacts on display so that they may also become precious curios for sale. One can take the commercialized artifacts out of the Indian desert, but we will never be able to take the desert of commerce out of the Indian artifacts.

The oddest quality of the Heard Museum is how thoroughly the state-sponsored violence resting at the center of today's Native American culture, or the brutal holocaust that befell the Americas after 1492, is virtually ignored. Unlike "The West as America" show, or even the Gene Autry Museum of the Western Heritage discussed in chapter 1, the "cowboy" operator of the infamous "Cowboys and Indians" equation is simply null and void. Instead of openly examining the reservation gulags that still contain most Native American tribes, where the survivors of this holocaust cope with indirect rule from European American society by building casinos, siting waste dumps, accepting strip mines, or selling religious spectacles mostly for the profit of non-Indians, the Heard offers only reinvented, inspiring visions of traditional ways. In this way, the museum mainly is a kind of "preholocaust museum," displaying fragmented survivals of ethnic values prevailing before Europeans ethnically cleansed North America of its native inhabitants. Moreover, the European influence on contemporary Native American practices is shown as being enriching, not annihilating. It brings better dyes to Navajo rug weavers, silver to Zuni jewelry makers, better kilns to Acoma potters, new designs to Yuman basket weavers. As the Heard Museum shows them, Native Americans are still Santa Fe Indians: essential for inventing today's Southwest as markers of primitive simplicity, exotic nobility, or wild freedom. They are the same/near/now as the rest of the United States, but they also anchor a hyperreal otherness that can be imagined as different/there/then to recharge the Southwestern mystique.

The "Native peoples of the Southwest" at the Heard Museum are not all human beings who have been born and raised as "natives" of this place: its indigenous white and black populations as well as Asian and Hispanic peoples all are erased in these narratives. The "true" native is from American Indian tribes chosen for aesthetic intensification by the museum's displays, particularly those with already existing image archives, like the Hopis, Navajos, or Zunis. Which Native American peoples, then, becomes an interesting question still defined by the Heard's prime directive. Those peoples who produced enough pottery, baskets, rugs, jewelry, or other arts to become commodified by the settler economy as "a cultural heritage" that, in turn, helped enrich the lives of the Heards and other local developers became "those" Native peoples worthy of museumic representations.

Indeed, a Native American people's profile at the museum seems to be a direct coefficient of their success at commodifying material culture: this factor for Navajos and Hopis (with many kachinas, rugs, pottery, baskets, jewelry, and studio artwork) is quite high, while for Mohaves and Cocopahs (with only a few pots and baskets) it is rather low. Moreover, there is a peculiar time-bias built into these categories at the Heard Museum in that "which" Native American peoples being displayed tends to be those living before the intrusion of wage labor into Indian economies or those who still escape wage work today. The Santa Fe Railroad tropes of simplicity, nobility, freedom still ring true. Thus, the Native American peoples of the Southwest who are now off the reservation, and in the cities and towns living among their Anglo, black, Asian, or Hispanic neighbors, also are ignored.

Consequently, the Heard Museum is quite selective about how Native American peoples are represented. On one level, its images of Native American peoples could be seen as being honestly presented in this way "to other Native American peoples" and "for Native American peoples." Clearly, the corrosive effects of cultural conformity in Arizona are rapidly eviscerating many of the old ways among younger Native Americans. To sustain the specificity of Indian life, something must be done to valorize the unique values and ideas embedded in their ways. And, to some extent, the Heard Museum is promoting some vital preservationist programs in reproducing these disappearing cultural practices. Yet, on another level, the fact that these cultures need a European American museum to aid in their reproduction is profoundly disturbing. It parallels closely the efforts of zoos trying to preserve a few remaining California condors or botanical gardens struggling to keep small patches of native environments unmarred by outside forces. If such museums are needed to keep a culture alive and treasured, then it most likely is already dying, or even dead, for many of its members. To slightly broaden this dangerous arts and crafts bent in its past displays, the expansion spaces added in 1999 now feature an exhibit titled "More Than Art." This display suggests that art is only the most visible part of Native American culture, which also embraces learning, patience, memory, family, song, stories, and prayers. In turn, the museum devotes a display case or two to indicate how its activities, as a major cultural institution, help individual Native American artists and specific peoples realize these themes in their artwork and communal activity.

Few cultural institutions simply advance one purpose; and in hosting this show on Santa Fe Railroad and the Fred Harvey Company, the Heard Museum proves that it is no exception to this rule. Nonetheless, it also illustrates how the Heard operates very effectively as a screen of power suitable for simultaneously putting certain things on view, while shielding many other things from view.[31] On the one hand, its displays have become a normative field on which self-affirming images of Native American people are projected, creating definitive categories for classifying and judging the cultural heritage of Arizona's Indian cultures. Here Native American peoples acquire an aesthetic, well-adjusted, satisfied image as tradition keepers and curio makers intent on fitting seamlessly into Arizona's mainstream society. All of the images captured from film and television about Indian life can be replayed at the Heard Museum, revalorizing these exotic qualities and mysterious features. At the same time, the museumification of Native American peoples' material culture disembeds artifacts from their own cycles of organic use-value within indigenous religion, family life, dress, culinary practices, shelter, or status hierarchies to circulate them within market-centered art exchanges off the reservation.

On the other hand, the museum as a screen of power capable of carrying normative images positively on itself also coexists with more negative ideological deployments as a screen for power, obscuring other things from view. Native American peoples—as most of them live much of the time in the Southwest today—are rendered invisible by the Heard Museum's operations. The repressive peculiarities of modern reservation society as an abject site of underdevelopment, exploitation, or detainment does not fit into the Heards' vision of "our cultural heritage," even though such sites also have enriched the lives of Anglo-Americans inasmuch as non-Indian Arizonans expropriated land and resources from Arizona's Indians via war, unequal exchange, or bureaucratic legerdemain.[32] Instead of showing how most reservation families now live miserable material lives in Third World poverty, the museum recasts itself as a special contemporary kind of Harvey House, positioning Indian life in the aura of tourist spectacles and railroading the values of Indian artifacts in specialized Santa Fe–styled art markets.

Native American peoples here in "the invented Southwest," at the end of the day, remain the latest, most sophisticated version of those popular natives invented by the Fred Harvey Company's "Indian Detours" or the Santa Fe Railroad's "Super Chief" advertising: the Hopi kachina dancer, the Zuni silversmith, the Navajo rug weavers, the Apache basket maker.[33] They are exotic fictions captured by the tourist gaze that seeks pure natural subjects creating primitive artifacts. And in these tourist forms, Native Americans continue to be those who can enrich the lives of all those outsiders who ever will either visit or set up shop in Phoenix, Arizona, or the Great Southwest.

CHAPTER SIX

Museum Pieces:
Politics and Knowledge at the
American Museum of Natural History

Giving some knowable, stabilized qualities to everyday existence requires things to be pieced apart, albeit in some clearly aesthetic manner, so that the play of power through discourses of knowing might piece those parts together again. This often grants us some fixity in our reality's givenness. Clearly, this can be seen as a hyperreal time, as chapters 3 and 5 assert, when models precede meaning or maps come before terrains, as chapters 1, 2, and 4 also illustrate. Museums function as vitally important modeling agencies or mapping centers that meld ontological meanings with cultural terrains. I want to suggest that if there is one museum on the North American continent that might singularly represent all of these activities, it is the American Museum of Natural History in New York City.

The American Museum has done much over the past 125 years to define and popularize the character of humanity's place in nature for all Americans. From its early days as a material beneficiary of New York's Gilded Age philanthropists to its current activities as an erstwhile defender of global biodiversity, this private scientific institution has been a central site for giving modern Americans their understanding of nature, history, museums, and even America itself since it first opened its doors to the public on Central Park West in 1877. In many ways, the American Museum of Natural History is the most well-known and highly regarded museum in the United States. Other municipal museums in Boston, Charleston, and Philadelphia are older; Chicago's Field Museum is nearly as impressive and innovative; the Smithsonian's many museums contain larger collections; but the American Museum of Natural History sits in New York, and many of its collections were gathered in wide-ranging, freebooting *Indiana Jones*–style expeditions that the city's media have celebrated for decades. Consequently, *Webster's Unabridged College Dictionary* uses the American Museum of Natural History, along with the British Museum in London, to exemplify its authoritative definitions of the word *museum*. As the noted biologist Edward O. Wilson observes, "The American Museum of Natural History: This is a museum that has thought big about the world."[1]

Because so many tangible pieces of the world—dinosaur bones, elephants, totem poles, whales, huge meteorites—are assembled here as the foundational pieces for many people's sense of the world's fundamental reality, the displays and storerooms of the American Museum or Natural History give us one of the world's best venues to reconsider the aesthetic politics of knowledge at museums. Therefore, I believe this chapter can be taken as "nothing more than a rewriting" or "a regulated transformation of what has already been written . . . it is the systematic description of a discourse-object,"[2] or, namely, the American Museum of Natural History. This rewriting of this discourse-object will trace how its displays produce power.

Reconsidering the politics, aesthetics, and epistemics of nature in museums is important, because of the ongoing culture wars that wrack the American body politic. Most battles in the cultural wars, as the 1996 and 2000 presidential campaigns illustrate, center on defining "a way of life" with moral authority. This chapter will not look at an obviously controversial one-off show, as do chapters 1 and 2, that ignited intense fighting. Instead, here I examine an essentially uncontested site—the American Museum of Natural History—to evaluate how its permanent displays mediate aesthetic and epistemic authority to define certain natural and historical realities such that they assure all who visit that their life "is as it should be" in "the American way of life." The American Museum of Natural History, then, illustrates how museums are much more than the depositories of culture: they are collective assemblies for power and the expressive effects of knowledge.[3] By operating as common carriers for power, museums must operate as ontologues, or definitive foundational scripts of what is "real," which they then work artfully and authoritatively to make rational. My analysis explicates how these ontologues are written, what the ontologues do, and whose interests the ontologues articulate in their rhetoric of relics and spectacle of specimens.

The American Museum's curators also have unified images and things from the outdoors expanses of many American states into representations of the United States' natural history. The museum is one site where all of "America" is imagined as a community.[4] Whether it is the origins and identities of "early Americans" from the Bering land bridge to Anasazi pueblos of the Four Corners region; the scope and duration of the Aztec and Inca empires; the exotic animals and peoples populating the Pacific Rim; the decline and collapse of Northwest Indian tribes; the location and characteristics of the North and South Poles; the distribution and extraction of the planet's mineral health; the diverse flora and fauna of Africa and Asia; or the ancient lives of dinosaurs from Mongolia to Montana, tangible evidence from all of these natural and historical realities rapidly enters American popular culture from this museum.[5] Facts are first extracted scientifically from the field, disciplined next technically in the laboratory, and then finally aestheticized formally as "knowledge" by the American Museum's many authorities. As the premier scientific institution in the major city of the twenty-first century's most enduring superpower, the halls of the American Museum are one of contemporary world culture's most consulted ontologues.[6]

The world of nature does exist independently of language. Its qualities precede and exceed all of our interpretations and explanations. These are realities, and they remain external to us. We can never know these certainties with final certitude, because we too are discursively constituted, language-using, and interpretatively constrained beings. Still, our external reality with all of its infinite qualities can be, in part, realized internally, finitely, qualitatively for us through the discourses, languages, and interpretations of any museum's shows of force. I will follow Foucault here, agreeing that "we must not imagine that the world turns toward us a legible face which we would only have to decipher; the world is not the accomplice of our knowledge; there is no prediscursive providence which disposes the world in our favor."[7]

Taking this position does not endorse schools of thought that reduce human thinking to a pure play of language, as some conservative pundits claim, where discourse is all there is, or nothing is real. Instead, I want to leverage Foucault's disclaimers to discover how the world has been given a legible face, why our knowledge of it comes from certain accomplished practices, where its favors are disposed discursively to us, and then recognize how much of this process happens at museums. Within these spaces, as Campbell observes about discursive practices,

> some statements and depictions come to have greater value than others—the idea of external reality has a particular currency that is *internal* to discourse. . . . investments have been made in certain interpretations; dividends can be drawn by those interests that have made the investments; representations are taxed when they confront new and ambiguous circumstances; and participation in the discursive economy is through social relations that embody an unequal distribution of power.[8]

Meanings, then, circulate through many venues: schools, theaters, churches, sciences, technologies, and states all mediate the exchange of this discursive economy.

Museums, however, provide a decisively important conjuncture for such discursive forces. They give us narrative glue to assemble totalizing oversight out of fragmentary facts. Museums are much more than entertaining destinations for family outings on weekend afternoons, but they also become so powerful because so many families visit them voluntarily and frequently. Thus, museum sites are key ontotopes, museum discourses generate many ontonyms, and museum curators act as powerful ontocrats. The political dynamics of their aesthetic and epistemic practices, then, are well worth studying in far more detail.

The Origins of the American Museum of Natural History

In the eighteenth and nineteenth centuries, many cities featured "cabinets of curiosities" and "academies of sciences" in which nature and society were poked and prodded by the accumulation of vast collections of oddities, curiosities, and relics culled from all over the world.[9] Most of Europe's great cities built such institutions during the Enlightenment, and by the mid-nineteenth century so too had Philadelphia, Boston, and Washington, D.C. New York, however, was often dismissed "as merely a center of crass commercialism, incapable of producing a museum of note," even though it featured Delacourte's Cabinet of Natural History as early as 1804.[10] Yet this small institution experienced financial difficulty, and closed soon after opening, and Delacourte sold the bulk of his motley collection to Russia.

The founder of the American Museum of Natural History, Professor Albert S. Bickmore, created this unusually influential institution mostly by the force of his extraordinarily entrepreneurial personality. Born in St. George, Maine, in 1839, he attended Dartmouth, and then graduated from Harvard after studying chemistry and geology. After a brief apprenticeship under Louis Agassiz at Harvard's Museum of Comparative Zoology, he set off for the East Indies on a collecting expedition in 1863, which was to accumulate specimens that might stock a new natural history museum in New York. Indeed, this museum project was, as one colleague noted, "that incessant preoccupation of his mind, the new museum building, its future, its uses, how it should develop, how it would feed school, college, and university... how it would expand commensurately with the new continent's metropolis until it outrivaled... the collective shows of all the world."[11]

In 1868, other New Yorkers were thinking along the same lines as Bickmore. Andrew Green, who headed the Board of Commissioners of Central Park in New York City, resolved to build a Paleozoic museum fashioned after the great dinosaur panoramas of London's Sydenham Park. To be devoted to "specimens of animals of the pre-Adamite period," the Paleozoic museum was intended by the commissioners to be "a museum devoted to *American* beasts" so that those modern Americans, who would visit the Paleozoic museum, could be reminded of the many divisions and passages of time by feasting their eyes on concrete simulations of the flesh that once hung on prehistoric beasts like those that left behind recently discovered fossil bones: "for thousands of years men have dwelt upon the Earth without even suspecting that it was a mighty tomb of animated races that once flourished upon it... Generations of the most gigantic and extraordinary creatures... huge fishes, enormous birds, monstrous reptiles, and ponderous uncouth animals."[12] The project, however, never came to full fruition, because William "Boss" Tweed came to power in Albany. Tweed could not find a means of getting monetary kickbacks from its contractors, so he had its already constructed foundations plowed under and its main planner, Benjamin Waterhouse Hawkins, harassed by thugs until he abandoned the idea.

Bickmore admired Agassiz's Museum of Comparative Zoology, but he regretted its out of the way location in Cambridge. "In Europe," he argued, "the institutions of this character are placed in the political and monetary capitals of the several empires," so it stood to reason that if

New York was America's "city of the greatest wealth" it probably was "the best location for the future museum of natural history for the whole land."[13] To realize this vision, he resolved to set about making it happen himself. Bickmore's fundraising among wealthy New Yorkers, including J. Pierpont Morgan, Theodore Roosevelt Sr., Morris K. Jesup, and Samuel J. Tilden, soon garnered enough pledges to support a world-class institution. Apparently with kickbacks assured by such august supporters, "Boss" Tweed ran its charter through the state legislature in 1869, and Albany gave Manhattan Square, a sixteen-acre parcel of land adjacent to Central Park on 79th Street, to the museum. On 2 June 1874 President Grant laid the cornerstone for its new building in a ceremony attended by three members of his cabinet, the governor of New York, and the mayor of New York City, all of whom wanted to help launch a national institution devoted to accumulating "a collection of objects of scientific interest second to none other in the world."[14]

Donna Haraway's fascinating analysis of the American Museum of Natural History as one expression of shared anxieties about the death of organic nature and racial contamination percolating through the upper crust of Gilded Age America's robber barons deciphers many of its more famous displays as object lessons in race, gender, class.[15] These interpretations are compelling, but they do not begin to exhaust all of the museum's meanings. The multivocal polyvalence of the Theodore Roosevelt Memorial, lurking behind its declared institutional engagement with TRUTH, KNOWLEDGE, VISION on the walls around the American Museum's Central Park West entrance, does much more than simply deploy the arts of taxidermy or politics of eugenics against decadence. Consequently, this chapter looks beyond Haraway's intriguing reappraisal of the statics of American social class structures in the museum's accounts of nature's historical dynamics to consider how it manufactures a new ontological program for modern industrial society. Its chronicles of natural history, in fact, unfold within various narratives that all historicize nature, giving us "the givens" of an Americanized natural reality.

This museum is one mechanism by which the disorder of beings, ordinarily known as "life," has been reshaped into an industrial order of natural things by the collected displays of its holdings. Most importantly, this museum-based order of things expresses and enforces one institutionalized means for coping with disorderly beings in the life of the state by normalizing "a way of life" through their aesthetic and epistemic representations of nature. The highly touted accessibility of the museum's many exhibits, for example, derives from the explicitly political intentions of its influential founders, like Morris J. Jesup, a wealthy railroad magnate and banker who was one of the museum's most important presidents. A self-made millionaire who left school at age twelve, Jesup saw immediately how the museum could become "a power of great good" in New York, and he set himself up as the measure of its teachings, claiming, "I am a plain, unscientific man; I want the exhibits labelled so I can understand them, and then I shall feel sure that others can understand."[16] Great power and wealth in New York's ruling elites, then, demanded from the outset simple accessible statements about the reality they sanctioned.

The American Museum of Natural History has embodied Jesup's unsophisticated pursuit of plain scientific truths for more than 125 years: "cataloguing species, describing their distribution, and enumerating their familial relations and physical evolution—the primary scientific tasks of the Museum."[17] Yet this fixation on "the facts, just the facts" reveals a very factualized sense of survivalistic justice, whose fair play in the many markets beneath "the American way of life" assures us all that "life is as it should be." As a vast observatory of disciplined life-forms, which are, in turn, subjected to the always ongoing disciplinary investigations of science, the American Museum's many collections constitute a catalogue of beings—past and present, animal and plant, human and nonhuman—whose scope and depth try to represent contemporary humanity's socio(onto)logy out of the paleo(onto)logy of dead dinosaurs once native to America to the neo(onto)logy of moribund Native American tribes.[18]

History will be written by the winners, while nature will be defined by the survivors. Ancient artifacts and prehistoric fossils serve as some of this nation's visible signs of supreme survival, revealing the creative destruction of history and the destructive creation of nature. At the museum, "American natural history" is what becomes New York City, and "if you can make it there, you can make it anywhere." The dynamics of these power plays cannot be made more manifest. In the last analysis, "the Museum was, first of all, a repository of facts—tangible, visible evidence of a world beyond New York City that many of the visitors would never see. Somehow, seeing the Great Auk, its founders believed, would make New Yorkers and all Americans better citizens, more diligent workers."[19] By finding and then displaying a Great Auk, the American Museum affirms a specific political vision of national survival and success as it has created its new epistemic order out of many artful representations of nature.

Politics and Epistemics: Death as Life

The American Museum of Natural History was chartered in 1869 with a clear mission: "For the purpose of... encouraging and developing the study of Natural Science, of advancing the general knowledge of kindred subjects, and to that end of furnishing popular instruction."[20] Simply stated, its basic goals are both totalizing and particularizing: "Museum scientists have sought to identify and describe the Earth and its life forms and to explore human culture."[21] With this agenda, the American Museum has helped to systematize all of the disparate knowledges that later came to be known by new disciplinary names, like zoology, geology, botany, archaeology, and anthropology, as well as mobilize productive power through their worldwide operations.

As Castañeda argues, the power/knowledge operations of a modern museum can be reaffirmed "as a 'theater of the real' (versus of memory-images) in which the representation of the world is triangulated by the categories and qualities of Nation, Civilization, and Man that are not displayed directly in images, but *evoked* through realist images of objects."[22] So it is, of course, a very Americanized "Man" and "Civilization" whose knowledges, actions, hopes, and identities are being (re)presented on Central Park West in New York City. The divisions and disciplines of the museum's collections reflect Americanizing knowledges about the history of human and nonhuman nature that all need to be defined or discovered in order to understand man.

"Discipline 'makes' individuals," Foucault argues; "it is the specific technique of a power that regards individuals as objects and instruments of its exercise."[23] The disciplines of natural history, which many activities of the American Museum of Natural History show, are so remarkable because their scientific analyses are regarded as the "killer applications" of ontological determination. Each discipline oddly remakes collective statements about the living out of individual specimens that are dead as it exercises its institutional explanatory powers. Whether one sees dinosaur fossils, leopard skins, conch shells, gorilla carcasses, or pickled fish, wherever one looks, the natural multiplicities that the museum surveys, assesses, classifies, and judges are dead.

Ironically, then, the self-understanding of life given to the human populations living in the world's greatest modern metropolis has been grounded on building one of the planet's most extensive necropolises. In celebrating its disciplined collectors, Douglas J. Preston naively inventories this dark side of discipline's enlightenment:

> Any attempt at enumeration of the items in the collections quickly becomes absurd. Butterflies? The Museum has 2 million of them (in addition to its 1.6 million beetles, 800,000 flies, 1 million spiders, and 5.5 million wasps. Bones? The Museum stores roughly 50 million of them, including 330,000 fossil vertebrates, 100 complete elephants, and the largest skeletal collection of Manhattan aborigines, among others. It also has one million birds, 600,000 fishes in jars of alcohol, one thirty ton meteorite, eight million anthropological artifacts, one balding tarantula named Blondie, two skulls of *Tyrannosaurus Rex,* several dozen dinosaur eggs, 4,000 Asian shadow puppets, 264,000 amphibians and reptiles, a stuffed gray parrot that once belonged to Houdini, the skeleton of Jumbo the elephant, 120,000 rocks and minerals, the Star of India sapphire, a grasshopper found on the observation deck of the Empire State Building, 8.5 million invertebrates, one Copper Man, 250,000 mammals, and one dodo bird. . . . it has the largest hippo on record (Caliph, who died in a zoo in 1908 of acute indigestion); the largest collection of skunks in formaldehyde, the largest collection of non-Western smoking pipes; the largest crab (twelve feet from tip to tip); Raffles, a starling that spoke more languages than any other bird; the longest elephant tusks; a hermaphroditic cloth (about 4,500 years old and replete with mummified lice); the most slowly cooled meteorite known (the Emery, found by sex researcher Alfred Kinsey); the finest collection of birds of paradise; the finest uncut emerald; the largest piece of polished jade; the largest azurite specimen (the Singing Stone, weighing 4.5 tons); the only red topaz; the largest cut gemstone (the Brazilian Princess); the only two *Pachycephalosaurus* skulls in existence; and the best fossil horse collection.[24]

This inventory is as startling as that Borges passage from a certain Chinese encyclopedia, which anchors Foucault's *The Order of Things,* because it too demonstrates the exotic charm of another system of thought: one that has pieced together a comprehensive vision of life by piecing apart that problematic out of so many things and beings set in the domain of death.[25] What system for thought and unthought would chronicle the history of nature by filling, in defiance of "reasonable description and enumeration," vast storerooms with "the most spiders, the most beetles, the most dinosaurs, the most fossil mammals, the most whales, the most plant bugs, and the most birds of any museum in the world?"[26]

The organic reality of preindustrial traditional societies, which Haraway rightly criticizes the American Museum for struggling to document, was dying, if it was not indeed already dead, when the American Museum reached its national apogee from the 1880s to the 1950s. Imperialism had by 1885 parceled up every last corner of terra incognita among the major capitalist powers; machinic industry and agriculture were already polluting vast regional ecologies; and most terrestrial biomes featured tremendous anthropogenic changes of remarkable scope, depth, and duration. From the beginning, then, the American Museum has been a memorializing monument, indeed, a headstone marking the passing of precapitalist nature with its vast accumulation of dead bits and pieces from that nature's not yet fully mortified corpse. Its conservatorial intentions are to accumulate the best or the greatest from a dying nature so that its methodical morticians in "the Museum's numerous scientific departments"[27] might put them on display under glass in perfect taxidermic order.

With the dying of precapitalist nature, modern science and technology can recombine elements of its still-vital properties out of our "global environment" from which contemporary expeditions of discovery out in the field or operations of recovery back in the storerooms find new natural resources, unknown biodiversity assets, or lost genetic information. The American Museum's taxonomic collections become today's treasure troves because such repositories of historicized dead nature are now regarded as "not only more fragile than previously thought, but also far more valuable."[28] After the death of nature, the dead from nature "have become absolutely priceless from a scientific point of view, since they could never be replaced or duplicated," and many artifacts or specimens "have become highly sought after by private collectors and dealers who pay hundreds of thousands of dollars for even mediocre artifacts."[29] Indeed, Merchant's distraught rendering of "the death of Nature" could be moved into the far more concrete realms of material practice by reexamining how the collections of natural history museums are built.[30] Piece by piece, specimen by specimen, the death of nature is registered as bits of dead nature as it is pinned, picked, or pressed in the storage cabinets of countless taxonomical tombs. In the catacombs of classification, out of the morticianship of morphological categorization, through the crypts of conceptualization, the dead define the not yet dead that the museum's various displays use to depict "Earth and life forms."[31]

Because Foucault asks us to consider how power exerts its effects through the unfolding of life, "death is power's limit, the moment that escapes it; death becomes the most secret aspect of existence, the most 'private.'"[32] Natural history museums, like the American Museum, constitute one decisive means for power to deprivatize and republicize, if only ever so slightly, the realms of death by putting dead remains into public service as social tokens of collective life, rereading dead fossils as chronicles of life's everlasting quest for survival, and canonizing now-dead individuals as nomological emblems of still-living collective biopower in nature and history. A very peculiar politics of human and nonhuman bodies is sustained by the curators, who are engaged accumulating, classifying, and displaying such necroliths in the museum's performances. Thus, the American Museum's thirty million cultural artifacts and scientific specimens can serve as strange superconductive conduits, carrying some of the *elan vital* of contemporary biopower between "the disciplines of the body and the regulations of population," or those "two poles around which the organization of power over life" directs "the performances of the body," either living or dead, to supplant sovereign power's classical ministrations of death with modern disciplinary power's "calculated management of life."[33]

Manufacturing Nature

Nature, however, is not simply discovered on the American Museum's many scientific expeditions. Instead, it also is manufactured meticulously out of an endless series of methodical measurements and disciplinary decisions. Being included in the collections of the American Museum of Natural History virtually canonizes anything as part of "nature" and/or "history." The work of Henry Dybas, a curator from Chicago's Field Museum, who painstakingly defined *Bambara intricata*—a minute feathering beetle from Bimini—for the American Museum demonstrates how this manufacturing of nature occurs.

During 1951, American Museum entomologists spent four months on the Bimini cays collecting nearly 110,000 insects and 28,000 arachnids.

In their traps they discovered six species of feathering beetles among thousands of specimens. By sorting, examining, and classifying them, Dybas "was able to illuminate the complex workings of a small corner of the natural world."[34] Borrowing many of the American Museum's specimen vials in the mid-1960s, Dybas conducted morphological studies of the feathering beetles that turned up a species hitherto unknown to science. In turn, he selected a "type" specimen to represent this species, or *B. intricata,* in the American Museum's collections, in complete conformity with his scientific sense of normalizing disciplinary practice. To select, shape, and stabilize "a small corner of the natural world," Dybas chose "the most normal, the most *average* individual he could find, and designated it the type. In doing so, he made an utterly insignificant beetle—an almost invisible brown period—a scientifically priceless specimen.... locked in its cabinet, resting in perpetuity as the official representative of all its kind."[35]

This strategic alliance of scientific experts from the Field Museum and American Museum of "Natural History" shows how the museum is little more than a vast observation machine, classification engine, or preservation apparatus. As Preston asserts, the American Museum of Natural History takes the chaotic, irrational prehistory of nature to the bar of scientific examination and creates a calm, rational history for Americans, and all other modern humans, of nature. That is,

> The Museum is the guardian of thousands of such seemingly insignificant specimens, but as each bone in the mighty *Tyrannosaurus* is just a piece in the puzzle of the whole, each tiny bug is an indispensable link in the chain of knowledge that exists in the collections of the American Museum. Like the beetle, virtually every Museum specimen is invested with significance and a history. (Indeed, specimens without a history are often thrown out).... *B. intricata*... is an example, in microcosm, of what the Museum is.[36]

Preston is dead right with these observations. Typing specimens from nature to specify the significance and history of nature anthropogenically *is* what the museum is about. Those specimens without a history then can be thrown out of this historicized nature by the guardian of these well-disciplined dead beings. Nature, however, is never "wild nature" per se. It is a pastiche of historicized representations, whose specific identities and various commonalities emerge from the normalizing judgments of hierarchically authorized examining powers, who deputize one typical specimen, which "becomes the physical and legal representative of all of its kind" to serve in the cabinet of definitions permanently constituted in the museum's storerooms.[37] In turn, these highly disciplined dead delegates are entrusted "to describe what the new species looks like," and it is these individuals "that all others will be compared or contrasted with, and measured against, for the rest of time."[38]

Preston's celebratory assessment of the American Museum of Natural History as a center of natural science valorizes these death-dealing taxonomical practices:

> More than anything, natural scientists of the late nineteenth century believed deeply in the value of *collections*. To them, collections were *facts*. They held secrets about the world; secrets that could be extracted through careful study. Collections would reveal the relationships among all life on the planet, including human beings. They would be a resource for scientists centuries into the future, long after such things no longer existed in the wild.[39]

Such disciplined museumological practices are the foundation of the American Museum's "positivity." Each fragmentary piece of dead nature in every collection becomes a factual bit of still living reality, making possible various scientific statements about natural beings and their many relationships with the earth. The museum's self-professed goal of showing "the natural history of our planet and its species" "in more than forty exhibition halls"[40] enables such enunciative modalities in all of its displays and collections to work on the museum's professional employees and visiting patrons.

These death-dealing dynamics of definition, however, are applied to much more than tiny insects, common songbirds, or ordinary plants. Charismatic megafauna, like elephants or gorillas, also are invested with historical significance in the taxidermic theater of habitat groups. The museum's world-renowned Akeley Hall of African Mammals, which includes the infamous Gorilla Group that inspired Haraway's attacks on the museum's "teddy bear patriarchy,"[41] was modeled on the smaller habitat studies in the museum's Hall of North American Birds. Begun at the turn of the century, such "habitat groups" were meant to show animals and plants in their native surroundings. "By 1909 the techniques of duplicating plants, flowers, rocks, trees and backgrounds had been per-

fected,"[42] and Carl E. Akeley, a remarkably innovative taxidermist working for the Field Museum in Chicago, was commissioned by the American
Museum in 1909 to procure and mount a habitat group of elephants.

In planning this display, Akeley pushed his aesthetics of duplication
beyond technically perfect taxidermy in static unreal settings into the
realm of hyperreal simulation, creating habitat groups "on a huge scale,
and he wanted them to be bursting with vitality and spontaneity, to be
aesthetically beautiful as well as scientifically accurate."[43] Instead of
stuffing animal skins like old sofas, he remodeled them over realist armatures, whose lifelike subsculpture gives the skins the hyperreal role of
natural costumes in a materialized play of concrete organic matter. The
American Museum had African exhibits already on display when Akeley
signed on to create its new elephant group. However, they were the usual
static showings of dead animals, killed and stuffed for exposition, as
representative examples of the many more live ones still on the hoof
out in the wild.

After nearly dying in Kenya of injuries he received from an old bull
elephant he had hunted down for the exhibit, Akeley experienced a rev-
elation about animals, taxidermy, Africa, and nature during his lengthy
recuperation. Things were changing in Africa too quickly. Indeed, on
the eve of World War I, Akeley realized that far too much had changed
since his first trips there as a young man. Farming and ranching rapidly
were displacing game, and the wildlife of Africa was doomed by the on-
slaught of agriculture, herding, mining, and town building brought by
European colonialism. Therefore, the premise of the American Museum's existing African exhibits, namely, that its few specimens were
simply indoor tokens of a much greater outdoors reality, was becoming
invalid. As Akeley told a friend, "everything that has been done in the
American Museum of Natural History in the way of African exhibits
must be thrown out and completely discarded: we must start over again."[44]

Hence, Akeley's bizarre taxidermical skills were mobilized to manufacture a prehistorical African nature with a series of hyperreal *tableaux
mordant*. Africa's once vast biomes and robust biota had to be remembered for representation as they perhaps were before being dismembered in the global capitalist markets brought by European imperialism. Akeley's galleries of charismatic megafauna would be microcosmic
skits that could realistically reproduce representative groups of once-

unendangered wildlife in new macrocosmic dramas. By memorializing their disappearing habitats, and sacrificing handfuls of the precious few remaining live examples to serve as signs of the now-lost millions of dead beings, nature's identity could be stabilized and preserved.

Before he died, Akeley corresponded with the museum's director, expressing even greater shock over how rapidly things had slid since 1921, when his safari collected the gorillas he needed for the Gorilla Group: *"The old conditions, the story of which we want to tell, are now gone, and in another decade the men who knew them will all be gone."*[45] Here in the Akeley Hall, the mordant energies of the museum reach their perfect pitch. Like the Akeley Hall of African Mammals, the Hall of North American Mammals, the Hall of Reptiles and Amphibians, or the Frank M. Chapman Memorial Hall of North American Birds manufacture static simulations of "the old conditions" of real beasts living unclassified and free—a state now long gone virtually everywhere for animals in their natural habitats. Preserved to be observed, these scientifically stabilized models represent to the urban millions "a way of life" being taken away from other forms of life, like these real dead beasts, by proliferating human populations meeting their material needs in many new world cities, like New York. Strangely today, these displays, which were once designed and built to represent the raw promise of nature's wild fecundity at the dawn of the twentieth century, are being releveraged at that century's dusk to alert the urban masses of the twenty-first century to the far more pressing threats of nature's contemporary exhaustion in the Hall of Earth's Diversity.

The dioramaturgy of such habitat groups freezes time, producing an exemplary vision of wildlife outdoors for human life indoors. Thus the museum as a conservatory of nature functions doubly as an observatory for history. Museums, like the telescope, the lens, or the microscope, emerged in the early modern era as one of science's most important "observatories," because they too are "an apparatus in which the techniques make it possible to see induce effects of power, and in which, conversely, the means of coercion make those on whom they are applied clearly visible."[46] Curators serve, in keeping with a key original meaning of the term, as "overseers," whose oversight is arrayed concretely through the galleries of their institutions in accord with "the minor techniques of multiple and intersecting observations, of eyes that must see without being seen."[47] Shrewd curating, then, designs these displays so that every gaze cast by any visiting patron would see through specific sorts of eyes, which always see without being seen, and form "a part of the overall functioning of power."[48] Likewise, the entire problematic of museum architecture after the Enlightenment shifts from representational registers of the aristocratic dynasty of a royal sovereign—royal storehouse, curiosity cabinet, or family hoard—to one of a national state of some people—open exposition, chambers of chronological progress, or discursive display—as the disciplinary intentions of museum observations diffuse into society's built rhetorics as concrete logics for more modern modalities of power. Architectural design functions within calculated economies of disciplinary power inside of which one sees

> an architecture that no longer is built simply to be seen (as with the ostentation of palaces), or to observe the external space (cf. the geometry of fortresses) but to permit an internal, articulated and detailed control—to render visible those who are inside it; in more general terms, an architecture that would transform individuals: to act on those it shelters, to provide a hold on their conduct, to carry the effects of power right to them, to make it possible to know them, to alter them. Stones make people docile and knowable. The old simple schema of confinement and enclosure . . . began to be replaced by the calculation of openings, of filled and empty spaces, passages and transparencies.[49]

Like schools or hospitals, which were erected as pedagogical machines or therapeutic operators, the museum is remade into a observatory of remembrance whose walls are arrayed to make people more docile and things more knowable.

What once was merely a hoard of precious keepsakes or exotic curiosities becomes a nationalized place for modern humanity's training, recording, and observing in which the objects to be known, and the knowing subjects who must gain knowledge, can be combined at one site where normalizing judgments and disciplined examinations are hierarchically organized by formally authorized overseers. "The perfect disciplinary apparatus" makes it possible "for a single gaze to see everything constantly."[50] The nature museum approaches this perfection as what were once only chaotically intermingled curiosities are subdivided into topically dedicated galleries, thematically focused centers, or theoretically reorganized expositions. The nature museum emerges, in turn, as "a sort of apparatus of uninterrupted examination" whose disciplinary power is exercised "through its invisibility; at the same time it imposes

on those whom it subjects a principle of compulsory visibility" where-
by disciplinary power "manifests its potency, essentially, by arranging
objects."[51]

Remaking Present Practices as Memory

Museums are apparatuses devoted to the disciplinary training of memory. By organizing what are "moving, confused, useless multitudes of
bodies and forces into a multiplicity of individual elements," dismembered
pieces emerge from museums as memorable fragments to be remembered purposely through careful curatorial intervention in "small, separate cells, organic autonomies, genetic entities and continuities, combinatory segments."[52] Once collected and displayed, the museum as memorial
reveals the modalities of disciplinary power—hierarchical observation,
normalizing judgment, and routinized examinations—in their everyday operations.

The aesthetics of memory at the American Museum distance industrial America/New York/international modernity from the subjects and
objects it dismembers, and then remembers, within its displays. In order
to "furnish the popular instruction" of "Natural Science" and "of kindred
subjects," a commonly shared time and space is ruptured by the overseeing analytical classifications of its curators. The referents of its min-
eralogical, paleontological, zoological, and anthropological discourses
are otherized by relegating them instrumentally all to "a Time other
than the present of the producer" of such scientific discourses, slowing
and fixing their images apart from the globalized economy's fast capitalist times such that they hold "still like a tableau vivant."[53] These moves
are pitched to place the museum visitor/viewer simultaneously in spaces
of acceleration, activation, and appropriation, whose difference author-
izes the symbolic and material utilization of these otherized observa-
tional objects.

This allocentric pose saturates the entire American Museum of Natural History. Almost all of its more than forty halls depict images and
dictate stories fixed in registers of "long ago" and/or "far away." The
Arthur Ross Hall of Meteorites show lost fragments of the extraterrestrial cosmos that have impacted life on earth. The Harry Frank Guggenheim Hall of Minerals shows how earth's inorganic formation brings
useful materials from earth's genesis into our daily economic transactions
as treasured gems in the suitably named John Pierpont Morgan Hall of

Gems. The Hall of Human Biology and Evolution shows humanity evolving through lost millennia into the sentient consciousnesses of the present. The Eastern Woodland Indians, Plains Indians, Northwest Coast Indians, Eskimo, Mexico and Central America, South American Peoples, African Peoples, Asian Peoples, and Pacific Peoples halls mix contemporary ethnic and geographic labels to freeze frame all of these exoticized humans in otherized times/spaces/ecologies/economies before, beyond, or beneath the moment at which the universalizing transformative influences of North Atlantic capitalism erase them through trade or war. And, of course, the dinosaur and Extinct Mammal Halls resurrect the *Sein und Zeit* of nonhuman beings known only through the arcane hermeneutics of fossil analysis.

In its displays of the human family in all of these ethnological and paleontological halls, the American Museum of Natural History privileges the nation-state, or, in particular, the American nation-state, in a naturalized history of social progress. Its collections are the definitive point of classification, documentation, and interpretation by which a modern nation-state reimagines all other forms of human community—groups, bands, tribes, races, cultures, civilizations—in grades of growing complexity, sophistication, and power. Likewise, all of nature is reaffirmed in memory/knowledge as "native to America" or "foreign to America" in the process of revealing how Americans' biophysical environments came to be what the contemporary nation-state finds as its standing reserves of technoscientific action.

As Castañeda suggests, the modern museum rewrites earthly existence as "a natural history in which Man is simultaneously centered in the universe yet decentered through naturalization."[54] The tone of the American Museum's *tableaux vivant,* however, resonates with an externalization of biopower in which an expansive American multinational commercialism finds "the natural history of our planet and its species"[55] as an ontogenic space of movement for its economy and society to assume "responsibility for the life processes and undertook to control and modify them."[56] The lifetime of the American Museum begins at that moment when

Western man was gradually learning what it meant to be a living species in a living world, to have a body, conditions of existence, probabilities of life, an individual and collective welfare, forces that could be modified, and a space that could be distributed in an optimal manner. For the first time in history, no doubt, biological existence was reflected in political existence; the face of living was no longer an inaccessible substrate that only emerged from time to time, and the randomness of death and its fatality; part of it passed into knowledge's field of control and power's sphere of operation.[57]

Not surprisingly, the American Museum's focus is on "fundamental issues that concern us all," that is,

- the evolution of the human species and of human culture
- past and present extinctions of plant and animal species
- patterns of social and biological adaptation
- processes that shape the earth and provide the environmental framework for the evolution of life.[58]

The American Museum's dioramas, then, rationalize the randomness of fatality, redirecting the outcome of extinction and evolution into knowledge's control and power's intervention. Its ontotopic chambers teach what it means for modern Americans to have a body, conditions of existence, or probabilities of life by showing all of the forces they have modified—other human and nonhuman—and all of the spaces—present, past, and future—that they might redistribute in an optimal manner.

Gems, minerals, plants, animals, and all other races are taken control of through the geoeconomics and geopolitics of American nationhood—a historicized nature becoming a naturalized history—worldwide on expeditions of discovery and accumulation. Capitalist efficiency plus imperial effectiveness recast Marx's famous dictum, taking all that was solid and vanishing into thin air, or life and its energies, by reconjuring its presence out of the extinct, the dying, or the dead from long ago and far away in the solidified narratives of this museum's thick descriptions of "bio-history." At this juncture in time, the American Museum illustrates, first, why anthropogenic changes are the most powerful forces at work on earth, as globalized ecological colonialism causes the extinction of nonhuman life and economic imperialism initiates an eradication of many human life-forms, but, second, it also positions America at the center of these shock waves of destruction. Its displays provide another rich archive about the regulation of populations, surveillance of energies, or understanding of bodies that arise when we apply "the term of *bio-history* to the pressures through which the movements of life and the processes of history interfere with one another," forcing us "to speak of *bio-power* to designate what brought life and its mechanisms into the realm of explicit calculations and made knowledge-power an agent of transformative of human life."[59]

This exposition of life on earth at the American Museum also is shot through with the history of sexuality and its population-centered system of survival. Patterns of biological adaptation, sources of extinction, or origins of evolutionary shifts are sexualized registers giving the museum's curators and scientists "a means of access both to the life of the body and the life of the species."[60] Its polyvalent natural/historical discourses implicitly embed the Malthusian couple in virtually every diorama of human and nonhuman life, just as procreative behavior is socialized by the American state to support population dynamics. Whether it is the dioramas depicting the *Australopithecus afransis* couple leaving footprints in the ancient mud, upland gorillas in the mist of Mount Mikeno, the African elephants in their taxidermic charge through the Akeley Hall, or the Komondo dragons preying on the stuffed wild boar, the fertility of couples in family groups interlock individual bodies and collective populations in biopower histories of extinction-avoidance/evolution-continuance as the American Museum's exhibits maneuver to "furnish the popular instruction" in nationalized stories of survival.

The Hall of Human Biology and Evolution continues these nationalized/statalized metaphors in its dioramic discourses about "the human body." The human body is explored in exploded machinic diagrams, like an engine or transmission, to reveal all of the componentialized subsystems that contribute to its overall physiological workings. Joints and muscles are explored in a video of baseball players, revealing how joints, muscles, and tendons function like simple machines composed of fulcra, pullies, levers, and hinges. The interplay of organism and environment shows how humanity evolved from other primates mostly by demonstrating incremental increases in brain size, unusual abilities for tool use, and conjugally based family societies. The natural history of humanity is recast in these historicizations of human anatomy as one of geoeconomic forces: muscles are energies, joints turn into machines, brains are information engines. Nature reveals itself as a cosmic collection point of intelligent/energetic order as the human body's evolution in an Americanized history of the natural is one of the controlled insertion of machineries of production into natural bodies caught in vast technoscientific processes.

To display the wonders of the human bone structure, the very American game of baseball stabilizes the hardball of modern biopolitics, which needs to grow, domesticate, and access such biopowers among individual bodies and population bodies. By using computer-generated dioramic guides to represent reality, reality is made as rational as machines in baseball-game-playing movements. So dioramas of skeletal human families watching computer-generated cyborg cartoons in their suburban home distill the Hall of Human Biology and Evolution down into DNA-driven chronicles of an evolving biotechnologized humanity. Here dioramaturgy reveals how even dead bones can be charged with biopower—one more exercise of biopolitics in its many forms, or "the investment of the body, its valorization, and the distributive management of its forces."[61]

The American Museum of Natural History proves to be a key capacitor for biopower in the development of capitalism inasmuch as its allocentric representation of reality segregates various types of life and nonlife, otherizes living beings as instruments of exploitation or species for extinction, and classifies remote societies or distant lands as likely sites for further progressive development. The ontonymic machinations of museum dioramas and ontocratic judgments of museum curators are biopolitical acts, helping to manage "the controlled insertion of bodies into the machinery of production and the adjustment of the phenomenon of population to economic processes."[62] Many American Museum examples are quite suggestive: the Hall of Ocean Life depicts how even vast populations of marine life must be managed carefully to economically/ecologically sustain the insertion of these bodies into machineries of production; the Akeley Memorial Hall of African Mammals guarantees that zebra, gorilla, or elephant life might survive as representations even as encroaching human populations displace them from their habitats with maladjusted economic processes; and the Guggenheim Hall of Minerals presents the earth's inorganic substance as useful minerals and crystals, which must be extracted to create many of the products we use. Turning all of the universe under observation into a storehouse of treasures charges economies and ecologies with the disciplinary logics of biopower. Most impressive of all, however, is the new

Rose Center for Earth and Space, which takes visitors beyond the solar system to faraway galaxies, black holes, and cosmic nebulae. The aesthetics and epistemics of such dramaturgies in the American Museum allegedly reveal "processes that shape the Earth and provide the environmental framework for the evolution of life"[63] in highly disciplined representations, which serve, in turn, as "methods of power capable of optimizing forces, aptitudes, and life in general without at the same time making them more difficult to govern."[64]

The paleontologies of the American Museum, however, carry many other meanings. At first blush, dinosaurs, like the concrete casts from Andrew Green's planned Paleozoic Park, might be seen as moralistic tokens of human origins, representing pre-Adamite life's highest attainments. Yet two other lessons seem to follow from the vast scientific expeditions of American Museum dinosaur hunters, scurrying out across Mongolia's or Montana's outbacks. First, these small-scale searches for fossilized bones mimic the quest of large-scale sweeps by American capital through every remote expanse of the world in search of other organic goods from the Paleozoic era, like coal, oil, gas, or pre-Paleozoic inorganic minerals, like gold, silver, copper, bauxite, or iron. Just as the American Museum of Natural History excavated dinosaur fossils to bring ancient life to modern human awareness, so too would Amoco, Asarco, or Alcoa extract other long-buried ancient treasures from other lands to let them dance in the markets of America's major cities. And, second, the fixation on dinosaurs, as fossilized megafauna, provided a uniquely scientized tombstone for organic life itself in the dawning age of human megamachines. Like man the hunter or gatherer, dinosaurs as hunter/gatherers were truly awesome beings, which were worthy of remembrance, but now they are Paleozoic.

Yet neozoic cyborg life-forms, like the vast corporate collectives of capitalist men and corporate machines that actually exhume, exhibit, and explicate them, are not singularly organic life forms, and they will not leave these sorts of traces.[65] In an era of global corporations, national states, and international markets, individual men and women also may become dinosaurs whose remaining traces will appear most legibly only in museums. Otherwise, they are collaborating cellular elements of the new multicellular beings of contemporary technoscientific capitalism. On these paths, "paleontology" simply parallels the implicit guidance laid down for human beings by the neoplutocracies of modern corporate institutions.

Natural History as Historicized Nature

The fact that many people probably learn much more about art, culture, history, nature, and science from museums than they do at universities recenters our attention on the stakes of culture war. Museums are ontologues, because their displays create, control, and circulate what are taken as "our" representations of other people's history, environment, and culture. How identity/difference, superordination/subordination, value/ valuelessness, and origins/ends are represented at any museum creates terrains of contestability where, not too surprisingly, culture wars can break out anew as opposing interpretative blocs mobilize all of their symbolic and material forces to induce their opponents to do their will by accepting the power of their knowledge.

As centers of scholarly research, museums train both museum-visiting publics and museum-managing professionals to accept particular representational practices as actual realities. Most importantly, as repositories of human artifacts and/or nonhuman specimens, museums resocialize people to accept artful displays of material objects and natural specimens as authoritative and legitimate means to understand the world. Museums develop a shared sense of particular spatial and temporal order, which emerges and then endures in specific national places and historical chronologies. As one product and producer of national modernization for the state, museums are intimately involved in fabricating a mass consciousness of the nation's shared spatial context and temporal chronology. In this way, as its founders asked, the American Museum has been "furnishing the popular instruction"[66] through five generations, as Bickmore wished, "for the whole land."[67]

Museums should not be viewed as aloof, isolated enterprises. They are frontline fortifications in an unending war of position whose expositions continually reposition the channels of power and conduits of knowledge to produce societies of subjects as well as collectives of objects that are capable of circulating easily with the disciplinary demands of modernity. Natural history museums are perhaps the most central of these emplacements, because they seek to collect, classify, and conceptualize everything from all of the time to reposition "man," as national communities of men/women, in territorially containerized expanses of "nature." Our naturalized familiarity with this project comes from museums, and their natural history dioramas depicting prehistoric man evolving into what is taken to be the "us" where we first, or most frequently, gain our powerful forms of productive subjectification. Without museums like the American Museum of Natural History, or the Missouri Botanical Garden and Arizona–Sonora Desert Museum, as chapters 6, 7, and 8 suggest, these ontological constants could not construct and circulate power with any sort of effectiveness.

My approach to the American Museum of Natural History has not sought to uncover hidden essences or recover lost treasures underneath the discursive dust coating all of the museum's displays. Instead, I simply have worked to systematically describe the objects and practices of the museum's discursive reification of American nature vis-à-vis parallel currents in American history's discursive representations for a highly nationalized group of humanity. Nationhood, possessive individualism, progress, technoscientific knowing, and reality are all energized and enabled by the museum displays of this historicized American nature at the American Museum of Natural History, because it is, as Wilson asserts, the museum "that has thought big about the world."[68]

CHAPTER SEVEN

The Missouri Botanical Garden: Sharing Knowledge about Plants to Preserve and Enrich Life

The Missouri Botanical Garden sits in striking incongruity amidst the rough neighborhoods on the south side of St. Louis that now surround it. Sitting not far from old sprawling railway yards, decrepit industrial factories, and rundown inner-city houses, where everything distressing about America's urban decay is jumbled together cheek by jowl with crime and chaos, the garden is a small oasis of Victorian order penned up behind limestone walls and chain-link fences. Next to the world-famous St. Louis Arch over the Museum of the Western Expansion, the Missouri Botanical Garden is one of the city's most recognizable icons. The *New York Times,* for example, in an April 1999 story, ran a color shot of bright yellow tulips in the big beds before the garden's Ridgway Center entry as a "sign of Spring" in a heroic effort to cast St. Louis as an attractive destination for bored Manhattanites.[1]

Few photos of the garden disclose the beleaguered urban position of its grounds, perhaps because these decaying old brick homes and dying business strips have been starting and stalling toward redevelopment for nearly three decades. When Henry Shaw began building his botanical gardens in the 1850s, the site was a treeless prairie far removed from the city of St. Louis. After Shaw died in 1889, St. Louis continued to prosper. Its strategic position along the Mississippi and Missouri rivers allowed the city's business and financial elites to enrich themselves on east-west and north-south trade in America's booming Gilded Age economy. By 1904, St. Louis had developed into the nation's fourth-largest urban center, and it used this rising preeminence to stage the Louisiana

Purchase Exposition and host the first Olympic Games held in the United States. Afterward, it grew even richer as a manufacturing center for aircraft, beer, cars, chemicals, foods, and shoes, reaching its peak population in 1950 at 857,000. During the Cold War era, however, the city slumped tremendously.

Beer continues to be important, and a few airplanes are still assembled there, but most of the automobile, chemical, food, and shoe factories have left town.[2] In 1990, only 397,000 people called St. Louis home, and this number fell to 348,000 in 2000. The city once grew up around Shaw's estate in the years after his death, and now it also is falling down around it into shabby disrepair. For local residents who often tire, as Mark Twain noted, of the "solid expanse of bricks and mortar" reaching off "into dim, measure-defying distances" that make up St. Louis, a walk through the garden can be highly restorative. Yet, these walks pass through a stilted Victorian vision of nature that casts trees, bushes, and grasses as a tonic for humans who live too much of their day on hot concrete in stale air surrounded by noisy machines.

I want to argue here that the Missouri Botanical Garden, like the American Museum of Natural History, now serves as one of the world's most definitive distilleries of nature discourse. What is regarded as "the botanical" at this privileged place differentiates what most people understand as "nature" from what they regard as "society." On the one hand, more than a million visitors come to the garden to "see" its rich verdant plantings, but on the other hand, the site is also "the unseen garden," a place where landmark work in many fields of botanical research is, in the words of its curators, "of the utmost importance if we are to understand plants properly and use them, enjoy them, and conserve them in a rapidly changing world."[3] For "the seen garden" in St. Louis, however, definite architectural barriers, like limestone walls and cyclone fences, divide what is feared by many as "society" on the hard-luck streets of south St. Louis, and what will be revered by others as "nature" in the wood thickets and plant beds of the Missouri Botanical Garden. Nature both does and does not exist, as such, and exhibitions such as this one are staged in order to constitute it discursively and materially where it does not exist for those who need it to somehow organize their lives. Of course, all of these divisions are drawn by botanists or horticulturalists in "society," who intentionally shape these spaces by putting the why, where, when, and how of "nature" in its place. This too is "the unseen garden."

Nature parks like this one essentially put nature "in park," stabilizing, containing, decoding, and showing it in very specific immobilized forms. Because many urban residents have little contact with nature above and beyond their experiences in such parks, the nature of whatever nature is discussed and presented at such sites becomes quite significant. The rhetorical pose of many botanical gardens is one of scientific objectivity; yet most of their operations indicate that nothing could be farther from the truth. In the hyperurban expanses of St. Louis, a permanent exhibition like the Missouri Botanical Garden stabilizes nature—or whatever is somewhere "out there," over the fence, beyond the boundary, away from the city, past the limits—as what has been rooted "in here" by the garden's management. The chaotic profusions of plant life captured from many wild sites are brought safely back into the city as the orderly, but also totally unnatural, biomass of a botanical garden. Once it is organized as a botanical garden, nature acquires an identity from global markets that mobilize its trees, plants, and soils to serve the ends of human use.[4]

Representations of "nature," "plants," or "botany" at the Missouri Botanical Garden are not objective copies of stable truths that exist as such. On the contrary, they are historically variable constructs that serve the cultural needs of variously evolving museum institutions and their audiences. Instead of regarding museum sites as sustained attempts to prove the veracity of enduring independent truths, we should regard them as permanent campaigns to verify certain contingent propositions with enough truthfulness for their place and time. When looking at their thematic foci, such as plants, the natural, or the technoscientific, I look at which past, which nature, and which technoscience are being represented. I also examine for what purposes these representations are made and to whom they are important. As chapter 8 suggests about nature and deserts at the Arizona–Sonora Desert Museum, the contextual reticulation of such rhetorical expositions always must be considered.

The contradictions of "first nature," or what is usually treated as nonsocial, ahuman, and pretechnical raw planetary stuff, and "second nature," or what is seen as socialized space, culturalized resource, historicized place for human use, soon attain an odd reconciliation in botanical gardens. The worst aspects of each can be suppressed to exalt the positive moments of both. Nature's often random poverty and plenty can be effaced in the ordered luxuriance of botanical displays. Rare plants can be cast as the green signs of an always abundant nature in the artifice of designated display plots. Planted to exemplify the findings of botanical science, plants are used to squeeze historicized meanings from their natural life-forms. In turn, a spectacular image of nature is fabricated out of natural stuff in order to highlight its potential as industrial resources, and this spectacle of use allegedly represents the substance and form of nature as such.

Origins and Operations

The Missouri Botanical Garden began in 1859 as the dream of Henry Shaw, an English immigrant from Sheffield who had made his fortune in St. Louis before the Civil War by selling tools and hardware. After accumulating a small fortune, he toured Europe extensively during the 1840s, garnering ideas about how to build his homes in downtown St. Louis and on a country estate southwest of the city in the Prairie des Noyers section of St. Louis County. On his last trip to Europe in 1851, Shaw attended the London Exposition and visited the estate of the Duke of Devonshire. The gardens there at Chatsworth as well as the Royal Botanic Gardens at Kew inspired him to establish a similar botanical garden on his suburban country estate, which soon was called Tower Grove because of the way his house towered through the trees.[5]

To design his garden, Shaw solicited advice from Sir William Jackson Hooker at the Royal Gardens at Kew in a correspondence during 1856. Hooker, in turn, advised him to contact Dr. George Engelmann, a gynecologist and naturalist, who had a practice in St. Louis. With Engelmann's assistance, Shaw made contact with Dr. Asa Gray at Harvard University, who was regarded as the leading botanist in the United States. With the guidance of these three outstanding experts, Shaw devoted nearly twenty acres three and a half miles southwest of central St. Louis to his gardens in 1856–1857. Following Hooker's advice, Shaw agreed to combine beauty and science in his project, and admired Sir William's "magnificent establishment at Kew... [as] a wonderful means of promoting a taste for horticultural improvements in the multitudes of people that frequent it."[6] Engelmann was instrumental in purchasing the herbarium of Johann Jakob Bernhardi in Germany in 1857 as well as in building a library for the garden. Gray, in turn, advised Shaw on prospective curators, the nature of the garden's plantings, and layout of the facilities.

The Missouri state legislature chartered the garden on 14 March 1859, and the first visitors to Tower Grove and the Botanical Garden were admitted on 15 June 1859. The garden featured an arboretum and fruticetum as well as a number of plant houses, an entrance gate and limestone perimeter walls, and a museum—modeled on the museum at Kew—that opened in 1860. The first greenhouse was built in 1868, the Linnaean House was designed in 1882 for the palm collection, and a granite mausoleum was designed in 1885 where Shaw was interred after his death in August 1889.

Shaw regarded botany "as the branch of natural history that related to the vegetable kingdom," including such pursuits as "the naming and classification of plants, their external form, their anatomical structure, their functions, their distribution over the globe, and their uses."[7] A botanic garden, in turn, must operate as the focal point for "the collection and cultivation of all species and varieties of plants that thrive in a given climate with or without the aid of glass."[8] The Missouri Botanical Garden, in turn, moved this technoscientific theory into operational practice, giving experts the space to display the functions of plants by external form or anatomical structure as well as by name, their distribution around the world, or use to society. The garden enabled botany to advance its work, while popularizing the profit potential in "the Vegetable Kingdom" in this scientific enterprise against the backdrop of beautiful landscape, artful gardening, and park architecture.

Shaw's vision of a botanic garden conformed closely to Hooker's original suggestions to him, and the Missouri Botanical Garden's displays are an odd example of international technology transfer. In fact, Shaw's desire to combine "beauty and science" in order to celebrate the aesthetic and economic uses of nature closely parallels the ways in which Kew served the purposes of Victorian agribusiness. For Shaw, the Royal Botanic Gardens at Kew were the best exemplification of how humanity might combine botanical science with beautiful gardening: "Great Britain and its colonies yield a most interesting and useful exhibition of this kind. The museum in the Royal Botanic Gardens of Kew is the object of national patronage, and is rapidly increasing in magnificence and importance...."[9] A year after Shaw's death, the garden's director, William Trelease, acknowledged the salience of Kew as the model for Henry Shaw inasmuch as "the Missouri Garden took...a step in advance of its prototype, adopting as its model, the public garden at Kew...the leading institution for scientific botany in the world . . . Mr. Shaw hoped for a somewhat similar career of usefulness for the Garden founded by him."[10] In this regard, Shaw's Victorian botanical garden implicitly celebrates the Enlightenment narratives of production, profit, and progress resting at the heart of England's Georgian agriculture. By the eighteenth century, England's enclosure of its lands during the sixteenth and seventeenth centuries was paying off mightily with improvements to its land and people as good husbandry of soils, crops, and animals in Georgian agricultural capitalism made Great Britain a leading economic force. Given Shaw's fascination with the Royal Botanic Gardens at Kew, some consideration must be paid to this institution to trace how its workings influenced the Missouri Botanical Garden. Begun in the 1750s as Britain struggled with France for world supremacy during the Seven Years' War, the Royal Botanic Gardens at Kew provide a unique expression of human technical power over nature while assuming the aesthetic forms of a royal park.[11] It was at Kew that King George III won his nickname "Farmer George," but Kew is also where one can find the best traces of nature as it came to be shaped by British commercial imperialism. In creating a world empire via naval intervention, industrial revolution, and cultural domination, Great Britain represented the scope and variety of its territorial control with a profusion of exotic plants. Plunked down in the western suburbs of London along the Thames, Kew is a fascinating puzzle whose pieces reveal much about how the world's natural environments have been fabricated, represented, and manipulated by the modern nation-state, capitalist technology, and scientific culture.

Kew's modern gardening imitates ancient European gardens, appropriating their antique grandeur while at the same time equating their primitive powers with those of exotic orientalisms represented by foreign gardens replete with pagodas, Ming temple lions, palms and divine water lilies. Otherness and oldness are integrated into the grids of royal authority. From the Rose Pergola to the Palm House to the Rhododendron Dell, Kew now stages a script of plant appreciation that ties visitors to observing and walking through theatricalized landscapes designed to display particular types of plant life or peculiar qualities of vegetation in their most edifying, and hence mostly unnatural, ways along many pleasant footpaths.

As an imperial artifact, then, Kew plainly embodies a botanical orientalism in all of its glory. Otherness, elsewhereness, oddness, ancientness are attributes that plants can carry as botanical traces of exotica. Bizarre plants from far away are kept in bizarre hothouses as hostages of imperial horticulturalists intent on showing how mighty the Crown is. So great is its power that it can command plant life from the tropics and deserts to exist in England, thanks to capital, science, and technology. Indeed, the greenhouses themselves become ironic embodiments of imperialism as these technoscientific housings of bits and pieces from an uncontrolled nature overseas capture and contain living fragments of an imperialized earth. The antipodes are proven to be under the control and cultivation of the Crown on Kew's grounds, and all are invited to enjoy this power on celebratory holiday jaunts of appreciation via the tube to Kew.

Not all species are corralled in Kew's greenhouses, but those that are can be seen as the royalty of many plant worlds invited before the British court as England rules over their home ground indirectly from afar via technical surveillance, scientific domination, commercial exploitation, and botanical policing. As a living representative of the world that the British have imperialized, Kew is the one place left in the Commonwealth where the sun never sets on the life-forms of a world empire. Plant emissaries from each corner of the realm obey their keepers at Kew, and some of this plant matter in the hothouses of royal power may live even after natural extinctions occur at home.

In a suburban space where the native grass cover is cut off periodically to manage butterfly habitat for the edification of park visitors, people from around the world visit Kew to commune with what passes for "an authentic Nature." Three hundred landlocked acres of trees, water, bushes, soil, and grasses amidst the sprawl of West London's bedroom suburbs is a tad small for all nature, but this small simulation sustains many fictions about "wild nature" outside of this exclusive park. Here the modern tropes of nature/culture, the wild/the social, and rusticity/domesticity are continuously rebalanced in an elaborate play of myth and illusion.

But the spectacular vision of nature posed by the Royal Botanic Gardens at Kew is being eclipsed by newfound commitments to denaturing plants into economic feedstocks for high-tech enterprises bent on discovering new medicines, foods, and fuels. Today Kew is all about "vital scientific work that benefits mankind."[12] As a repository of plant matter for scientific accumulation, classification, and exploitation, the garden once staged its many ongoing spectacles of plant life to simulate nature's profusion under highly disciplined conditions, reflecting the grandeur of one human empire in little botanical skits.

Nature here is represented by plant matter, but this plant matter is tightly controlled, closely organized, and rigidly planned by human experts to accentuate an unreal verdant profusion, which convinces many that it grows as if it were still "wild." Empire is naturalized as nature is, at the same time, imperialized. After the end of empire, these plants are now depicted as packages of DNA, bundles of exchange value, or subservos of ecosystems needed by transnational capital to sustain the globalized megamachines supporting human life on the planet. Courtaulds, the chemical and fiber concern, touts its concern for the world's cellulose in "The Thread of Life" exhibition at Kew to underscore its support of Kew and all of the good work Kew does to find useful purposes for plant material.[13] Kew, in turn, portrays itself today as a scientific steward of nature's bounty for all humanity rather than as one warden over many botanical retainers in the Court of St. James where nature was once called to pay tribute and respect to the Crown. In fact, Kew Gardens openly admits to its far more economistic purposes for today's operations. In the 1990s one of Kew's main slogans was "finding plants to meet mankind's future needs."[14] Such applied practical engagements, in turn, were placed at the heart of Shaw's Missouri Botanical Garden from its very beginning.

The metaphor that now organizes the Missouri Botanical Garden is that of "a house." A visitor soon senses, as its *Guidebook* suggests, that "the Garden consists of a series of 'rooms,' each with its own special role in the overall design."[15] Each separate garden and landscaping feature reflects a historical period, a national gardening style, a special species, a family of related plants, or a unique interest in Henry Shaw's life. After steering visitors on tours through this expansive greenhousing of so many different botanical displays, the garden takes pride in how many leave its grounds seeking "more horticultural information through the Garden's educational program" in which they "learn about their own gardens as well as the world's."[16]

Not surprisingly, one of the garden's most popular and larger displays is the William T. Kemper Center for Home Gardening with extensive exhibits on the ins and outs of home gardening and residential landscaping. This facility, in turn, is nestled up to a small Chinese Garden (the Grigg Nanjing Friendship Garden), the larger English Woodland Garden (which provides a peek at the back acres of Chatsworth and Kew), and a much larger Japanese Garden with its four-and-a-half-acre lake, drum bridge, and lotus bed, where visitors can see at least how some of the world's gardens might look. All of these features extend to the west from the Victorian Area in the garden that once constituted Shaw's original nineteenth-century garden. Shaw's 1851 home, Tower Grove House, the 1859 museum building (modeled on one at Kew), the observatory, and Shaw's 1887 Mausoleum are scattered through this area along with a Victorian Garden and Maze Garden.[17]

To the north of the original Shaw grounds the garden's very modern iconic building, the Climatron, the 1882 Linnaean House, and Ridgway Center are clustered around extensive sculpture gardens, where fountains and reflecting pools, rose and bulb gardens, iris and daylily gardens, and expansive outdoor plazas break up the garden's spaces. The Ridgway Center is the main entrance to the garden as well as its gift shop, visitor's center, main auditorium, and educational area.[18] The Linnean House was constructed under Shaw's guidance to honor Carl Linnaeus, whom he saw as the world's greatest naturalist. Two other prominent naturalists who advised Shaw on the garden's construction also are featured there: Thomas Nuttall and Asa Gray. This traditional Victorian greenhouse is devoted to camellias, and it is surrounded by traditional European gardens of perennials and bedding plants. The 1960 geodesic dome building, the Climatron, now houses more than 1,400 species of plants on multilevel terraces that cover more than a half-acre. Featured here are "plants important to the economy of the tropics: banana, cacao, coffee and rubber, plus a selection of the Garden's large collection of orchids . . . pools and waterfalls give the sense of lushness of a tropical forest."[19]

To the northwest of the Climatron is the Temperate House, which replaced the 1913 Mediterranean House in 1989. It displays plants from temperate coastal regions. To the south is the 1914 Desert House with cacti and spurges from the world's arid lands. With its swaths of lawns, woodland, and plazas, the garden holds a very large tract of land that also contains the 1972 John S. Lehmann Building for research on tropical botany and partial storage of the garden's vast herbarium specimens—a collection of nearly four million carefully preserved specimens—and the Emerson Conservation Center that focuses on plant conservation. These research facilities are quite capacious, but the garden also owns the modern Monsanto Center two blocks further west on Shaw Boulevard.[20] This building holds the bulk of the garden's herbarium and now serves as the headquarters for its botanical research programs.

A Florapower Regime

As they are discursively constructed in contemporary technoscience, government often now finds "the principles of its rationality" and "the specific reality of the state"[21] in ecological programs, such as the policy programs of sustainable development, balanced growth, and ecological harmony championed by the Missouri Botanical Garden, as vital services for the earth's many constituent populations of human, and nonhuman, beings. Government comes into its own when it has "the welfare of a population, the improvement of its condition, or the increase of its wealth, longevity, health, etc."[22] as its object, and the Missouri Botanical Garden has found its target populations in St. Louis, the state of Missouri, and the United States, which it designs to improve by connecting their survival to plants. The expansive reach of transnational commerce gives scientific agencies and national governments all of life's biodiversity to administer as "endangered populations." And plant life can be the perfect beneficiary of various state ministrations inasmuch as plants are ignorant of what is being done to them as part of "the moment when it became important to manage a population . . . in its depths and details."[23] Preserving biodiversity in the plant world, then, simply crystallizes the latest phase of the "three movements: government, population, political economy, which constitute . . . a solid series, one which even today has assuredly not been dissolved"[24] in the formations of contemporary green governmentality.

Over the past generation, the time-space compression of postmodern living has brought the biopower of the entire planet, and not merely that of human beings, under the strategic ambit of administrative authority and state power. The environment, and particularly the goals of its protection in terms of "sustainability" or "security," has become a key theme of many political operations and ideological campaigns to raise public standards of collective morality, personal responsibility, and collective vigor. To organize and direct this global regime of biopower, however, reliable information is needed about plants and plant life. Henry Shaw's mission at his garden was "to discover and share knowledge about plants, in order to preserve and enrich life,"[25] and the Missouri Botanical

Garden continues this quest today by supporting a project of defining, developing, and deploying a specific type of biopower, namely, "florapower" to preserve and enrich human life. The Missouri Botanical Garden seems to follow Foucault by exploring how botanical gardens might articulate "a whole series of different tactics that combined in varying proportions the objective of disciplining the body and that of regulating populations"[26] through this florapower.

Botanical gardens, then, can be seen as power/knowledge formations that cloak science in beauty or wrap technology in landscape to reconstruct first nature systematically as second nature. What occurs autochthonously in many different environments around the world as "natural vegetation" gets reprocessed as collections of "domestic plants" arranged in the garden. Raw terrains are remade into landscape gardens, vegetable gardens, flower gardens, as well as arboretums and fructicetums. Nature is recruited into a spectacle in which new, useful, or odd plants can be introduced to human beings for ornamentation, cultivation, and exploitation.

The transition from nature to society via myths of contract shifts the register of power/knowledge operations by transforming the basis of disciplined inquiry. Centering discourse and practice on plant life covers nature with a new historical a priori or "a series of complex operations that introduce the possibility of a constant order into the totality of representations. It constitutes a whole domain of empiricity as at the same time *describable* and *orderable*."[27] The green chaos of forest, jungles, or prairies is redescribed, measured, reordered, and mediated by botanical science to define florapower and help it serve human populations. As Foucault suggests, the "framework of thought" in this historical a priori is what "delimits in the totality of experience a field of knowledge, defines the mode of being of the objects that appear in that field, provides man's everyday perception with theoretical powers, and defines the conditions in which he can sustain a discourse about things recognized to be true."[28]

One can argue that the modern regime of biopower formation, as it was described by Foucault, has not been especially attentive to the role of nature in the equations of biopolitics.[29] The controlled tactics of inserting human bodies into the machineries of industrial and agricultural production emerged as part and parcel of strategically adjusting the growth in human numbers to the development of industrial capitalism.

Policing the development of large human populations did generate systems of biopower. Under this regime, power/knowledge systems brought "life and its mechanisms into the realm of explicit calculations" and turned the manifold disciplines of scientific knowledge and discourses of state power into a new type of productive agency that led to the "transformation of human life"[30] into populations with the industrial revolution. Once this threshold of control was crossed, social experts recognized how the environmental interactions of human economics, politics, and technologies continually placed all human beings' existence as living beings into question.

Foucault essentially divides the environment into two separate, but interpenetrating, spheres of action: the biological and the historical. For most of human history, the biological dimension, or timeless forces of nature acting through disease and famine, dominated human existence with the ever-present menace of death. Developments in agricultural technologies as well as hygiene and health techniques, however, gradually provided some relief from starvation and plague by the end of the eighteenth century. As a result, the historical dimension began to grow in importance as "the development of the different fields of knowledge concerned with life in general, the improvement of agricultural techniques, and the observations and measures relative to man's life and survival contribution to this relaxation: a relative control over life averted some of the imminent risks of death."[31]

As the historical gradually started to envelop, circumscribe, and surround the biological, plants often marked these interlocking disciplinary expanses for "the environmental." And such environmentalized settings quickly dominated all forms of concrete human reality: "in the space of movement thus conquered, and broadening and organizing that space, methods of power and knowledge assumed responsibility for the life processes and undertook to control and modify them."[32] While Foucault does not explicitly label these spaces, methods, and knowledges as such as being "environmental," such disciplinary maneuvers are the origin of many forms of ecological activity. As biological life is refracted through economic, political, and technological existence, "the facts of life" pass into fields of control for many disciplines of technical knowledge. So the spheres of intervention for the management of biopower are generally also sites for cultivating faunapower (animal populations) and florapower (plant populations) specifically.

Foucault recognizes how these shifts implicitly raised "ecological issues" to the degree that they disrupted the understandings provided by the classical episteme used to define human interactions with nature. Living could become environmentalized as humans, or "a specific living being, and specifically related to other living beings,"[33] articulated their historical and biological life in profoundly new ways within artificial cities and mechanical modes of production, which deeply endanger faunapower and florapower reproduction. Environmental intervention into the plant world arises from "this dual position of life that placed it at the same time outside history, in its biological environment, and inside human historicity, penetrated by the latter's techniques of knowledge and power."[34] Strangely, even as he makes these linkages, Foucault does not develop his ecological insights, suggesting "there is no need to lay further stress on the proliferation of political technologies that ensued, investing the body, health, modes of subsistence and habitation, living conditions, the whole space of existence."[35]

Even so, Foucault finds the conjunctions needed for "the environment" to emerge as an anchor point for knowledge formations and/or an operational cluster of power tactics to discipline nature. As human beings consciously chose to wager their life as a species on the products of their biopolitical strategies and technological systems, a few also recognized how they were now wagering the lives of other, or all, species as well. While Foucault regards this shift as just one of many lacunae in his analysis, everything begins to change as human biopower systems interweave their daily operations in the biological environment, penetrating the workings of faunapower and florapower in many ecosystems with the techniques of knowledge and power.

Henry Shaw is one of the first North Americans to recognize that ecological knowledge about nature's power can become, through naturalistic science, a strategic technology to reinvest human bodies—their means of health, modes of subsistence, and styles of habitation as strategies for integrating the whole space of existence—with biohistorical significance.[36] With new institutions like botanical gardens, nature museums, and zoological expeditions, societies and states began to reposition their peoples within newly historicized biophysical environments, which are now also filled with various animal and plant bodies populating geophysical settings in a faunapower and florapower regime. What is varmint, and what is good critter; what is a weed, and what is useful plant are distinctions that must be made as the biological and historical are redefined.

Botanical gardens mobilize the forms and substances of first nature in second-nature terms to serve agendas set by social forces. Soil, plants, water, and stones are artificially combined in heavily cultivated, purposely engineered, and specially dedicated plots as representations of nature's bounty. Taming technologies are used to theatricalize the wild, turning wildernesses into plantings of representative trees, typical bushes, or common flowers. Just as zoos often decouple animals from their environments to cast wild nature as sad bags of feathers, fur, or fins in little pens for city dwellers to watch, so too do botanical gardens frequently misrepresent wild earth by plunking down a few plants in intensely gardened plots for cultures and societies to walk around in parklike sideshows. Real nature with its wild vegetation and untracked vistas turns into proper little paths paved through a gardener's tableau verdant.

But one cannot trail the traces of nature down the paths and through the plazas of the Missouri Botanical Garden without facing a far more troubling proposition. A trip along these tracks through families of plant life leads "beyond good and evil," because it soon exposes how putatively "discovered natural truths" are basically invented social constructs, or, at least, heavily processed conventional codes. The ultimate truth of any botanical knowledge is no less than what we believe to be "true" about nature at some critical juncture. Hence our systems of truth arise out of the instrumental distinctions made between plant and animal, wild and domestic, weed and crop. Truths, then, are only intelligible, significant, or believable statements, and truth can only be grasped as "a system of ordered procedures for the production, regulation, distribution, circulation and operation of statements."[37] Installations like the Missouri Botanical Garden are needed to give these statements naturalized material quiddity in rose beds, woodlands, and tropical greenhouses. By inventively constructing nature as "gardens," society uses natural myths to establish social truths of use, exchange, and profit.

The world-changing authority of botanical gardens rests on the same foundational conceit of all modernist Enlightenment philosophies: "a state of nature." From Hobbes to Rawls, there has been the presence of a somewhere, somehow, and something anterior to the state of civil society,

which is known as the "state of nature." This term provides the initial conditions for modern individuals: (a) to uncover the guiding principles of
modern rational living; (b) to organize a new civic order to leave a state
of nature; and (c) to enter some civic condition that justifies an atomic
individualism in commercial societies centered on attaining life, liberty,
property, or happiness by choosing various material goods from a basket of material/immaterial utilities. Whether these contracts are with
each other or a designated third party to serve as sovereign enforcer, these
agents are motivated by: (a) some fear of lives solitary, nasty, brutish, and
short; (b) some guarantee of an impartial judge to enforce the rational
laws of nature; (c) some desire to recapture some of the freedoms of nature in society; or (d) some concern for a justice for all acceptable to
each.

Modern Enlightenment reasoning must put these terms in practice
and position them in space, while modernized cultures constantly purify
these conceptual products by presuming two paradoxical principles,
namely, (a) "even though we construct Nature, Nature is as if we did
not construct it"; and (b) "even though we do not construct Society, Society is as if we did construct it."[38] Modern individuals can construct a
civic social order that protects some of the freedoms once held in the
state of nature, while alleviating many of the liabilities raised by living
in a purely natural condition with social alternatives. Still, a domain of
pristine natural givenness must also be found to frame where and how
such freedoms might thrive. Nature and society are kept pure and distinct although their continuous mediation is the daily work of modernity.[39] In markets, botanical gardens, and urban centers, plants evince
the unconstructedness of nature and the ungivenness of society.

Never entirely convincing, the modernist myths of this state of nature become utterly surrealistic at this conjuncture in history. After two
centuries of industrial revolutionization, nature as vast expanses of un-
tamed wildness has mostly vanished into modernity's commercial mediation of social/natural action. Enmeshed in complex networks of scientific rationalization and commercial exploitation, nature obviously
becomes contingent clusters of constructions. The entire planet now is
increasingly either a "built environment" or a "planned habitat." These
sites of "economic development" are what botanical gardens always have
been, even though they have pretended to be merely illustrative displays
of wildness.

As Foucault portrays the arts of government, they are concerned essentially with how to introduce rational economy into the management of things, including now the living animal species and plant material of nature, into the policy regime of the state. Rulership becomes in the eighteenth century the designation of a "level of reality, a field of intervention, through a series of complex processes" in which "government is the right disposition of things."[40] It evolves as an elaborate social formation, or "a triangle, sovereignty-discipline-government, which has as its primary target the population and as its essential mechanism the apparatuses of security."[41] Most significantly, Foucault sees state authorities mobilizing governmentality to bring about "the emergence of population as a datum, as a field of intervention and as an objective of governmental techniques, and the process which isolates the economy as a specific sector of reality" so that now "the population is the object that government must take into account in all its observations and *savior,* in order to be able to govern effectively in a rational and conscious manner."[42] The networks of continuous, multiple, and complex interaction between populations (their increase, longevity, health, etc.), territory (its expanse, resources, control, etc.), and wealth (its creation, productivity, distribution, etc.) are sites for governmentalizing rationality to manage the productive interaction of these forces.[43] While many see these observations pertaining to people, all of these insights are equally true of animals, plants, and all biomass in the world's growing capitalist economies.

Ecological disciplines, like botany, horticulture, and genetics, must mobilize particular assumptions, codes, and procedures in enforcing specific understandings about the economy and society. They generate useful knowledges, like those embedded in notions of sustainability or development, which create significant reserves of legitimacy from faunapower and florapower management.[44] Inasmuch as they classify, organize, and vet larger understandings of our natural reality, such discourses either authorize or invalidate the possibilities for constructing particular institutions, practices, and goods in society at large. They simultaneously frame the emergence of collective subjectivities—nations, animal species, and plant types as dynamic populations—and collections of subjects—individuals as discrete units in such nations, populations, and biomasses. The parameters of ecological discipline, in turn, can be reevaluated as the operational elements of control "in which are articulated the effects of a certain type of power and the reference of a certain type of knowledge, the machinery by which the power relations give rise to a possible corpus of knowledge, and knowledge extends and reinforces the effects of this power."[45]

Gardens and Governmentality

In its green governmentality, the Missouri Botanical Garden's disciplinary articulations about sustainability and development follow Henry Shaw's dicta about using plants and knowledge of plant material "to preserve and enrich life" by establishing and enforcing "the right disposition of things" between humans, plants, and their biophysical environment. In this capacity, the Missouri Botanical Garden has a five fold organizational mission: "*Research:* exploration, discovery, and classification of plants; *International Scientific Collaboration; Education:* for children, adults, and graduate students; *Low Impact Horticulture:* integrated pest management, water conservation, composting, and more; *Conservation:* The Missouri Botanical Garden is part of the Center for Plant Conservation, a national network that works to preserve our endangered species of the United States. The Center has its headquarters at the Missouri Botanical Garden."[46]

The application of such botanical discipline expresses the authority of knowledgeable forces to police the fitness of all biological organisms and the health of their natural environments. Master concepts, like "survival," "preservation," and "sustainability" for species and their habitats, empower technoscientific managers at the Missouri Botanical Garden to enscribe their biological/cultural/economic agenda on the earth's many territories in an elaborate array of closely cultivated environments. Hence there is no surprise in what the Missouri Botanical Garden declares to patrons in its *Visitor's Guide:* "Plants are essential to life on Earth. The quality of human life, our very survival, depends on the health of our global environment. Everything we do affects our environment, and we are all responsible for protecting it."[47] Still, some of us, like the botanical experts at Shaw's garden, will be much more protective and responsible than others.

When approached from this direction, our planet becomes an immense engine, or "ecological life-support system," for the human race that has "with only occasional localized failures" provided "services upon which human society depends consistently and without charge."[48] As an environmental engine, the earth generates "ecosystem services," or those products and functions derived from natural systems that human societies perceive as valuable, faunapower and florapower reserves.[49] This is what must survive. Human life can continue only if such survival-promoting services continue. They include the generation of soils, the regeneration of plant nutrients, capture of solar energy, conversion of solar energy into biomass, accumulation/purification/distribution of water, control of pests, provision of a genetic library, maintenance of breathable air, control of micro- and macroclimates, pollination of plants, diversification of animal species, development of buffering mechanisms in catastrophes, and aesthetic enrichment.[50] As an environmental engine, the planet's ecology requires ecoengineers to guide its sustainable use, and systems of green governmentality must be adduced to monitor and manage the system of systems that produce all of these robust services. By preserving and protecting florapower, the Missouri Botanical Garden aims to be in the vanguard of this movement. Plants are after all quite important. They sustain humanity's supply of oxygen, food, fair climates, economic goods, and medicine.[51] Just as the sustained use of technology "requires that it be maintained, updated and changed periodically," so too does the "sustainable use of the planet require that we not destroy our ecological capital, such as old-growth forests, streams and rivers (with their associated biota), and other natural amenities."[52] Florapower, then, is the key value.

The Missouri Botanical Garden speaks to the ecological conscience of the contemporary era by presuming to be one of the planet's advocates for all plants. Every *Visitor's Guide* received by patrons with their paid admission spends one quarter of its coverage on pointed ecological briefs: "Why are Plants Important? What is Biodiversity? Why is Biodiversity Important? What You Can Do."[53] In fixating on plants, the garden finds a way to espouse implicitly the teachings of Barry Commoner's three laws of ecology, but it does so in ways that beg the question of nature with the presumption of society.

Commoner's first law of ecology is "everything is connected to everything else," and the whole depends on "each part doing its part to sustain these complex habitats."[54] Everything for the garden becomes "biodiversity," or "the total variety of all living things on Earth," and it is connected to population growth, the global economy, and modernization of the tropics. Biodiversity, however, cannot do its part, while rapid population growth, spreading poverty, and greater industrialization undercut all biodiversity by destroying plant species and habitats. Life is a jigsaw puzzle in which "every species has value and each one depends on many others for survival. If we lose too many parts of the puzzle, our entire global ecosystem is threatened."[55]

Commoner's second law of ecology says "everything has to go somewhere,"[56] and the garden confirms that plants and plant services go many places to sustain the development of markets. Forty million acres of tropical forests are destroyed each year to fill markets with goods; more than half of all human food comes from three grasses, wheat, rice, and maize; and out of 250,000 species of flowering plants on earth, only 25,000 have been evaluated for their potential uses to humans. Ecologies are merely the supply side of economies, and botany shows how everything in them can go somewhere quite profitably.

Finally, Commoner's third law of ecology is "Nature knows best,"[57] and the garden guarantees that this tip-top knowledge in nature is well displayed in its exhibits. What constitutes nature's best knowledge is simple: plants serve humanity in countless ways: they generate oxygen, they are food, they moderate climate, they provide shelter, they give medicines, they are commodities.[58] Everywhere nature gives, and botanical gardens collect and concentrate its gifts by discovering and applying the best knowledge from nature of its plant life. Plants left on their own cannot produce these outcomes; but, once captured in gardens, they become vital relays of florapower. These technologies should not operate autonomously, but rather as rational circuits in the world system of producing and consuming commodities.

Boundary Functions

The Missouri Botanical Garden draws a border for humanity between inside and outside, defining the spaces where, when, and how either "nature" or "society" occurs. In here, plants and soils must constitute nature by design, socializing wild ecologies to serve artificial ends. Out there, plants and soils might continue their random haphazard becomings, naturalizing tame ecologies in gardens by serving the autochthonous ends of wilderness. Botanists mobilize such gardens to operate as continuous grids of rolling judgment, naming this a "useful plant" and that a "noxious weed." Gardening, in turn, becomes mostly planting for use. These designs always are historical/cultural/social in their economy, not timelessly neutral or suprahumanly objective. Hence, the Missouri

Botanical Garden works as much to define and eliminate useless vegetation as it does to cultivate and propagate useful vegetation. Its program on home gardening is simultaneously an evangelical campaign for useful nature and an endless pogrom against useless nature as determined by science and aesthetics.

On the one hand, as director William Trelease observed, "it is impossible to divest the idea of a garden from the idea of park, a place to which people go for their recreation; a place where the love and the taste for the beautiful may be at once cultivated and gratified."[59] Yet, on the other hand, as Trelease asserted, "the Garden also had scientific and educational uses. . . . It furnished materials for the study of fruitful and medicinal plants."[60] The garden, then, helps soft sell science as landscaping. And nature—once disciplined and deployed in the landscapes of an urban park—allows gardeners and botanists to bring its fruitful and medicinal plants into cities as material furnishings for industrial parks, home gardens, and planted landscapes.

Foucault is correct about the modern state. It is not "an entity which was developed above individuals, ignoring what they are and even their very existence," because it has evolved instead "as a very sophisticated structure, in which individuals can be integrated, under one condition: that this individuality would be shaped in a new form, and submitted to a set of very specific patterns."[61] Missouri is one such state, and the Botanical Garden slices and shapes its visions of nature there around the individuals molded by this state. Biopower is meant here to coevolve rationally with the faunapower and florapower of a sustainable society. Producing discourses of ecological living, articulating designs of sustainable development, and propagating definitions of environmental literacy for many individuals on personal visits to the Botanical Garden simply add new twists to the "very specific patterns" by which the state formation helps constitute "a modern matrix of individualization."[62] The regime of human biopower, in turn, operates through character-shaping systems of technoscientific identity as much as it does through the policy machinations of governmental bureaus within any discretely bordered territory. Botanical gardens merely echo the effects from "one of the great innovations in the techniques of power in the eighteenth century," namely, "the emergence of 'population' as an economic and political problem"[63] for states to administer the health of their animal and plant life alongside humanity.

Once demography emerges as a science of statist administration, its statistical attitudes can diffuse into the numerical surveillance of nature, or earth and its nonhuman inhabitants, as well as the study of society, and its human members.[64] Government—and now, most importantly, statist modes of ecological technoscience—preoccupies itself with "the conduct of conduct." Previously, the ethical concerns of family, community, and nation often guided how conduct was to be conducted; yet, at this juncture, technoscientific scans of the environment emerge as a new anthropocentric ground for normalizing each individual's behavior. Environments are spaces under police supervision, expert management, or technocratic control; hence, in the taking of environmental agendas into the heart of state policy, one finds the fullest articulation of the police state. Inasmuch as the conduct of any person's environmental conduct becomes the initial limit on others' ecological enjoyments, so too does the conduct of the social body's conduct necessitate that the state always work as an effective "environmental protection agency." The ecological domain is the region of being that science, society, and the state must now produce, protect, and police in eliciting biopower: it is the center of environmentalizing discipline, knowledge, and power.[65]

Mobilizing the biological energies of florapower, then, accelerates after the 1970s along with global fast capitalism. The concern for biodiversity in ecology becomes a formalized disciplinary mode of paying systematic "attention to the processes of life . . . to invest life through and through"[66] in order to transform all living things into biological populations for transnational commerce. The tremendous explosion of material prosperity on a global scale in the twentieth century would not have been possible without ecology to guide "the controlled insertion of bodies into the machinery of production and the adjustment of the phenomena of population to economic processes."[67] A new politics of all plants and animals also can emerge out of ecology as biotic resource managerialists, like those at the Missouri Botanical Garden, acquire "the methods of power capable of optimizing forces, aptitudes, and life in general without at the same time making them more difficult to govern."[68]

Human populations must coevolve in markets with plant populations, and the Missouri Botanical Garden provides the means to attain that outcome. The main mission of operations like the Missouri Botanical Garden is to define and defend florapower. This adjusts the accumulation of valuable plants and valued animals to suit capital, while at the same time seeking to check whatever unsustainable growth that could threaten these assets. In becoming an essential subassembly for transnational economic development, florapower generation helps rationalize the conjoining of "the growth of human groups to the expansion of productive forces and the differential allocation of profit."[69] To preserve and enrich human life by discovering and sharing plant knowledge, population ecology, environmental science, and range management are now, in part, very representative expressions of "the exercise of bio-power in its many forms and modes of application."[70] Indeed, turning nature into society's botanical garden might signal that a postmodern condition perhaps has been reached, because, as Jameson concludes, "the modernization process is complete and nature is gone for good."[71] Following Foucault, the curators of the Missouri Botanical Garden now claim that the lives of all species are being wagered in all of humanity's new economic and political strategies. At the same time, when guided, in part, by Missouri Botanical Garden experts, modern societies and states also assume "responsibility for the life processes" as they undertake "to control and modify them"[72] by permitting the vegetable kingdom, as Shaw once directed, to preserve and enrich life. With this strategy, then, Shaw's garden concretely exemplifies the instrumental rationality of Georgian agriculture in Great Britain, the watchwords of which were best expressed by the King of Brobdingnag in Swift's *Gulliver's Travels:* "whoever could make two Ears of Corn, or two Blades of Green to grow upon a spot of ground where only one grew before, would deserve better of mankind, and do more essential service to his country, than the whole race of politicians put together."

CHAPTER EIGHT

Southwestern Environments as Hyperreality: The Arizona–Sonora Desert Museum

The ideological profile of nature has remained a perpetual object of contestation in American culture and society, as chapters 6 and 7 have maintained, during the 1990s and the early twenty-first century. Even after centuries of Enlightenment rationalism, the currents of mysticism, conservatism, and romanticism are quite strong in Western philosophies of nature. Consequently, the ideological meaning of nature remains unstable, ineffable, or indeterminate in much of the contemporary world.[1] In turn, the collective imagination of nature often serves as a screen for other displaced social contradictions or cultural affirmations, which seize on discrete signs in the environment, enduring cycles of the cosmos, or persistent tendencies among life on earth to stabilize various political ideologies.[2]

As Foucault suggests, power in everyday life must work through many different cultural discourses and technical disciplines in order to have any effect, and the construct of nature always has figured importantly in this process.[3] This disciplinary force propounds indirect systems of ideological legislation, which operationalize themselves in cultural productions like museum exhibits by simultaneously forming new planes of productive power.[4] Such power helps to construct and police modern publics by managing the nodes of knowledge, regimes of rules, and spaces of subjectivity endorsed by museum displays.[5] This indirect ideological guidance helps to order social and personal behavior from below by tacitly steering systems of cultural inclination and making their impact often far more powerful than the direct legislation of sovereign agencies attempting to impose order from above by coercive acts.[6]

The ideological dynamics found in most nature museums, I believe, are no different at the world-famous Arizona–Sonora Desert Museum in Tucson, Arizona. While arguably there has been much to admire in the development of this museum institution in America's Southwest, I want to suggest that the Arizona–Sonora Desert Museum over the years also has cultivated a contradictory set of ideological positions in its displays. On the one hand, it combs through the biological diversity of the local deserts, gathering together a dazzling display of wildlife and plant species in imaginative museum exhibits, which have become a potent imaginary force operating symbolically as an internationally recognized iconic representation of Southwestern desert ecologies. On the other hand, this institution increasingly depends on economic support from visitors, residents, and developers tied to a destructive land-development economy in order to maintain these particular types of "civilizing rituals."[7] The everyday operations of the region's economic growth continually consume more undeveloped desert lands to build contemporary Sunbelt cities, like Tucson, El Paso, Albuquerque, Las Vegas, Phoenix, or Los Angeles, while they destroy the deserts and wildlife habitat the museum would preserve.

As David Harvey suggests, all places, including the Arizona–Sonora deserts, are constructed out of intricate networks of social relations. Consequently, as the Desert Museum illustrates, these networks become "the focus of the imaginary, of beliefs, longings, and desires," in which their substance and shape capture intensely concentrated discursive activity "filled with symbolic and representational meanings" that are "a distinctive product of institutionalized social and political-economic power."[8] The Arizona–Sonora Desert Museum, then, has become ensnared in a dangerous dialectic that plays for audiences in both the national and the local.[9] While it poses as the protector of the real desert, all of its displays hyperrealize Arizona's desert ecologies in a unique desert imaginary, the many little ecological minispectacles put on exhibit in the museum's displays. Still, the hypercapitalistic growth economy of the Arizona–Sonora region works by exploiting the mystique of the desert imaginary to produce the concrete deserts of Sunbelt urbanization.

Indeed, the Desert Museum's "themed environments" for artfully displaying desert plants and animals are widely acknowledged by tourism promoters, local officials, and many residents as extremely powerful symbolic attractors, pulling millions of new tourists and migrants into the

Southwest to enjoy the mysteries of desert living. Each of them brims with specific symbolic meanings that are a distinctive product of the region's institutionalized images of balanced growth and concentrated cultures of outdoor living that power Arizona's economics, politics, and society. Not surprisingly, then, *Frommer's Arizona '95* tourist handbook, for example, touted the Desert Museum as one of Tucson's top attractions—a site to see even if the visitor has only a day to spend touring the city. And it assured the would-be visitor, "don't be surprised by the name," in other words, this is not another boring museum; instead, "this is a zoo and it's one of the best in the country."[10] This analysis begins to explore some of these ideological conflicts and material contradictions as they are expressed by the representational workings of the Arizona–Sonora Desert Museum as a "nature" museum.

Origins and Operations

The Arizona–Sonora Desert Museum occupies twelve acres in the Tucson Mountain Park about fifteen miles west of downtown Tucson, and, as the "Winter City Guide: NOT TO BE MISSED" section of *Tucson Lifestyle* records, "recognized worldwide as a leader in natural history interpretation and exhibitory, this 'living' museum houses over 1,300 kinds of plants and 300 species of animals that live in enclosures designed to replicate their niche in the wild."[11] In many ways, it is a uniquely sui generis attempt to represent the unusual Sonoran desert biome; and, in other respects, it simply continues familiar representational philosophies for museum exhibitions first tested during the 1920s and 1930s in New York State at Bear Mountain Park for a museum system centered on trailside exhibits of nature, wildlife, and historical material. Instead of New York's eastern woodlands, however, the local Sonoran ecology is displayed at the Desert Museum in an idiosyncratic system of nature representation that eclectically combines elements of a zoo, botanical garden, geological park, nature museum, and ecological simulation. Open every day of the year, it welcomes visitors from around the local Arizona–Sonora bioregion and the world at large to learn about desert wildlife and vegetation from exhibits that mix and match rhetorical elements of zoology lecture with nature mysticism, environmental rant with land-planning brief, botanical disquisition with boosteristic spiel.

The museum had its beginnings in post–World War II Tucson during the early 1950s. At an October 1951 meeting of the Pima County Park

Committee, Arthur Newton Pack and William H. Carr proposed that some portion of the 15,000 acres set aside as the Tucson Mountain Park in 1929 be used as "a leading educational center for the purpose of acquainting the public with their rich but vanishing heritage in wildlife, plant life and scenic values, to the end that, through knowledge, will come appreciation and a better attitude toward all resource conservation."[12] Taking a recreation facility built by the Civilian Conservation Corps and Works Progress Administration in the 1930s and then known as Tucson Mountain Park Lodge, Pack and Carr were authorized by the Pima County Park Committee to use ten acres around the lodge buildings "to present a rounded exposition of conservation and natural history factors through the development of an outdoor museum and in combination with zoological and botanical gardens and nature trails."[13] With $10,000 from a small foundation in Carr's family and work contributed by many volunteers, the Desert Museum opened on Labor Day 1952 with its founders hoping to provide "a means of helping man to recognize and assume his responsibilities toward nature in order to gain some hope of assuring his future."[14] Within two weeks it was being touted in the *Tucson Daily Citizen* as "one of the outstanding assets and attractions of our community for the use of local residents and visitors to the State alike."[15]

The Desert Museum has indeed proven to be a very valuable asset and attraction for both Tucson's and Arizona's economies. From 1950 to 1995, Tucson's population grew from 46,000 to nearly 450,000; and, during the same four decades, its urbanized areas expanded from less than 40 to more than 155 square miles.[16] Further north, the Phoenix metropolitan area's growth has been even more remarkable. Counting 107,000 people in residence during 1950, Phoenix grew to nearly 1,100,000 residents by 1995. Its developed area increased just as exponentially, rising from less than 60 square miles in 1950 to 420 square miles in the mid-1990s, while the entire Phoenix metropolitan area grew to more than 1,000 square miles.[17] Growth in these highly concentrated urban areas, at the same time, does not count the thousands of other acres chewed up out in the desert by ill-conceived land-development schemes all across the state where only a few ramshackle houses or double-wide mobile homes quickly can reduce once pristine desert habitats to dusty wide-spots in the road. From the early 1950s to the mid-1990s, Arizona's human population rose almost five-fold from 750,000 to more than 4 million.[18]

As William Claibourne observes, "the relentless assault of encroaching development" is so intense that "the Sonoran Desert in central Arizona is vanishing at the rate of an acre an hour."[19] The economic development payoff of cultural assets like the Desert Museum has been considerable.

As its enabling resolutions required, this institution has been much more than merely a museum, a zoo, an aquarium, or a botanical garden inasmuch as it always has worked to generate a pointed environmentalistic interpretation of the Sonoran bioregion by demonstrating the complicated interplay between terrain, climate, plants, animals, and history in the evolution of this desert environment. As Carr admits, even local residents had very little appreciation of the desert when the museum opened in 1952.[20] Outside of their small urban oasis in Tucson, most residents espoused a "pioneer ethic of *subduing* nature. . . . in the march westward, most natural things had been considered hostile if they were not of immediate use, or at best inconsequential."[21]

Carr had worked at the American Museum of Natural History as well as at the Kanawauke Regional Museum in Bear Mountain Park, New York. At the invitation of George H. Sherwood, the director of the American Museum, Carr put together the Nature Trails and Trailside museums at Bear Mountain, which were unusually organized outdoors with living objects themselves in order to complement, but not duplicate, the formal exhibits of indoor city museums. Coming to Tucson in 1944 after eighteen years at Bear Mountain, he became involved in the local conservation community and was elected president of the Arizona Wildlife Federation in 1947. As an exercise in conservation education, the Desert Museum under Carr's guidance stressed the importance of treating the Sonoran Desert with great care: its rare flora, sparse fauna, precious water, and fragile soil in the region's unusual basin and range ecologies are very easily destroyed, but very difficult to restore. Carr's vision of the Desert Museum as a bulwark against runaway growth was approved grudgingly by the world-renowned naturalist Joseph Wood Krutch, who admitted in the early 1960s that growth cannot be stopped. Therefore, Tucson had to accept a "partial solution—namely the reservation of some sections of it as public land explicitly reserved in Parks, Monuments, and Wilderness Areas. It is far more rewarding to be able to *live* in the desert than merely to visit it. But that is at least better than nothing."[22]

Over the past four decades, the Desert Museum has stuck to Carr's original conservationist principles, and it has done much to enhance many people's visits to the desert. Approaching the Arizona–Sonora Desert Museum from the south on Kinney Road, visitors drive through the mostly pristine hills and arroyos of Tucson Mountain Park. A huge billboard sign admonishes visitors and residents alike: "Removal of Natural Rock and Vegetation Strictly Prohibited." Within the spare few thousand acres of the park, this injunction is obeyed so that it can be sanctified fully on the twelve tiny acres of simulated desert habitat inside the Desert Museum. Outside the park and the adjacent Saguaro National Park, however, the local real estate/banking/land development industries relentlessly box up and blade off all natural rock and vegetation to manufacture "Arizona As It Is Supposed to Be," namely, verdant golf courses, vast water parks, crosstown connector parkways, and spray stucco subdivisions. The Phoenix metroplex alone already covers more than 1 percent of the Sonoran Desert's 100,000 square miles, and the cities of Tucson, Yuma, Ambos Nogales, and Hermasillo are rapidly effacing more of its lands every day. Consequently, the Desert Museum's permanent gold reserves of twelve pristine acres of museumified desert anchor the circulation of millions of other desert acres as fast capitalist commodities in boom-town economies.

Still, after being open and active for almost fifty years in a state now well known for its destructive cycles of rapacious land development, the Desert Museum largely has failed as a corrective device, which Carr thought would help Arizona and America "to recognize and assume its responsibilities toward nature."[23] Although many of its local boosters still pretend that it serves such educational purposes, this point can be pushed even further. In addition to failing to fulfill its original conservationist goals, the "imaginary desert" being produced at the Arizona–Sonora Desert Museum actually has acquired, implicitly and explicitly, an important symbolic role in anchoring the regional political economy of rapid growth. Amidst the growing expanses of these concrete deserts, it now serves as an authoritative symbolic depository of the Southwestern desert's cultural and ecological mystique, which is now being paved over rapidly by urban sprawl.

The Museum as Desert Walkabout

To appreciate the possible personal impact of a visit to the Desert Museum, one must recognize how its design aims to simulate a walkabout through the Sonoran Desert, concentrating its entertainment effects by cramming the signs of many real desert habitats into a relatively small space. As Carr admits, the museum essentially is designed to give "visitors who otherwise would not risk wandering in the desert an opportunity to see its flora at close range."[24] Therefore, it combines zoolike habitat displays with museumlike natural history narratives with botanical gardenlike concentrations of plants with parklike rambling walks. These slightly odd combinations and contradictions give the museum its unusual educational potency. Within its small boundaries, an indoor zoo, an outdoor museum, a natural zoological park, a desert botanical garden, and an arid region's celebration of water are all jumbled together amidst the saguaro-dotted foothills of Tucson Mountain Park.

At the museum's entrance, one is drawn immediately into one of two cool dark halls containing exhibits of the fishes and amphibians as well as the reptiles and invertebrates that inhabit the Sonoran Desert from the coasts of Baja California to the small creeks draining into the Gila and Colorado Rivers. Immediately below the low stone-and-timber structures of this main building, an elaborately landscaped cactus garden with more than 140 species of cacti and other desert vegetation stretches out below the visitor, illustrating the strange adaptations of plant life to this bioregion. To the right, a winding path invites the visitor into a geology ramada to observe the basin and range topography of the Sonoran Desert by looking out over the Avra Valley to the Santa Rita Mountains and Baboquivari Peak to the south. Then the path runs underground into the Cave and Earth Sciences Complex, which simulates a live limestone cave and displays a broad spectrum of mineral specimens common to the area.

Here visitors can experience firsthand the concrete rhetoric of the artificial rock emulation technology pioneered at the museum, whose simulated boulders compose 90 percent of all enclosures and structures in the Desert Museum's habitat displays. The walk also invites one to envision the museum site in the Precambrian Era (1.6 billion years ago), when it was in a mountain range; the Paleozoic Era (350 million years ago), when it was on the seabed of a shallow ocean; the Mesozoic Era (180 million years ago), as it sat in a river delta and volcanic zone inhabited by dinosaurs; and the Cenozoic Era (11,000 years ago), as it occupied a cool moist landscape full of prehistoric megafauna and pinõn-juniper vegetation. This particular display stresses the enduring realities of contingency and change in nature, which today often is seen by many contemporary environmentalists as being totally timeless or fixed in some frozen perfection. Yet the Desert Museum accurately indicates how the present biophysical guise of the Arizona–Sonora Desert actually is only about 4,000 years old.[25] As the visitor leaves the Earth Sciences display hall, the path then leads out to the Mountain Habitat display.

There one finds the large mammals and birds of the "mountain islands," which dot the Sonoran Desert flatlands, displayed in very natural "open habitats." Black bears, for example, are shown in canyonlike settings complete with cottonwood, ash, and Arizona cypress trees that they have ripped out and eaten, as they do in the wild, since first put on exhibit at the museum. Along with them there are enclosures with Coues' white-tail deer, Merriam's turkeys, Mexican gray wolves, mountain lions, and jaguars to illustrate the various animals occupying the mountain habitat of oak-pine-juniper woodland at the 4,000-to-7,000-foot level in elevation. The adjacent Desert Grassland ramada shows the nature of the environment at 3,000 to 5,000 feet of elevation. A prairie dog town and enclosures for coyotes, kit foxes, javelinas, and coatis showcase some of the animals in the region, but the path quickly runs through the Small Cat Grotto (with margays, ocelots, bobcats, and jaguarundis in natural settings) and the riparian habitat (with beavers and otters in an artificial canyon stream) that is joined by a bighorn sheep display in a mini–box canyon, which all composes the beaver/otter/sheep complex.

The walkway meanders by a desert tortoise pen and an immense aviary with more than three hundred species of desert birds all coexisting inside an immense open-air cage. Then it turns back toward the main entrance halls, going past the desert garden display, another underground exhibit (which was quite innovative during its development in 1956), illustrating how desert animals retreat underground by day to cope with the desert's intense heat; the enchanting walk-through hummingbird aviary with its eight different species flitting from flower to bush to tree for the visitor; and then finally the saguaro cactus exhibits. The path finally circles back to the cactus garden, bringing the visitor again to the steps of the main entrance with all of his or her imaginary impressions from this walkabout through the desert's ecology, landscapes, and wildlife. A visit to the Desert Museum after a few days in Tucson or Phoenix allows one to visit "the real desert" at one discrete site of hyperreal concentration without really leaving the urban complex, releasing one from facing a real desert environment and recharging all of the symbolic ideologies about the unique attractions of "desert living." Michael Logan aptly observes that the Desert Museum has served an invaluable service to Tucson's residents and visitors inasmuch as it has provided "safe sojourns into the incredible variety of vegetation and animal life in the desert."[26]

Themed Environments: The Hyperreal Desert

The Arizona–Sonora Desert Museum has been in the aesthetic vanguard of developing "themed environments" at zoos and museums thanks to the early work of Merv Larson, who spent the years from 1955 to 1976—supported by museum cofounders Carr and Pack—designing artificial "natural environments" to represent different aspects of the desert's geology and ecology to museum visitors. Coming to the museum with a background in museum operations rather than zoo management, Larson wanted to fabricate "nature dioramas, like in a museum, only with live animals instead of dead animals."[27] With this aesthetic agenda, the Desert Museum's hyperreal simulations were first successfully launched, like Disneyland, in the 1950s. The museum's model, "nature dioramas" with "live animals," became the theoretical template for organizing every visitor's activities in these desert territories, the built environments of the museum's grounds. As Baudrillard suggests, "simulation is characterized by a *precession of the model*, of all models around the merest fact—the models come first, and their orbital (like the bomb) circulation constitutes the genuine magnetic field of events."[28]

The rigors of the desert environment force many animals underground in the summer heat, leaving most visitors to the museum in its early days wondering where the wildlife was. When Carr heard about schoolchildren dreaming about going underground to see them, he proposed, not long after the museum opened, that a subterranean display be built to include views of mammals and reptiles in their daytime burrows, plant roots underground, and native Arizonan-Sonoran bat species in a special manmade cavern. To make these settings realistic, the museum began experimenting with plaster-latex cast "rocks" that, under the eye of Merv Larson, were scaled up to build "natural enclosures" for larger desert mammal, fish, plant, and bird species. By 1957 the tunnel was opened to visitors and immediately became a benchmark installation for similar exhibits elsewhere around the world.

Inspired in part by a friend who worked at Disneyland, Larson used the rock technology invented by Disney imagineers for Skull Island in the Anaheim theme park when he began working at the Desert Museum. However, Larson created an ideal ecological map of all the desert's environments rather than the actual territoriality of the desert, creating, as Baudrillard might observe, a hyperreal simulation of places and spaces that do not, in fact, really exist. This process is "the generation by models of a real without origin or reality: a hyperreal."[29] By using steel rebar, wire mesh, fiberglass, and sprayed concrete, Larson fashioned entire rock formations, cave complexes, and canyon habitats at the Desert Museum in order to, ironically, "put every animal there into a natural environment."[30] These animal display sites, instead of being the old-wave steel-bar, concrete slab pens of traditional zoos, simulate the realities of some natural site with new-wave hyperreal, concrete sites of imagined sights for which no original actually exists in nature. These new habitats, in turn, are quite flexible. Rather than killing and stuffing real animals for display inside urban museums, like Tucson's International Wildlife Museum a few miles back toward the city's downtown, the Desert Museum with a "combination of real and unreal rocks and trees and real dirt" now can "put animals together in groups similar to their groups in the real world."[31]

Whether they are designed as royal menageries for aristocratic trophies or public art galleries for Mother Nature's living artworks, most zoos have been little more than concentration camps for unfortunate animals condemned to run around in small pens or cold cages as zoological traces of their native habitats.[32] Zoos pretend to represent "nature" to "society," but they often basically do little more than incarcerate a select cross-section of nonhuman beings outside of their native habitats in cages amidst human cities. They suggest that the societies that build them have the power and wealth to take these creatures from their natural settings, but they do not successfully emulate where the creatures come from beyond grouping all of the cages of those animals taken from each continent or bioregion together. Nature and its environments rarely are represented realistically in zoos, although some of their feathery, furry, or fishy denizens are held hostage against the wild as people stare at these bags of skin and bundles of neuroses to learn allegedly more about "the wild animals" of nature. Much of this continues at the Desert Museum, although the more natural designs of its hyperreal "open habitats" make some slight improvement in animal detainment technology.

In addition to enhancing the condition of the animals, Larson's fabrication of simulated rock formations was partly environmental and partly aesthetic in its motivations. If real rock was removed from the Tucson Mountains or somewhere else nearby, it would, of course, scar the terrain as much as any other earthmoving project intending to build a trailer park or a waste dump out in the desert. But more importantly, the use of fake rocks to represent the desert holds more true to the essential hyperreality underpinning much of contemporary American life in which most environments are cinematically or televisually themed products.[33] That is, when confronting the question of moving real rocks to the museum, Larson realized it is "a case of the more-real looking less real than the not-real."[34] Imagineering the themed environments of the Arizona–Sonora Desert Museum, then, endorses the credo of Disney-style imagineers, namely, the imperatives of "an imaginary effect concealing that reality no more exists outside than inside the bounds of some artificial perimeter."[35] For Baudrillard, Disneyland (the fantasy) exists to induce popular belief in the United States (a hyperreality). Indeed, "Disneyland is there to conceal the fact that it is the 'real' country, all of 'real' America, which is Disneyland (just as prisons are there to conceal the fact that it is the social in its entirety, in its banal omnipresence, which is carceral). Disneyland is presented as imaginary in order to make us believe that the rest is real, when in fact all of Los Angeles and the America surrounding it are no longer real, but of the order of the hyperreal and simulation."[36]

In the themed environment of the Arizona–Sonora Desert, the Desert Museum's hyperreality envelops these arid spaces and begins reproducing mysteries of nature out of spray cement. "When you use real rock, it doesn't look like it was created by Nature," as one environmental imagineer notes, "it looks like a pile of rocks that somebody put there. Artificial rock work, if done right, you won't notice it. You'll assume it's real."[37] These remarks might be regarded as the fundamental watchwords of the Desert Museum's "desert experiences." One could search the entire desert region, but there is no one single site that could be roped off, and then vended to visitors as the quintessential Sonoran Desert reality. Reality just looks too dry, dead, and deserted to work. But at manmade sites, like the Desert Museum, the Sonoran Desert can be artificially imagineered, like Disneyland or Disneyworld, by concentrating real dirt, fake rock, real animal groups, fake plant communities on twelve acres of artificial caves, trails, cages, and habitats. It is a done deal, this manufacturing of nature, but when it is done right, no one notices, or, at least, protests against its hyperreal qualities, because most visitors assume it is "real." Indeed, many patrons of the museum record their astonishment in the guest book over how lucky its founders were to discover these caves, canyons, and springs all in one place.

Interestingly, Larson left the Desert Museum in 1976 to found the Larson Company, which reproduced many of his Desert Museum innovations at many zoos and aquariums around the world. After Larson sold the company in 1987, however, it has gone the next step to produce "naturescapes" as part of hotels, theme parks, and road projects in what it calls "themed environments." Just as it once engineered natural environments, like canyon streams or caves for beavers and bobcats to enjoy as their habitats, it now builds elaborate water theme parks as naturescapes for Sunbelt tourists at posh resorts. This transfer of impoundment technologies from zoos to resort hotels and upscale homes for hyperreal naturescapes within contemporary cities, however, raises some troubling questions about the Desert Museum and the environment it is dedicated to displaying. At some point, one wonders when and where these alluring hyperreal representations begin to undermine attempts to organize an effective defense of really wild nature. In comparison to the Desert Museum's tamed hyperrealism, real nature may seem quite barren, dull, and worthless, if indeed it is perceived as real at all. Lacking the hyperrealistic intensity of the Desert Museum's imagineered displays, the usually unattractive real state of Arizona's desert nature then much more naturally can become Arizona's attractive desert real estate.

Manufacturing the Southwestern Mystique

The Desert Museum is quite thorough in cultivating its careful representations of all the unique geological and meteorological qualities of the Sonoran Desert. From its visualization of the mountain highlands, desert grasslands, and desert flats, the museum has been very exacting about how each of these ecological niches has been colonized by particular animals and plants. Yet there is a tremendous void in all of the Desert Museum's displays, namely, the human communities of the Sonoran

Desert. Neither the prehistoric, the historic, nor the contemporary human being is brought systemically into this careful representation of these environments.

The Sonoran Desert, as it is conceptualized and represented here, is essentially the pristine desert as it historically has been, and still is fabricated, for the tourist's gaze. The Sonoran Desert in addition to being a place on the map also has become a bundle of potent icons, manufactured over the past century by railroad companies, pulp Westerns, land developers, travel agencies, Hollywood movies, naturalist writings, and chambers of commerce.[38] Its semiotic conductors and capacitors are coppery sunrises and pink sunsets, rocky mesas and saguaro cacti, vaqueros and Apaches, roadrunners and rattlesnakes, mountain lions and Gila monsters. Once again, this constellation of signs mostly is simulation, or a derivative imaginary generated, as Baudrillard claims, "in systems of signs, a more ductile material than meaning in that it lends itself to all systems of equivalence, all binary oppositions and all combinatory algebra . . . substituting the signs of the real for the real itself."[39] First the railroad, then the automobile and the airliner have served as the paths used by thousands and then millions of tourists to come and see the territories of "the desert" mapped by these hyperreal models of Southwestern space.[40] Just as Old Tucson, the well-known generic cowtown of a hundred TV shows and movies (first built nearby during 1939 in Tucson Mountain Park for the 1940 movie *Arizona*), represents "the Old West" for traveling visitors a couple of miles down the road from the Desert Museum, the Arizona–Sonora Desert Museum anchors a vision of "the desert environment" that has been artfully packaged as touristic practices of gazing upon cacti, animals, and rocks in their "natural habitats" during ten-day jaunts into the Western badlands.

Unlike the Copenhagen Zoo, however, where two human beings were put "on display" as higher primates in a plexiglass-walled apartment between the baboons and lemurs during August 1996,[41] the museum's displays feature humans only intermittently. On the one hand, they pop up in its geology dioramas as these histories recount different human cultures engaged at various times in hunting mammoths, cutting trees, and building dams. On the other hand, their food use of local plants is mentioned, and they are shown as restricting the range of big desert predators. And they are exhorted, as museum visitors, to replant their gardens with native desert plants. Still, the workings of contemporary human communities in the Sonoran Desert—whether it means Tohono O'odham villages, inner-city barrios, Air Force bombery ranges, global copper mining, or Sunbelt suburbia—are mostly quite conspicuously absent from the museum's displays. On one level, this phenomenon could be just one more expression of ordinary human exceptionalism with its anthropocentric visualizations of nature as an alternately benign and menacing otherness. Accordingly, the Sonoran Desert can be presented as a mystic zone to be loved and feared as the exotic embodiment of nature's ambivalent essence. On another level, however, this move recapitulates the typical hyperbole of traditional naturalists, erasing all corrupting traits of modern society in order to revel in the alleged purity of nature. Like Main Street, U.S.A., in Disneyland, where what Disney's imagineers create is "a 'Disney realism,' sort of utopian in nature, where we carefully program out all the negative, unwanted elements and program in the positive elements,"[42] the Desert Museum is an artfully crafted hyperreality.

The Arizona–Sonora Desert Museum purports to display the complete ecology of this entire biome to its visitors, but it too constructs a utopian site—heavy on positive elements, light on negative unwanted elements. Given Arizona's phenomenal levels of urban growth, the museum must purposely omit all traces of the one dominant subspecies now occupying the apex of the desert's complex food chains: human land developers, who now sit perched atop its home-building, leisure-resort, land-speculation, and retirement-community industries. The home builders, in particular, are interesting inasmuch as they interpret all of the many contingent social trends causing such rapid economic growth as inalterable natural forces. In summer 1994, for example, *Tucson Lifestyle* did a "Southern Arizona Home Builders Association Housing Update" that reported "Literally thousands of families are coming to the Old Pueblo due to corporate relocation, unfavorable weather conditions, urban sprawl, and the mystique of the Southwest. Area builders are pacing themselves to keep up with the demand."[43] While they tout the advantages of "sensible, planned growth" being ineffectively forced on them by the local, state, and federal governments, these human predators preside over the planned destruction of the natural Southwestern habitats mummified in the Desert Museum. And in the long boom of the 1990s, this sort of urban sprawl skyrocketed in the greater Tucson region.

Tucson Lifestyle aptly, if unintentionally, sums up the essence of the Desert Museum's hyperreal simulation of the desert biomes it purports to display:

> Wandering through the Desert Museum is like taking an enchanted walk through the desert—with no fear of snakes or critters. Lots of information, plenty of shade and water, and lots of close-up views of all the animals you've heard about: bobcats, prairie dogs, coyotes, hawks, Mexican gray wolves, scorpions, rattlesnakes, roadrunners, quail, and more. Trees and cacti are identified for you as well.[44]

The museum concentrates all of the desert's iconic animal and plant species at one hyperreal site. Fortuitously, in turn, any of the people who destroy the desert daily as a by-product of their everyday economic activities can get a few close-up views of the well-labeled critters and cacti whose habitats they are chewing up at record rates. The desert, of course, is actually something else: arid, mostly unshaded, full of fearsome snakes and unidentified plants. In other words, it is real wilderness—untouched, disorganized, unprocessed, desolate. What little range is still left for experiencing raw nature in the United States might still be found in the Arizona Sonoran and Mohave Deserts, as Edward Abbey has tried to convey in *Desert Solitaire* and *The Journey Home*. But, as he also argues in *Hayduke Lives!* and *The Monkey Wrench Gang*, these sublime spaces rapidly are being reduced to real estate or tourist parks where the average consumer is saddled with simulations of "what really was" in the hyperreal codes of the Arizona lifestyle that "now is." While intellectual integrity might more rightly dictate that the Arizona–Sonora Desert Museum follow the lead of the two Danes dwelling in a typical urban apartment in the Copenhagen Zoo and build a new Human Ecology Complex with a Tohono O'odham or Seri Village juxtaposed against a Sonoran Mexican pueblo or an Arizona Anglo upscale housing tract, these additions to the museum's survey of all the desert's ecological niches most likely will never happen. They would disrupt the flow of semiotic energy through the museum's paths, decentering and shifting attention to what really is happening to the desert rather than keeping the mysterious desert centered as a key semiotic source for many of these economic changes.

Hence, the Sonoran Desert at the Desert Museum serves as one of Arizona's hyperreal repositories of living natural objects to be seen "in their native settings," which supposedly will enable residents and visitors alike to gain more knowledge and understanding of nature's South-western desert mysteries. But, on another level, the omission of humanity from this "naturescape" is necessary to fully charge the imaginary desert as a "themed environment," because today's humans are the decisive factor that disrupts the ecological connections between the desert's natural communities. "When the real is no longer what it used to be" as Baudrillard argues, "nostalgia assumes its full meaning. There is a proliferation of myths of origin and signs of reality; of second-hand truth, objectivity, and authenticity."[45] The Desert Museum is a nature preserve where tourists and local residents can consume "nature preserves" no longer freely available in large supplies outside the complex. The tourist gaze desires the bedazzlement of secondhand Southwest icons, like saguaro-spotted bajadas, mountain lion dens, and desert bighorn sheep, and not stripmined mesas, dusty barrios, or plastic malls. The Desert Museum aptly illustrates how models must come first in hyperreal simulation, "concealing the fact that the real is no longer real, and thus saving the reality principle."[46]

Human beings are missing from the Desert Museum because they and their technologies are ruthlessly colonizing the desert everywhere else. To continue theming the Sunbelt Southwest with the complex natural mystique of the Sonoran Desert, a hyperreal exaggeration of some shards of a vanishing natural reality proves very useful in stabilizing the signs and symbols of simulations that the tourist, and, now increasingly, the local resident expects to hold true. The Desert Museum, in fact, is now trapped by this same political economy of tourism and land development as it struggles to survive financially.

As a private, not-for-profit organization, its operations are entirely financed by gate admissions, local memberships, and occasional contributions. With more than 600,000 visitors every year, the Desert Museum's major source of revenues continues to be paid admissions, which constituted nearly two-thirds of its annual budget in the 1990s.[47] Memberships, held by mostly local people, bring in another sixth or fifth of its revenues, and concession sales to tourists and local visitors run another twelfth or tenth of the annual cash flow.[48] The net from admissions rose considerably in the 1990s, but these major sources of funds have remained more or less constant in recent years.[49] Without a great number of tourists, the Desert Museum will fall quickly on hard times. During 1995, for example, annual giving contributions rose slightly from

1994 and 1993, but general contributions and special gifts fell quite significantly from 1993 to 1995.[50] With a $2.7 million reserve fund behind its $5.1 million annual budget, the Desert Museum has been forced to look aggressively at new funding sources to sustain its operations.[51]

Not surprisingly, the Desert Museum's directors resolved in 1995 to court the corporate sector more actively by happily announcing "a new annual membership program especially for the business community."[52] With three levels of membership, the Desert Museum promises some very useful benefits, including "recognition on the Museum's Annual Donor Wall," along with discounts on admission for company employees, discounts on the conference center rentals, and special family memberships for corporate representatives.[53] The Arizona–Sonora Desert Museum now features prominently in its Vista Ramada an extensive list of proud donors from the local construction, land-development, banking, public-utility, legal, and road-building communities—all of whom are eager to camouflage their pillage of the desert with handsome corporate donations to the Desert Museum. The survival of the Desert Museum in the twenty-first century is now fully ensnared by the economics of Arizona, even though it is Arizona's economic system that is destroying the very desert it hopes to preserve. Without the tourist traffic attracted to its displays or the local developers who cite it as an asset for their developments, the museum would fold. Yet if these tourists went elsewhere, and if the developers closed out their many construction projects, the Sonoran Desert might well thrive as it did during the four millennia prior to the Arizona territory's acquisition by the United States of America.

Open Habitats and the End of Nature

This discussion has considered which aspects of nature are being represented by the Desert Museum, by whom and how it has been presented as a themed environment, and for what social, economic, or cultural purposes this domain of nature has gone on display. The Desert Museum has proven a very mixed blessing for Arizona's environmental well-being. As a high-profile site for "nature appreciation" in the Sonoran Desert, it attracts thousands of visitors who otherwise might be out trampling down the arroyos and bajadas of the desert itself, ruining it for decades, if not forever. Here, the hyperreal oddly enough may promote the preservation of surviving desert biomes. Real deserts can be bypassed, because the Desert Museum is now an absolute "must-see" attraction. On the other hand, it also is a symbolic asset, providing an authoritative simulation of what the Sonoran Desert once was before, beyond, or behind the outer fences of Tucson as it began to creep out into Pima County from the base of what is now "A Mountain." As one of the Desert Museum's own visitor's brochures claims, "The Great Sonoran Desert region is a world filled with natural beauty and mystery. The Arizona–Sonora Desert Museum provides a unique opportunity to see a comprehensive collection of the plants, animals and geology of this area,"[54] because its hyperrealities consolidate a nostalgic vision of the desert at one complete, easy stop. In turn, those who would struggle to preserve much more real desert beyond the confines of the Desert Museum now have a harder sell to make, because few, if any, natural sites match the hyperreal intensity of these few acres of emblematic desert displays.

One must enter the museum's small "living world" because outside its fences increasingly there is only a huge development zone, a growing "dead world," no longer as full of such natural beauty and mystery. Krutch's hope to *live* in or with the desert is long gone; one now only visits it. All across the lands of Pima County, the plants, animals, and terrain of the Sonoran Desert continue to be either reengineered into a quasi-Mediterranean, quasi-Californian, quasi–Santa Fe resort city or they simply are trashed in acre after acre of bare dirt and tumbleweeds. A few animals—skunks, lizards, jackrabbits, coyotes, and ground squirrels—adapt to this new ecosystem as their native range becomes low-density housing subdivisions, golf courses, and parkways, but most others cannot. Likewise, some plant material, like the saguaros, palo verdes, and ironwood trees used so profusely at the Desert Museum, has been favored for landscaping, but most native desert vegetation is bulldozed over to make way for more concrete, asphalt, and thirsty turfgrass.

The creation of "open habitats" at the Desert Museum, then, is another sure sign of the ecological destruction sweeping across real natural habitats outside the museum's grounds. The animals, rocks, and trees on display are real, but the hyperreal "openness" of the wilderness it tries to simulate is collapsing under incessant human pressure in the Sonoran Desert's real habitats. A recent University of Arizona study of twenty-seven miles of State Route 85 in southern Arizona, for example, looked at the level of roadkill for a single animal: snakes. From 1987 to 1991, the researchers concluded that nearly a thousand snakes were killed every year on this piece of highway, or thirty-seven per mile each year.[55] Thousands of other animals, in turn, die along with snakes on the thousands of other highway miles knit across the Sonoran Desert's 100,000-square-mile expanse. Suggestive snippets and tatters of nature can be conserved for displays like those at the Desert Museum, but truly survivable natural habitats where animals and plants can live free from the threat of becoming roadkill are not being preserved today as truly wild habitations for all of nature's desert creatures.

The creation of "open habitat" zoos and museums, like the Desert Museum, could be taken as another indicator of the incipient end of nature.[56] From the staging of hyperreal simulations of entire ecologies to represent different facets of the Sonoran bioregion, it would appear that this bioregion, like most of the planet, is increasingly subject to radical reengineering.[57] Traces of nature can be memorialized in small, hyperreal ecological imaginaries, featuring representative collages of real plants, fake rocks, endangered animals, and artificial streams in engineered "naturescapes." However, much of nature itself—those open, untrammeled, wild, undeveloped, and noncommodified life zones beyond and before humanity—is either dying or dead. As human populations in Arizona push toward six million, the mountain lion, Gila monster, diamondback rattler, and bighorn sheep populations are falling to almost nothing. So the ecological essences of "nature" as "the Sonoran Desert" are translated into scientific simulations in the name of environmentalism, and then sold as day trips to suburban Arizona families, who often now have little more appreciation of the desert regions outside their city limits than those held by the tourists from Ohio mingling with them.

CHAPTER NINE

Superpower Aircraft and
Aircrafting Superpower:
The Pima Air and Space Museum

On the southeast side of Tucson, Arizona, Davis-Monthan Air Force Base continues serving into the post–Cold War era as the operations center of the 12th Air Force and headquarters of Southern Command Air Forces. Because of Tucson's remarkably mild climate year-round, Davis-Monthan also has become one of the American military's most important aircraft storage and demolition centers. This assignment began in 1945 when literally thousands of American fighter, bomber, and transport planes were flown to Arizona to be overhauled, mothballed, or scrapped after World War II. During the Cold War, Davis-Monthan's mothballing facilities worked almost continuously as many new generations of jet aircraft replaced, first, older piston-and-prop-driven and then earlier types of jet aircraft. During the Vietnam War a few examples of older World War II aircraft, which flew well into the late 1950s or early 1960s, were recommissioned here to fill close combat-support roles that the newer jets were either too fast or too expensive to undertake. And as the Soviet Union collapsed, Davis-Monthan became a final resting place for most of the strategic bomber and tactical fighter jet aircraft that allegedly kept communism at bay for nearly five decades. To guarantee the SALT II accords, 443 BGM-109 G ground-launched cruise missiles were dismantled at Davis-Monthan. And row after row of old B-52 bombers, now broken in two and placed wingtip to wingtip, are parked on the desert for Russian spy satellites to monitor. Today nearly 4,500 aircraft from all four military services are stored on the 3,000 acres of Davis-Monthan AFB's Aircraft Maintenance and Regeneration Center

(AMARC). Some units are treated solely as "hangar queens," or parts planes whose components are harvested to keep other rare types airworthy, while others could undergo a complete restoration when reactivated for new service with American or other foreign military units.

Over the years, then, thousands of aircraft have been recycled at Davis-Monthan, where they either were parted out, auctioned off, or melted down. But hundreds of others survive, waiting in the desert sun in a strange suspended animation for some possible future recall by Uncle Sam from mothballs. As long as some or perhaps even only one or two of each type survive, these machinic existences will not end. Consequently, I would maintain that the aircraft storage facilities at Davis-Monthan cannot be seen as "a graveyard" for military aircraft, because they are instead a site for their eternal preservation. Mothballing these machines, like cryogenic suspension for human beings, gives them a promise of some potential resurrection as well as a pledge of permanent remembrance.

Not too surprisingly, after a couple of decades of AMARC's operation, many servicemen, former pilots, and World War II vets who retired to the Tucson area, often after service at Davis-Monthan or the AMARC facility, saw merit in assuming a measure of personal and collective responsibility for keeping the promise of eternal life for such machines even more true by founding a private nonprofit educational foundation that would run a museum to preserve them. Knowing that the U.S. Department of Defense could easily eliminate all examples of any one aircraft-type to save money, rationalize its inventory, or simply create space for new arrivals, the founders of what would become the Pima Air Museum in the mid-1960s agreed to give perpetual care to certain historic aircraft on nongovernment property by using volunteer help from the local community. Accordingly, in 1967 the Air Museum was started on a patch of desert just beyond the ragged string of junkheaps, scrap yards, and refitters that had grown up outside Davis-Monthan on Pima County's Irvington and Valencia Roads. With seventy-five aircraft from AMARC and a small shack behind a cyclone fence, the members of the Air Museum Foundation spent ten years raising funds, repairing aircraft, rebuilding hangars, and refitting tools to open what is now the Pima Air and Space Museum on 8 May 1976 during the United States' Bicentennial year.[1] Unlike the largest display and collection of aircraft at the National Air and Space Museum, which is an important division of the Smithsonian, or the second-largest display collection at the United

States Air Force Museum in Dayton, Ohio, which permanently is part of the Air Force operations at Wright-Patterson Air Force Base, the Pima Air and Space Museum is, as the exhibit guide claims, "a self-supporting, non-profit, educational organization," which is "funded solely by gate receipts, gift shop sales, memberships, and donations" because it "receives no funds from any government agency."[2]

Clearly, there are strong presences here of many other less visible actors. Trans-World Airlines donated, and its retired employees in the area restored, a classic Lockheed Constellation, "The Star of Switzerland," from the 1950s New York to Zurich run; Hughes Corporation has backed an entire building to display rockets and missiles; other Arizona aircraft, avionics, or aerospace manufacturers occasionally contribute aircraft or funds; and the United States Department of Defense has donated items in the museum's collections, ranging from tools, engines, and maintenance gear to rare airplanes, strange helicopters, and an entire Titan II missile silo. For the most part, however, it is individuals and their families with their love for airplanes who power this institution's daily operations.

Aircrafting Agency: Cyborg Subjects/Objects

The sociology of technology argues that all successful technological innovation requires innovators to construct unbreakable complex linkages between humans and nonhumans.[3] Actor-network theory suggests that the terms of "actor" or "actant," should in turn refer "both to human beings and to nonhuman entities: electrons, microbes, or whatever. Our analyses, . . . should not privilege human beings by making them, *a priori*, the only active agents. Humans and nonhumans should be treated symmetrically."[4] Otherwise, all technologies too quickly become, as Latour argues, "black boxes," whose powers, origins, and workings in society are regarded as sui generis forces with little sense of how or why they actually function.[5] At the same time, however, it is the ways in which societies function that actually shape, darken, and inject these black boxes into the production and reproduction of our lives.

Mysterious forms of anthropogenic pseudomorphism in technology also fascinate Donna Haraway, who turns to "cyborg" mythologies as a means to unlock the mysterious (con)fusions of human and nonhuman in technological operations. Haraway asserts that we are now all cyborgs, living within "worlds ambiguously natural and crafted" such that "we are all chimeras, theorized and fabricated hybrids of machine and organism."[6] In other words, Latour's actor-networks seem to exist, and Haraway asks everyone to recognize how much "the cyborg is our ontology; it gives us our politics"[7] in their actancy.

Such interpretations of technology and society may seem very far-fetched from everyone's everyday ordinary existence until one stumbles on an unusual museum, like the Pima Air and Space Museum. While it is far removed from the mainstream of modern American life, as *The Tucson Official Visitors Guide* claims, the facility does not privilege human beings as the only active agents as it safeguards "more than 200 aircraft representing America's history."[8] It does this, however, because Americans are all, in part, hybrids of themselves, their nation's air power, and the histories of these two hundred different aircraft types, as these machines and their operators also have recrafted America as an aeronautical enterprise since 1941. Like the National Air and Space Museum discussed in chapter 2, the Pima Air and Space Museum is tangible sign of how America's history can be theorized, fabricated, and celebrated with flying machines by historicizing the hybridization of machines (aircraft/airweapons) and organisms (airmen/airwomen) with organizations (airlines/airforces) in their civil and military aviation forms. Whether they are touted as flying machines or fighting machines, these airplanes are presented as very active presences in the aircrafting of national superpower.

This "cyborganic" relation with flying machines is even more pronounced at the Arizona Wing of the Confederate Air Force, located at Falcon Field in Mesa, Arizona, because that smaller organization actually does focus on flying its war machines. Aircrafted subjectivity returns there to continue crafting airplanes that do fly in historic reenactments and revival tours of World War II war birds. As its official literature explains, this group has a special mission: "The Confederate Air Force, a worldwide, all volunteer non-profit organization, is dedicated to the preservation in flying condition of the great war birds that dominated the skies of WWII."[9] Instead of maintaining the machine form itself, like the Pima Air and Space Museum, the Confederate Air Force focuses on machine functionality by keeping its historic flying machines "flying" for dynamic displays of aircrafted agency. At the Arizona Wing, the Confederate Air Force operates a German Heinkel H-111 bomber (one of two still flying in the world today), a North American B-25 Mitchell bomber, a North American AT-6 SNJ trainer, a Grumman AF2 Guardian torpedo bomber, a Beech C-45 transport, and its most important icon, a Boeing B-17G flying fortress bomber (one of eight left flying in the United States of the 12,731 built during World War II) named *Sentimental Journey.*

Sentimental Journey was donated to the Arizona Wing of the Confederate Air Force in January 1978 by a California corporation that had used it as a borate bomber in suppressing forest fires since the 1960s. Like the B-25 currently under restoration by the Confederate Air Force in Mesa, the B-17 was disassembled and totally restored to its original World War II configuration, when it flew combat missions in the Pacific theater of observations. On display at its hangar during the winter months in Arizona, it leaves during the summer to go on tour, visiting "an average of 60 cities and towns across the United States each year as a patriotic and educational exhibit."[10]

At the Arizona Wing's hangar, visitors may wander into the machine shop where aircraft are recrafted, see extensive memorabilia displays from the "Home Front" and "War Front," and view other flying machines. Unlike the U.S. Army Air Force in World War II, all of the Arizona Wing's "members are volunteers who have a great love for maintaining these airplanes for the years ahead."[11] Like the Pima Air and Space Museum, the Arizona Wing does not receive any federal funds to support its activities. Instead, its members also raise their own money to maintain their "flying museum" of World War II aircraft and their small hangar museum facility at Falcon Field.

Back at the more static displays at Pima Air and Space Museum, Hangar No. 1 is the entrance hall for the museum, where the visitor is introduced to the early history of aviation. Walking into the displays, one passes a full-scale replica of an early Wright Flyer in the midst of exhibits that quickly survey aviation in the times just preceding and following World War I. Mainly using model aircraft and parts of actual airplanes, the museum highlights how rapidly new engine, airframe, propeller, and instrumentation technologies developed in the evolution of the airplane. The farside of the hangar holds exhibits that examine the fascinating variety of glider, helicopter, and small home-built civilian aircraft developed over the years since 1903, but this entire display mostly prepares visitors for the much bigger show of restored military aircraft in Hangars No. 2, 3, and 4 as well as the scores of planes parked outside in the sun.

Unlike the National Air and Space Museum in Washington, D.C., or the Air Force Museum at Wright-Patterson Air Force Base in Dayton, Ohio, the Pima Air and Space Museum directly accentuates the home-built aspect of American aviation. The 1903 Wright Flyer was the nation's first airplane, but it was pieced together in the home and shop of two young bicycle-store owners in Dayton. Most aircraft were constructed in this fashion, or in small artisanal shops, until World War I. Only during the war, and then afterward as civilian and military aviation blossomed during the 1920s, did corporate manufacturers displace the home construction of airplanes. In addition to highlighting these genealogical facts in the origins of aircraft, the museum has accumulated a significant number of antique and contemporary home-built aircraft, including a Bowers Fly Baby, a Pitts Special, and a Rutan Long Eze, which reinforce an awareness of airplanes as creatures spawned in American garages after being conceived on kitchen tables.

Hangar No. 2 is dedicated to a specific era in flight, the jet and space age, in its examination of aerospace technologies. Centered on an official NASA mock-up of the X-15 rocketplane, the exhibit presents many other models of experimental aircraft, like the X-14 VTOL plane, the X-29 fly-by-wire jet prototype, and the X-30 hypersonic transport, as well as representative examples of early jet engines, rocket motors, and spacecraft technologies. Materials technology, showing the vital roles played by aluminum, carbon composites, titanium, and ceramic components in spacecraft, also is examined as a vital part in humanity's realization of space travel.

One of the most intriguing considerations of military man/machine collectives is the public-service display from Hughes Missile Systems Group, which has operated for years in Tucson. Here company men and women in their corporate formations are depicted as the progenitors of the Hughes family of missiles used by military men and women. The "Missiles of Victory" exhibit on Operation Desert Storm in Kuwait includes the Phoenix, TOW, AARAM, and Maverick missiles. As the marvelous display of these weapons in full-scale mock-ups suggests, they were designed, developed, and proved in Pima county. The display depicts the Hughes Missile Systems plant in a color airphoto (as it might look to a AARAM shot in pursuit of some enemy ground-based radar) as well as a vast collage of candid snaps showing many of the Hughes workers at their workstations in the plant as they make these missiles.

Under the bold headline "Our Employees Make It Happen," this display celebrates other strings of (wo)man/machine collectivization in certain superpower aircraft, stretching from the shop floor to Desert Storm to these missile mock-ups, which are needed to create an aircraft superpower.

Along with these studies in aerospacecrafted subjectivity, Hangar No. 2 also features the Arizona Aviation Hall of Fame, with small memorials to individual Arizonans who gained fame around the world as aviators/aviatrixes. These celebrations couple portraits of the people with short accounts of their aircrafted subjectivity marked by small honorific mementoes, official certificates, or airplane photographs. Despite its peripheral location, Arizona has had a rich history as an American aviation center, ranging from Didier Masson's service as a $300-a-month contract air force for Pancho Villa in the Mexican revolution (Masson flew his Martin biplane in support of Villa all across Sonora in 1913) to Senator Barry Goldwater's service as a jet fighter pilot in Arizona's Air National Guard.

The displays of other older aircraft in Hangars No. 3 and 4 feature all of the major World War II icons. The famous war machines from the air battles of that war in Europe and the Pacific—a B-24 Liberator, B-25 Mitchell, B-26 Invader, and C-47 Skytrain in Hangar No. 3 as well as a P-63 King Cobra, F4U Corsair, C-46 Commando, and TBM Avenger in Hangar No. 4—are shown as well-restored first-line examples of the type. Most World War II aircraft were scrapped soon after the war. As a result, the museum does not have good representatives of every famous Axis, American, or Allied warplane. Its inventories of common and unusual jet aircraft from the Cold War, however, are quite extensive.[12]

Different aircraft are accorded various treatments at the Pima Air and Space Museum, but all of them are displayed in dignified realistic ways. Some, like the museum's SR-71 and B-17, get their own exhibit sheds and hangars. Others, like most of the Cold War jets, are parked on the desert floor, as if left there overnight by their crews. There are no gate guard sculptures or jet fighter signs at the museum, which abuse the bodies of warplanes by sticking their hulks up on poles or posts in silly or stilted uses, like those assigned to lawn jockeys or pink flamingos. Instead, every aircraft is treated with great dignity. Each type on display is flagged with its own stanchion with important data about the aircraft, including its museum inventory number, manufacturer, military designation code, official title and/or popular nickname, type of aircraft by design function, former and/or foreign service designations, and its operational lifespan in a military or civilian organization's actual use. In walking over the museum's grounds, then, visitors can get a fairly complete picture of each aircraft's history by closely examining the airframe on display and carefully reading the historical data. While the museum aspires to be a complete collection of all aircraft types, a walk around the ground can feel like a time-traveling visit back to a frontline airbase inasmuch as each one of these carefully described aircraft is sitting at ready in a place very much like that of its actual operational deployment.

The Pima Air and Space Museum's other side is to be found in the restoration section where old aircraft hulks, depending on their condition on arrival at the museum, receive either a nearly total resurrection or merely a new paint job. Here, in many ways, is what the museum most strongly aspires to be—a place for volunteers and staff to spend countless hours keeping the aircraft on exhibit "looking as fresh as they did during their operational days."[13] Many of the units on display are not in tip-top condition, particularly those out on the dirt. Quite a few aircraft are missing engines, control surfaces, propellers, rotor blades, or wings. A good number still look mothballed, like the thousands of aircraft that have been decommissioned at one time or another across Valencia Road on the grounds of Davis-Monthan Air Force Base. But a few, which sit inside climate-controlled hangars, are certainly as fresh as when they sat on the line ready for operations, especially the iconic planes of World War II, Korea, and Vietnam whose machinic forms aircrafted many of the best days in the lives of now-old airmen who visit them at the museum. The Pima Air and Space Museum's B-17, B-24, B-25, and B-29 types, for example, are all very operational, and they provide impetus for moments of contemplative time travel, in memory and imagination, for the thousands of vets who visit the museum annually.

In addition to displaying more than two hundred aircraft, the Pima Air and Space Museum as part of its operations hosts a special memorial for the 390th Bombardment Group and 390th Strategic Missile Wing (which operated around Tucson during the Cold War), and encompasses the Titan Missile Museum, complete with an entire, well-preserved Titan missile and launch silo in Green Valley, Arizona, a few miles south of Tucson. The museum also houses a number of well-known civilian aircraft, ranging from small civil aviation two-seaters and four-seaters from Cessna, Beech, Piper, Waco, and Ryan to large civilian transports built by Lockheed, Douglas, Boeing, and Vickers for the world's airline companies. Most of the aircraft are American designed and built, although there is a sprinkling of donated foreign types from MIG, British Aerospace, Focke-Wulf, DeHavilland, and Sud Aviation. Consequently, the Pima Air and Space Museum, like the National Air and Space and United States Air Force Museums, presents visitors with a very Americanized experience that stresses how much of America's technological prowess and military superpower are aircrafted phenomena. Those who are interested in knowing what $3 trillion of federal borrowing has purchased or how global superpower has manifested itself can see many of its most tangible signs here on the hardpacked dirt and gravel parking aprons of the Pima Air and Space Museum as well as in the rows of mothballed aircraft in the AMARC inventory on one of the museum's short trolley tours over to that facility.

To better understand the Pima Air and Space Museum, we should approach this site as one more location for what Latour calls "the proliferation of hybrids" where people increasingly might recognize how deeply "mixtures of nature and culture" become embedded in the technoscience artifacts, like old B-17 bombers, and are experienced through violent events, like World War II, that define our global community.[14] In contemporary global cultures, however, Latour wants to push beyond "social contexts and the interests of power" to address how we might understand "collectives and objects" as they form "delicate networks" amid nature/society/discourse relations.[15] Latour usually contents himself with tracing out the conditions of hybridization, or how networks interlace nature/society/discourse in such a way that "networks are *simultaneously real, like nature, narrated, like discourse, and collective, like society*,"[16] but he rarely assays the moral conflicts or political contradictions raised by different modes of collectivization. As he describes "collectives," they operate as "the association of humans and nonhumans" in which "society" usually designates "one part only of our collectives, the divide invented by the social sciences," because "the context and the technical content turn out to be redefined every time."[17]

This observation is quite useful. The "association of humans and nonhumans" between the aircraft and airmen of the U.S. Air Force or U.S. Navy from the 1940s through the 1990s is one context with a specific technical content. Yet a peculiar state formation—American superpower in the World War II Grand Alliance of United Nations as well as the victorious Cold War protagonist against the now vanquished USSR—has had a vested interest in associating all humans and nonhumans in many particular contexts with specific technical contents. These collectives of flight, war, travel, experiment, speed, and power, in turn, attained stable canonical forms in many social/political/moral/economic/cultural networks from 1945 to the present. These networks are real, like nature, narrated, like discourse, and collective, like society as their ideological frames have used aircraft to organize many political debates and social alliances for nearly fifty years.

Major national museums, like the National Air and Space Museum, have always played a significant role in the "collectivization process" by associating specific humans (Americans) and nonhumans (U.S. aircraft) in spectacularized historical performances to memorialize other networks of war, technical innovation, peace, and organizational development in the technoscience practices of flight. Museums are a central site where the discursive terms of "nature" (physics, chemistry, atomic energy) and "culture" (America, war, its allies, the enemy) can be "mixed" as well as "purified" in learned display discourses whose authors are intent on separating nature from culture so that their material evolution in different economies, technologies, histories can easily be traced to specific networks of hybrid elements drawn from each separate, purified domain.[18] The display of artifacts, the discourse of historical authenticity, and the development of individual agency for human beings all come together in aircraft history museums, as all aircraft series are depicted as evolving into the next, showing how "this presentness" followed from "that pastness." All too often, however, the exhibition of aircraft evolution at the museum rarely addresses bigger moral conflicts or political contradictions.

Nonetheless, these conflicts and contradictions are there. Latour argues that modernity "designates two sets of entirely different practices which must remain distinct if they are to remain effective," namely, *translation,* which "creates mixtures between entirely new types of beings, hybrids of nature and culture," and *purification,* which "creates two entirely distinct ontological zones: that of human beings on the one hand; that of nonhumans on the other."[19] Museums play a vital role in these purification projects by stabilizing continuously the metaphysical divisions of purified relations between the viewing subjects and objects on view. They are shown amidst a constant natural world and a fixed social world inside a predictable set of outcomes about technical momentum and human inventiveness that often hides the role of capital and commerce in their mixing. As translation centers, museums also mix new social identities out of the necessities of the political present and the contingencies of the historical past, while policing the contested identity of internal communities and the otherness of external groups. They are, in a sense, "socio(onto)logy" generators, which write the ontologues of individual and collective identity.[20] To discover the permissible political possibilities of "who, whom" in these equations of translation and purification, one must reread the ways in which the many possible hybridities of human/machine interactions are represented in museum practices.[21]

The contours of aircraft display at this exhibition of historic aircraft at Pima reveal many rituals for separation and purification used by American society to unify cultural objects and political subjects in which familiar social dynamics of attachment/detachment, objectivity/subjectivity, association/disassociation, and significance/insignificance all play out their possibilities in the many display cases of the museum's show.[22]

Aerospace history museums, like the Pima Air and Space Museum, are still deeply embedded in larger circuits of communication. These relays articulate many domains of scientific, political, or historical knowing into civil codes of specific "airplane" knowledge.[23] This historic knowledge often is believed to be conclusive, but of course it is not. Fresh visions of such aircraft knowledges are always evolving with society, and diverse cultural interpretations of these same bodies of knowledge are always seeking acceptance by museum institutions. History museums are effectively establishing authoritative rules for stabilizing regimes of both aesthetic and historic interpretation. Indeed, the careful curatorship exercised over preservation of technological artifacts in such museums affords experts their best opportunities to legitimate these everyday ontologies.[24]

I urge us to be extremely cautious, however, about how we exercise the governmentality mobilized in such power plays.[25] As Latour observes, any critical stance is now in crisis to the extent that all of these networks are unstable. As we cross and recross "the great fiefdoms of criticism," we must realize how much all of these networks "are neither objective nor social, nor are they effects of discourse, even though they are real, and collective, and discursive."[26] In criticizing how state power may work, one must not simply critique one set of political engagements built by established social formations in order to substitute his or her own apparently different ends to the service of these same means. Aircraft artifacts are cast by museums in specific performances, whose aesthetic impact can, in turn, mobilize both individual and collective subjects to repattern their behaviors in conformity with the normative goals highlighted by the exhibition with the artifacts on display.[27] Aircraft fuse airplane/airman/air force into one cohesive unit to operate as an actor-network. Not nature, not history, not culture: but an interoperation of all three. The Pima Air and Space Museum, in turn, memorializes airplanes, air men, and air forces by feting American airpower.

Divisions between the natural and social worlds, as Latour argues, can have a distinctly constitutional character as the founding writs of our reality. Indeed, relations of power and powerlessness in the world at large continuously script out the key ontologues at the core of what he calls "the Modern Constitution," which defines the key attributes of "humans and nonhumans, their properties and relations, their abilities and their groupings."[28] To keep with Latour's analysis, any museum devoted to explicating aircrafted technologies and events, like the Pima Air and Space Museum, must operate, in part, as a perpetually sitting constitutional court. Its exhibits provide judicial reviews of various human/machine links for the prevailing regime of psychosocial purpose, which draw the divides in nature/culture, subject/object, past/present, human/nonhuman relations in its displays of aircrafted human/machine interactions.

Aircraft Enthusiasms

Celebrating the aircrafted association of men and machines becomes quite explicit in the museum's display of a World War II barracks building. The surprisingly small dimensions of this building reveal the kind of space in which Army Air Force personnel lived during the war in Europe. Even when men and women were not directly interacting with aircraft, the war machine shaped and steered their daily interactions with a spare, uniform functionality that suggests these structures simply were small-scale hangars for humans. And to capture the full range of aircrafted subjectivity shared by the airmen in these barracks for any and all of its visitors, the museum has assembled a vast model airplane collection, as its exhibit guide observes, "arranged chronologically to show virtually all U.S. military aircraft from pre-WWI to the present,"[29] inside these barracks. For those airmen/airwomen whose real aircraft are missing outside from the collection as actual examples of their type, some token of reunification or remembrance is provided within the highly liminal spaces of an original military barracks where most of them would have spent many nights preparing to return to the flightline on so many wartime or peacetime mornings. The barracks, then, are another dream space to benchmark the aircrafted cyborganic identities of visitors and volunteers to the museum.

Such aeronautical cyborgs preserve national security, and the exhibit guide claims that the museum was conceived "in the interest of preserving tangible artifacts of our aviation history for the recreational welfare and education of our present and future generations."[30] Cyborg subjectivities of flight are one of these most tangible artifacts, and a plaque outside Hangar No. 3, dedicated to the aircraft of World War II, states the museum's working philosophies more forthrightly. That is, its exhibits "serve to remind us of the ingenuity, skill, and dedication of those who designed, built, maintained and utilized these tools of war." As a site of cyborg memory, the Pima Air and Space Museum also reminds us how these tools of war, when fused with humans in machinic systems, utilized/maintained/built/designed those whose dedication/skills/ingenuity are swirling everywhere around the museum's grounds as aircraft enthusiasm.

The Pima Air and Space Museum admits in its own publications that the aircraft enthusiasms of each visitor are "the Museum's most important asset," because it is the public's aircraft enthusiasm that keeps the doors open, by way of visitors buying admission tickets, purchasing gift shop items, or paying for annual memberships.[31] Unlike many other museums, where professionally trained staff set the narrative mood or denominate the display imagery, the Pima Air and Space Museum looks and feels like a local volunteer operation. Very little is slickly executed, many exhibits are overwrought with busy profusions of excessive technical information, and different things get jumbled together with little sense of historical classification, chronology, or commonality. Like many little aircraft clubs in which individuals get together as a group to renovate, operate, and possess an airplane that they all cannot manage alone, the museum bands hundreds of aircraft enthusiasts in southern Arizona in common cause to own lots of airplanes none of them could dream of keeping by themselves.

This pool of volunteer labor also accounts for the museum's strong fascination with airplanes as "flying machines." Most types of aircraft in the Pima Air and Space Museum's inventory are war birds; yet, unlike the National Air and Space Museum or the Air Force Museum, there is not much emphasis placed on "fight" in the displays, and very few guns, bombs, or missiles—either on or off their airplane mounts—are displayed. The focus falls directly on "flight," and almost all of the military airplanes are shown as purified flying, and not as fighting, machines. Of course, many World War I and World War II aircraft still have machine-gun barrels at their mounts, but little is made of big bomb bays, weapon payloads, or killing accuracies. Most Cold War jets are shown absent their weapons pods, gun stations, or nuclear payloads. Warriors come to see their old war birds, and kids want to see their favorite machinic characters from war movies, but the airplanes here are configured to be celebrated as the flying machines in which their human operators spent their best days in flight. Since so many airmen trained in Arizona during World War II, Korea, Vietnam, the Gulf War, and the Cold War, this association is natural. These are their airplanes as they learned to fly them. They want to remember how they became airmen or airwomen, not how they drilled to serve as carpet bombers, ground strafers, nuclear strike forces, or gun shippers. Thus, not all forms of cyborg subjectivity are celebrated as openly in equivalent proportions; it is essentially the awesome empowerment of flight that gets brought into fine focus by the museum's displays.

For those seeking that more violent side of military aviation, the Champlin Fighter Museum in Mesa, Arizona, is mostly about "fight" rather than "flight." Like the Confederate Air Force, the Champlin facility was located at Falcon Field for many years, and it also is the home of the American Fighter Aces Association. Devoted to "the glorious history of fighter aviation," this museum features more than thirty restored fighter planes from several nations that fought in World War I, World War II, Korea, and Vietnam.[32] Here the heritage of aircrafted cyborg subjects in air forces centers on air combat and combatant aircraft, as the visitor is invited

> to a share a unique movement of glory with the aces who flew these mechanical legends. Over 700 personally autographed photos of fighter aces from 15 countries spanning the history of aerial warfare together with countless pieces of military and personal memorabilia from the war years grace the halls and walls of this outstanding collection. As you listen to the strains of music from the war years, you may actually see

some of the heroes who navigated these war birds over enemy territory returning for a visit.[33]

The aircrafted subjects on display here are fighter aces: fusions of flying killers in deadly machines made glorious by propaganda and revered as national symbols in military adventures from 1914 to the present. If this privileged subtext at the Champlin Fighter Museum is not quite clear enough in the airplane hangars, one can visit its important ancillary display of "the most complete collection of historical military automatic weapons in the world! With over 200 weapons from 14 countries, our guests are treated to an educational experience covering the complete history of the machine gun from 1895 to the present."[34]

Cyborg Memorials

This imbrication of the war powers invested in human beings—through which technological practices, social organizations, flying machines, and sophisticated weapons interoperate as networks of cyborg subjects—is most obviously revealed at the heart of the Pima Air and Space Museum's grounds in the 390th memorial, which marks achievements of the 390th Bombardment Group, Thirteenth Combat Wing, Third Air Division of the Eighth Air Force. While all of the unit's members are celebrated in the memorial's displays, major attention is devoted in the central hangar area to the group's four B-17 bomber squadrons. Here the conditions of association during World War II of airmen and airplanes as air/force/ air/power/air/weapon are eternalized in the guise of historic memorabilia and crew remembrances.

Anchoring the display is "I'll Be Around," a B-17G which has been configured as a fully gunned World War II heavy bomber, even though it never served outside of North America. Because of its late manufacture, this B-17 flew with the United States Coast Guard until it was retired by the U.S. Air Force in 1958, when it was used as a slurry bomber by the United States Forest Service. While it was not an actual 390th bomber, this B-17 nonetheless is the sign that provides a symbolic center to the battles fought over Europe from 1942 to 1945 by American men/machines collectivized as the Eighth Air Force. Many forms of machinic human being and organic airplane service are portrayed by the memorial's various displays. Gunners and their guns, radio operators and their radios, navigators and their instruments, bombardiers and their bombsights, pilots and their cockpits all are studied to show how the bomber with its crew roamed over Europe in war to bomb the enemy. Likewise, the German opposition, with models of the fighter aircraft that hunted the B-17s and mementos from Luftwaffe flyers who fought against the 390th, also is displayed as an integral part of this war machine's life. Medals awarded, flight suits worn, battles fought, bombs dropped, guns fired, missions accomplished, friends made, comrades lost, hours flown, rounds shot, victories won, and bailouts made all are touted as moments in the life history of the 390th Bombardment Group in Europe.

Showing how its crews were barracked, its aircraft serviced, its heroes feted, its missions staged, and its foes vanquished, the memorial successfully remembers the men and the machines that worked together as a metamachine in this victorious network of complex cyborg agency. The men or machines alone could do nothing; only when they enmeshed in the quasi-subjective/quasi-objective capabilities of airpowered/aircrafted/airforced actancy did the 390th Group attain its effective operational existence. History often looks only at the men, technology mostly considers only the machines; hence, only visitations to memorials such as these can apprehend the symbiota created in such andromachinic collectives. And for those who now doubt that these beings existed, quips from many Allied and Axis wartime figures, from Winston Churchill to Albert Speer, testify to the historic importance of these American air force units in winning the war against Hitler.

B-17 crewmen who died when their aircraft were destroyed reveal their aircrafted subjectivies in their final explosive moments. Selected, trained, and deployed as a unit, men and machine were one battle unit, unified forever in the finality of burning fragments exploding in battle. The men were typically quite young, and what little mature autonomous life they had as human beings was led as B-17 pilots, copilots, gunners, bombardiers, navigators, radiomen. And they went to their deaths defined by, and (con)fused with, their life among these machines. For eternity, they are a fallen bomber's crew, B-17 airmen, World War II Army Air Force casualties whose living existence ended in a hail of meat and metal crashing to earth. Yet other B-17 crewmen, who survived when they and their aircraft finished their twenty-five missions, perpetuate their aircrafted subjectivities after being forced by peace or technology to find new cyborganized identities outside of those given in air forces, past aircraft, and beyond airmen. In their old age, they remember their (con)fusion with these complex collectives—Boeing's bomber, Hercules Corporation's 500 pounders, the U.S. Army Air Force, the United Nations Allies—in their wartime cyborganized existence as they all were tested against other machinic collectives—Focke-Wulf's fighters, Berlin's flak towers, the Luftwaffe, the Axis. When they stand before this B-17, tears of twenty-something angst and seventy-something experience commingle in memories of how they once lived as airmen, how their comrades perished as fliers, how their enemies died as targets, and how all of those flying/fighting cyborg subjectivities are now extinct save for such sites of remembrance.

The 390th Bombardment Group, however, has an even more unique tie to the Tucson area inasmuch as it evolved from a U.S. Air Force fighting unit into the 390th Strategic Missile Wing during the Cold War. This Strategic Air Command missile detachment operated the heavy, liquid-fueled Titan II ICBM from the mid-1960s to the mid-1980s. Based in huge underground silos, three detachments of these forces, each of which had eighteen missiles, were located in Kansas, Arkansas, and Arizona to launch heavy thermonuclear warheads into the Soviet Union. One of these Titan II missiles and its launch silo has been preserved outside of Tucson, and it too is now operated as the Titan Missile Museum by the Pima Air and Space Museum. The booster, of course, is no longer fueled, and the reentry vehicle has had its nuclear warhead removed. Still, it is otherwise accurate in every detail, and the entire site was designated a National Historic Landmark in 1994. Just as the 390th Memorial Museum commemorates the unit's World War II days, guided tours through the 390th Missile Wing's Titan II emplacement give America's many participants in the Cold War an opportunity "to view it exactly as it looked when it was being operated by the Air Force 390th Strategic Missile Wing."[35]

The Pima Air and Space Museum is not a cemetery for cyborg beings. Machines never truly die until either nature or society entirely destroys their form and substance by rusting them away or melting them down. The restoration section of the museum testifies to this truth: few aircraft are so far gone that their craftsmen cannot resurrect a new life from the shredded pieces of aircraft wreckage. The desert climate provides the perfect opportunity to place these machines in suspended animation, allowing those who flew them many visitations that also are an episodic return to their shared past.

Putting Machinic Collectives to Rest

The cyborg subjectivity presented at the Pima Air and Space Museum is, at the same time, a bit ersatz. We cannot, after all, climb into these machines' cockpits, turn over the motors, and taxi away for a sortie through the clouds. On an individual level, these meaning machines can spark a magical memory tour, imparting remembrances of missions past to those who flew, maintained, or built them in earlier days. Any visitor standing before them in the baking sun, the timelessness of the cacti and clouds in this desert environment, can easily believe that it is 1944, 1953, 1967, or 1991 again, can easily slip back into the role of pilot, bombardier, mechanic, builder. The aircraft object and airman subject can again become identical, if only momentarily in their memories, imaginings, flashbacks.

On more diverse collective levels, however, there are many other aircrafted cyborg subjectivities in America's history that almost everyone enjoys, and the museum also truly celebrates them: the megamachineries of modern industrial society, ranging from the giant corporations that fabricate aircraft, scientific institutions that refine their design, huge energy concerns that fuel their flight, to the military bureaucracies that operate them, the technical disciplines that design their components, the state apparatus that uses their power. Here, on the geographical edge of America, I see aircraft artifacts working as iconic generators of all these cyborg subjectivities, which almost all of the museum's visitors also possess as taxpayers, airplane enthusiasts, citizens, former servicemen, consumers, or wartime survivors.

Building these machines, operating them as weapons, and celebrating them as technologies concoct one of the more monstrous forms of modern Americanism because the power, security, and authority of the United States of America are mostly a product of coevolving with these machines. This man/machine fusion of collective subjects with a collection of aeronautical objects is another deep anchor for the Pima Air and Space Museum, as it draws in thousands of schoolchildren, ordinary citizens, foreign tourists, and day-tripping locals, all of whom have never set foot on an airbase as military personnel. They too come in awe of such collective cyborg subjectivity as cyborg citizens, or perhaps in fear as cyborg aliens, to view the flying machines that transmit the terrible powers of contemporary America's war machines anywhere anytime any way—Vietnam in 1972, Libya in 1986, Iraq in 1991, Bosnia in 1995, Serbia in 1999, Afghanistan in 2001.

As the world's super airpower, the United States has prided itself, first, during the twentieth century and, now, in the twenty-first century on its air forces. Indeed, much of its power projection, whether in Afghanistan, Yugoslavia, Iraq, Libya, Vietnam, Korea, Japan, or Germany, has been air powered, aircrafted, and airplaned. To revel in American superpower is to celebrate the flying machines that produce and maintain it, and vice versa. As a result, a visit to any American air and space museum, whether it is the Pima Air and Space Museum, the National Air and Space Museum, or the United States Air Force Museum, becomes a celebration of, or a confrontation with, the air forces that the United States uses to impose its will on other nations.

These collectives are purposely memorialized in other aircraft accumulations and displays at the National Air and Space Museum in Washington, D.C., and the United States Air Force Museum at Wright-Patterson Air Force Base in Dayton, Ohio. The airpowered essence of American superpower at the National Air and Space Museum celebrates how fully America is the air and space nation: first in flight, first to the moon, first in air force, first to strike with atomic weapons. America's national image and substance is shaped out of its coexistence with, and codependence on, powerful aircraft, which its leaders use to craft their authority and America's prosperity through swift strikes by air against others.[36] Similarly, the collective agency of humans and machines in the U.S. Air Force is given perfect rendition at Wright-Patterson with its spit-and-polish array of past and present American aircraft punctuated with representative enemy types from vanished foes.[37] In the prosperity and peace that this air power brings, one also can find at the Pima Air and Space Museum the civilian airliners and airplanes that give Americans part of their high standards of living in flight time and air service. Those actor networks of airplanes/pilots/designers/makers/passengers, then, also anchor the networked actions of an entire nation made perhaps more indivisible, free, and just by its aircrafted qualities. These seemingly innocuous metal hulks, in fact, are the plastic hulls of shape-shifting warriors transforming ordinary everyday flying machines into deadly fighting war birds. With these machines, air forces can be aircrafted out of airmen/airwomen/airplanes. Major corporations, modern nation-states, machine technologies, and mass media work their transformative powers, molding people and aircraft into hard-bodied warriors and deadly warplanes.

This relationship to machines is enhanced, if not reemphasized, in the museum's huge gift shop. It offers the visitor a choice of hundreds of different model airplane kits of various sizes, styles, and systems, which youngsters of all ages can take to model their time and energies around the construction of this or that aircraft relica. Small boys, eager to be fliers, begin by fusing their minds, hands, and imaginations with miniature aircraft, piecing together little machine copies in anticipation of coexisting with big machine originals. And grown-ups, hoping to recapture concretely their time as airmen, reassemble their memories of aircrafted subjectivity in the most faithful model they can create as a totem of their time as aircrafted beings.

There are few miniature dioramas with models here, because the entire site is a living diorama set down by an air force base, modern city, and timeless desert caught up in the reproduction of American's aviation machineries to model how to coexist with aircraft. The hangars, the parking slips, the barracks, the maintenance shops all are living, breathing, moving creations of many aircrafted beings—organic and machinic, individual and corporate, human and nonhuman. The site itself is a model meaning-machine, humming with the flow of cyborg subjectivity.

Museums and cemeteries share in one respect society's assignment to care for the material and moral remains of human beings. In museums, one finds the dead labor left behind by the dead laborers who fill the cemeteries. Each artifact can serve as a cenotaph of the artificers/owners/users who lie buried elsewhere. By disassociating man and machine, modern society sustains the dreams of the anthropological sleep under which, as Foucault asserts, contemporary subjects continue to pretend that someone like "Man" discretely comes into existence as the intelligent agency behind the many machinic creations of modernity.

Arguably, the real creations of modernity are not the sophisticated "Men" or refined "Women" of enlightened progress, as the purified anthropogenic/anthropocentric myths of modernity maintain. They are instead hybrids of women/men/machines, brought together by market

forces, technical imperatives, and personal volition in the cyborg subjectivities of human/machinic operations. Had many modern death rites
maintained some ancient practices, human tool users would be buried
with their tools. We might combine junkyards, cemeteries, museums,
and crematoriums at one site. Car and driver would be melted down together, popular mechanics might buried together with their tools, hand-
gunner and handgun could be interred as one. Cyborg subjectivity, however, is stridently denied in modern death rituals. Dead people go to
cemeteries for human subjects alone, and their used-up tools go to junkyards or museums to become dead objects suitable only for natural de-
composition, industrial recomposition, or museumic disposition unless
they wend their ways into some secondhand shop for another (con)fu-
sion with new sets of human hands.

Because human beings, and not cyborg beings, fill memorial parks,
whatever sense of cyborg subjectivity we can garner today can be had
only obliquely at certain museum venues. While the pretext of any museum's collection is the accumulation, preservation, and display of dead
objects as artifacts, as in the inventory in any automobile, firearm, railroad, or aircraft museum, these sites also occasionally cleave open some
of their hidden cracks through which we catch glimpses of the cyborganized agencies that really have cooperated, coevolved, or coincided as
collectives of hybrids amidst modern societies.

The Pima Air and Space Museum, then, is not the final end for these
aircraft; it is instead their eternalization. At this site, one sees an ever-
evolving assembly of old aircraft, but, more importantly, one also finds
the penultimate renditions of certain cyborg subjectivities, once constructed to conduct warfare in the air. Men by themselves are rarely so
interesting, and aircraft alone are only apparatus. But when positioned
in such museum settings with their aeronautical antecedents and suc-
cessors, the cyborg war machines of World War I, World War II, Korea,
Vietnam, Kuwait, Afghanistan, or the Cold War acquire tremendous personality. They again rest in their military niches where—in machinic uni-
son with so many other units, components, or crews—these aluminum/
steel/plexiglass contraptions served as battle stations in grand historical
dramas staged by the missing men and women not now strapped into
their seats.

CHAPTER TEN

Strange Attractor:
The Tech Museum of Innovation

In this chapter I want to explore how San Jose's new museum, The Tech Museum of Innovation, originated in a stark moment of civic envy, much like New York's American Museum of Natural History, St. Louis's Missouri Botanical Garden, and Phoenix's Heard Museum before it. When most Americans think of San Jose, if they think of it at all, they may replay in their heads Dionne Warwick's plaintive musical question of 1967, asking "Do you know the way to San Jose?," because it always has been an indefinite point somewhere out there on San Francisco Bay amidst truck gardens, military air bases, and electronic plants. Known for nothing special at all, San Jose, like Oakland, was known for having "no there" there. In the nearly thirty-five years since that song topped the pop charts, however, San Jose has developed into the fourteenth-largest city in the United States as well as the unofficial capital of Silicon Valley: the world's greatest concentration of high-tech computer, telecommunication, and networking industries.

Like the citizens of so many other American cities, the citizens of San Jose have celebrated their growing economic prominence by developing new civic spaces, museum institutions, and public buildings to mark their city's coming of age as an important urban center in the national and international economy. Because so many of its movers and shakers are connected to high-tech industries, The Tech Museum of Innovation is now becoming the centerpiece of this urban public-relations strategy for San Jose and Silicon Valley. At the same time, as a work of public architecture, The Tech Museum's noteworthy new, electric mango and azure building, which was designed by Mexican architect Richard Legorreta, is meant to serve as an icon of the city's most famous industry.

Most of San Jose and Silicon Valley's economic growth has been created by thousands of engineers and entrepreneurs who have invented and installed the boxes and wires, chips and cables, relays and routers of the computer industry.[1] I would agree that "innovation," as a process of continuous technological improvement, or, at least, constant technical upgrades, sustains this industry. However, it also leaves behind mostly unimpressive material signs of progress if one is trying to find things to fill a computing museum. Genealogies of circuit miniaturization, processing speed or memory growth in computers, can be documented, but displays of their technical development would show only increasingly smaller silicon chips, denser circuit masks, or more compact storage devices. Making such clumps of computers, tangles of transistors, and pieces of plastic seem exciting in a museum display as their manufacture evolves in complexity over time would be a bit of showmanship beyond human ingenuity.[2] So The Tech moves technology a degree or two past just "things" to put "processes," or what it labels "innovation," on display.

Inasmuch as technology is making new things, The Tech shows many new things, but very few old ones, in order to examine more closely the hows and whys of the innovative process behind their design and manufacture. Innovation ironically is far more a mostly sociological process than a purely technical one; indeed, close continuous collaboration between supposed competitors is what keeps the technological systems of high-tech informational capitalism humming. Therefore, I want to reconsider how the very social process of defining the need for The Tech Museum of Innovation, fund-raising for it, developing displays to put it in, and using it for regional self-promotion reveal as much, or even more, about the authentic essence of technological innovation in Silicon Valley than do many of its boxes-and-wires exhibits in the museum.

The Tech's Origin and Organization

Twenty years in the making, The Tech Museum of Innovation began in 1977–1978 when Carol Schwartz, a member of the Junior League of Palo Alto, returned from a visit to Chicago's Museum of Science and Industry. Just as Chicago once represented the old-wave technologies of smoke and steel at the dawn of the twentieth century, Silicon Valley, she believed, should house a fresh new museum to celebrate the technology tied to computers and communications.[3] The Junior League began pushing the idea with various Silicon Valley CEOs, and in the early 1980s San Jose's new mayor, Tom McEnery, made this high technology museum project a centerpiece of his redevelopment plans for the rundown central business district of the city. By 1984, San Jose won a regional competition to serve as The Tech Museum's host city by pledging to provide a site and new building. The publisher of the *San Jose Mercury News*, Tony Ridder, was welcomed as chair of the board for the new museum in 1985; and during this same year the redevelopment agency of the city of San Jose, developer Jack Wheatley, architecture critic Alan Temko, and Lucille Packard all chose Legorreta to design a new building. With launch money from Intel's Dr. Gordon Moore and Apple Computer's Steve Wozniack, the technology center began a sustained campaign of community outreach education with mobile technology shows in Silicon Valley as a means of getting visibility and raising more money in the late 1980s.[4]

By 1989–1990, Bill Hewlett of Hewlett-Packard pledged $2 million for permanent museum building and an interim fixed display site, The Garage, in honor of all of the Valley's famous garage-based high-tech start-up companies. The Garage opened in November 1990 just down Market Street from the permanent museum site in McCabe Hall at the city of San Jose's Convention Center. The institution changed its name to The Tech Museum of Innovation in 1991, and fund-raising started to roll in earnest from 1991 to 1996. Ground was broken for the new building in 1996, and the scope of the museum's fund-raising campaign expanded until its capital campaign hit the $100 million by October 1998 with $42 million from the redevelopment agency of the city of San Jose, $30 million in cash contributions from individuals, companies, and foundations, and $28 million of in-kind product and service contributions from Silicon Valley companies.[5] The Museum of Science and Industry in Chicago pioneered expansive corporate partnerships with private industry, but The Tech Museum has taken this form of fund-raising to new levels of sophistication.

The Tech's striking museum building opened on 31 October–1 November 1998. Peter Giles, The Tech's president and CEO, observed, in keeping with Carol Schwartz's original idea, that The Tech Museum's "mango-colored building, fusing San Jose's Mexican heritage with its Silicon Valley destiny, represents the highest form of investment an individual, corporation, and community can make" that should, in turn, "inspire future generations to realize their dreams in the Silicon Valley of the future."[6] This new 132,500-square-foot building holds four major fixed display galleries—Communications: Global Connections; New Frontiers: Exploration; Innovation: Silicon Valley and Beyond; and Life Tech: The Human Machine. A temporary display space, The Center of the Edge, The Robert H. Noyce Center for Learning, The Hackworth IMAX Dome Theater, as well as Tech Store and Tech Cafe, complete the array of public spaces at the museum. There is neither a strongly determinate path of access nor a clearly articulated narrative of presentation unifying the messages of each gallery area. So visitors are encouraged to visit any gallery in any order, not unlike channel surfing on cable TV or the Internet. Displays at The Center of the Edge are scheduled to be replaced every eighteen months, while the other four "permanent exhibits" are designed to remain open for five to seven years. The Tech wants to emulate the Museum of Science and Industry, but contemporary high technology has little to rival the display of a real Stuka dive-bomber, Spitfire fighter, Boeing 727, or German U-boat that visitors can see at the Chicago museum. Consequently, there is no commitment, as befits the museum's theme of "innovation," at The Tech to maintain extensive genealogies of technological innovation with explications of ancient computers, old telephones, and original biotech experiments. Without this accustomed archaeology of things that might explore the real challenges in engineering high technologies, The Tech's displays often seem entirely weightless, ahistorical, and context-free. Consequently, a visit to its existing galleries is much more like experiencing a computer trade fair extravaganza, particularly in light of the nearly $25 million in special equipment and proprietary services donated by more than five hundred firms to The Tech.[7]

The museum's first gallery on Life Tech explores "the ways science and technology help us to investigate and expand our understanding of life and the human body."[8] The Med Tech area, for example, opens a high-tech operating room with orthoscopic surgical instruments coupled with TV monitors to allow visitors an opportunity to perform operations on dummy patients. Life's New Frontier looks at DNA chemistry, biotechnological innovations, and genetic engineering, while The Transparent Body section displays the various ways that thermographic, x-ray, ultrasound, and MRI technologies provide imaging "to see, hear, quantify, record, and model the human body."[9] The Curiosity Counter exhibits new biotech innovations, ranging from synthetic foods to surgical tools, and Beyond Our Limits focuses on human bodies in motion in need of protection and/or rehabilitation from injuries. The benign images of biotechnologies and medical informatics on display here are underwritten primarily by big private entities like the Valley Foundation, IBM, and Genetech. As each visitor has been tipped off on his or her entry, these experiences in such places are what The Tech curators "hope will inspire the innovator in everyone!"[10]

Clearly, Gallery 2 on Innovation is the core area of The Tech inasmuch as this area in the museum highlights what Silicon Valley is all about today. The Miniature Revolution opens up a condensed microchip fabrication clean room, illustrating the intricate manufacturing processes involved in making microchips. Pushing the Limits provides visitors openings at experimental miniworkstations in sensor, circuit, and laser design as well as studies in nanotechnology. The Virtual Worlds section lets visitors create a new roller coaster, design a new bicycle, and make 3-D computer-assisted portraits. The most intriguing section here, on Robot Tech, enables visitors to see how robot mechanisms actually function in contemporary workplaces, while permitting them to separate "robot fact" (how hypermachinic robots really help us and supposedly do not threaten widespread human job losses) from "robot fiction" (anthropomorphic robots are threatening forces that will cause human unemployment, misery, and insecurity). Sponsored by Intel, SGI, and Applied Materials, the messages here about innovation are what big Silicon Valley firms would wish to convey to twelve-year-old boys and their apprehensive parents: "Don't worry, be happy."

Gallery 3 on the museum's lower level is organized so that visitors can see how communications technology enhances our capacity to work together, create communities, and keep informed about the workings of the world. The Digital Studio section lets visitors create a digital multimedia presentation at one of six workstations, while The TeleVideo Tower connects patrons to one another in a mobile teleconferencing system. The Electronic Cafe area introduces users to the virtual sociologies of online avatar interactions as well as the dynamics of e-mail or webchats at the twelve tables in the cafe. The other zone attempts to introduce a measure of reflexivity into the displays with its discussion of The Information Explosion. Beyond pondering abstractly "the deluge of information" from twenty TV monitors, five LED panels, and a montage of print material swamping everyone inside, not much critical distance is being created here. The highest level of sponsorship in these galleries comes from Hewlett Packard, AT&T, and the *San Jose Mercury News.*

Just adjacent to Gallery 3 is Gallery 4 on Exploration with its mix of displays on Land, Sky and Sea, and Space. Since The Tech is located in the earthquake-prone San Francisco Bay area, the Land section looks at plate tectonics, the San Andreas Fault, and quakeproof architecture. Sky and Sea examines the technology of geophysical imaging from satellite platforms as well as the many robotic and manned systems for exploring deep marine environments. Museum patrons here can design their own satellites and pilot remotely operated underwater vehicles to simulate some of the innovative performances embedded at the core of these technologies. Finally, the Space section explores the workings of the Hubble Telescope, NASA's space shuttle, and the new international space station. Simulated trips to the Moon and Mars are matched up with high-tech listening stations where scientists wait for signs of intelligent extraterrestrial life to appear as radio waves, visual images, or data transmissions. In keeping with the substantive themes of this gallery, the primary sponsors are NASA's Ames Research Laboratories, Lockheed Martin, and the David and Lucille Packard Foundation.

Implements as Innovations

To remain inspirational, The Tech essentially follows in the narrative footsteps of middle school science classes by representing "technology" as discrete individual devices, which, fortunately enough, local corporations invent and sell. This emphasis on high-tech artifacts mostly occludes their equally significant status as commodities. "Know-how" is connected with "own-how" only to the degree that a donor can be credited with generosity to The Tech Museum. Technology as commodity— goods and services with special privileged qualities circulating in great quantities that can be bought and sold by willing and able purchasers— is ignored in the flashing lights, ringing bells, moving parts of the hands-on display of The Tech. As is the case at most science and technology museums, the commodity dimension disappears into a realm of givenness with a taken-for-grantedness that is barely worth mentioning.

Like that of the paleotechnic displays at Chicago's Museum of Science and Industry, the neotechnic tenor of The Tech Museum also is celebratory. Simply visiting The Tech, as its visitor guide exclaims, helps it "to inspire and engage people of all ages and backgrounds in the technology changing our lives."[11] The Tech, however, is not in the business of distributing the same forms of awe vended at the Chicago museum where whole jet airliners, coal mines, and old fighter planes are hung, opened, or set up inside the museum's exhibition halls. Instead The Tech aims at engaging people in simulations of the creative processes of knowing/working/selling innovation with what it calls "hands-on" and "minds-on" activities. The Tech's slogan, "Be Amazed. Do Amazing Things and Discover the Innovator in YOU,"[12] aptly expresses the uncritical "gee whiz" narrative tone embedded in all three floors of its displays. Yet, to be amazed here, one must accept The Tech as a maze with so many wonders that always must be taken at face value. Ironically, today's fixation on robotics, computer technology, and software-driven special effects, which are so prominently featured at The Tech Museum, prompted even Chicago's Museum of Science and Industry to reemphasize its hands-on fun approach to science by hosting a Universal Studios display on how high-tech amusement parks are created in its 1999 exhibition "Theme Park: The Art and Science of Universal Studio's Islands of Adventure."

With this approach to technology, The Tech mostly fixes the viewer's attention on the quiddity of particular devices. The creative acts of inventing, producing, and popularizing technologies, as "how technology works and how it affects our daily lives,"[13] are centered on thing-production and thing-consumption. Technology, in turn, is thing-invention and thing-popularization. Larger background concerns—like how such things are owned, who controls thing-production, what limits thing-consumption, and why only some things are popularized by those who own lots of things, while many others are not—are social processes that are attributed here, at best, to innovative pizzazz, and, at worst, are ignored completely. The black boxes of technology are kept stable and secure, but their museumification is only meant to render them slightly translucent and not transparent. The enlightening rays of innovation reveal some of "the creative energy and spirit that makes Silicon Valley special,"[14] even though they also occlude most of the financial mass and corporate organization that work within the abstract force of "technology" to actually change our lives.

The Tech's celebration of innovation also pretends to explain the workings of technological devices to workers, and would-be workers, who already buy into the wonders of working on the real work of innovation. The Tech here shines the light of change on many things, but its translucence still casts many shadows. The makers and owners of innovation do not want fully transparent clarity, only a warm glow behind the workings of technology to convince new workers of the merits of having such allegedly wonderful work. Like the processed world that now emerges from postindustrial modernity, where, as Jameson suggests, "the modernization process is complete and nature is gone for good,"[15] The Tech shows the transnational/ hyperindustrial/interdisciplinary networks of big business as our second nature. The titanic class struggles of the industrial era between labor and capital are long ago and far away.

Instead the self-referential projects of human creativity are identified here with capital's autogeneration after the end of history, and labor is what comes out of creative people constantly developing new technologies, which then (re)create the people who made them. Technology is innovation: innovation is technology. Whatever transcendent *logos* or ultimate *telos* might have brought humanity to this point in its history, The Tech Museum suggests that technology is itself, of itself, for itself. Thus, The Tech becomes an excellent case study in the new postnational forms of civic education advanced by the global networks of information, energy, capital, labor, and value intertwined with major corporations. Those whose creativity, energy, and spirit will be lost in the rush to develop and ship the next generation of devices to the market are essentially ignored at The Tech. Commodification in markets is neglected here: it is not for commodities, but rather by devices, that we are amazed, and why we do amazing things.

Innovation essentially transmutes itself within these terms into a virtual attractive reality that can embrace all of the untested, unproven, and unrealized potentials lying within today's already realized technical objects and subjects. Even if only for a moment, and perhaps only as a simulation, The Tech projects a multiplicitous virtual reality of beaming technological progress. The Tech's curator, Peter Giles, implicitly concurs with this virtually real reading of The Tech when he asserts, "The Tech will have a long-lasting effect crossing cultural, social and economic boundaries. People of all ages now have the opportunity to hold technology in their hands, to put it up to the light of their curiosity and seek an understanding of how they can made a difference."[16] By bouncing the possibilities of so much technology off so many technologically curious visitors, The Tech becomes the ultimate virtual reality generator of a sunny progressive future for Silicon Valley's many visitors and rising younger generations.

While The Tech may not be "a technological marvel unlike anything the world has been before,"[17] it is, as suggested above, a remarkable bricolage of narrative displays and interactive exhibits. Its four themed galleries mostly accentuate fun-based experimental learning, but there are some twists and turns for deeper intellectual reflection and corporate public relations interspersed throughout the entire museum. Still, entertainment by technology and propaganda for the technologists are what every patron encounters first at the door. Visitors enter The Tech on the ground level where the Hackworth IMAX Dome Theater is the main attraction along with the New Venture Hall. All of the major display spaces are located one floor down and one floor up. To get to either one, all visitors pass the New Venture Hall (for experimental and yet to be developed shows) and the Sponsors Wall, which commemorates the support of Silicon Valley's greatest public and private powers: Intel, the Noyce Foundation, the city of San Jose, Microsoft, Phillips, and the San Jose Mercury News Corporation.

The lower level features two galleries—Communications: Global Connections and New Frontiers: Exploration—that connect visitors to the aerospace and telecommunication networking industries of Silicon Valley and its environs. With only a few exceptions, there is little here that is real, old, or substantial. The processes on display are quite generic, "communication" and "exploration." And the artifacts used to typify them are either quite ordinary, if authentic at all, or mostly models, if too big and complex to put inside a building. In this respect, The Tech is not a cabinet of true curiosities as much as it is a chamber for the curious.

Exploration's emphasis on "New Frontiers" falls most heavily on space and oceanic exploration, but a large section is devoted to seismic activities, space walks, deep submersibles, interplanetary probes, and extraterrestrial searches. All of these foci rely heavily on numerous video-mediated experiences. Communications, on the other hand, pops visitors into the Information Explosion in which a crude collage of newspapers, TV monitors, product posters, news magazines, and print flyers from around the world lead down a small tunnel to confront the World Wide Web. A bank of computers and wall captions details what the Internet is, how search engines work on the WWW, what homepages are, and how to "take charge of the Information swirling around you," but all of these ordinary artifacts can be found in any Radio Shack store. Beginning with the first electromechanical Ansa-Phone in 1958, which actually is one of the few historic things on display here, in the manner of a conventional technology museum, and moving to today's cell phones, the displays push a form of active, informed technological agency, not unlike being a *Wired* reader, as the best way to cope with the Information Explosion. As the wall captions suggest, "we need new skills and new tools to take control of the information pouring into our lives." And The Tech's displays are there pretending to know why the information is launched at us in massive semiotic strikes as well as how countermeasures might be mobilized to staunch the rush of information coming at us from so many global networks at the local, individual level of use.

The lower level also features the flexible Center of the Edge Gallery for traveling or temporary exhibits. In its opening months, two very engaging shows were installed. One, labeled "Boundary Function," borrowed its title from the Ph.D. thesis written by Ted Kaczynski, the Unabomber; and it explored the spatial relations between people with an interactive spatial cell-mapping program that draws spatial insulating zones around visitors stepping onto its display plane. The other, titled "Portable Effects," looked at the "nomadic design" exercises involved in very ordinary everyday activities when people dress, pack their book bags, fill their pants pockets, and stuff their purses for a trip out of the house. A project of the Interval Research Corporation, "Portable Effects" is a study of new market opportunities coming together at the operational intersection of technology, consumers, and popular culture that plays with new media to display both human forms and business products. This space also featured a virtual-reality trip through Virtual Jerusalem, Timbuktu, and Dubrovnik, where visitors simulated a walk in these places by donning a pair of 3-D glasses and ambling along a moving circular platform.

The upper level of The Tech, however, really gets down to the heart of Silicon Valley and beyond by introducing visitors to CAD (computer-assisted design) simulations of a new roller coaster, mountain bike, and computer chip as well as experiments in 3-D computer body-scanning industrial-laser operations, and manufacturing robotics systems. Sponsored by SGI, Applied Materials, Intel, and Ultratech Stepper, this gallery focuses on the uses of infotech not looking to the things of technology themselves but rather looking at simulations of such things, images of such thing use, and emulations of thing effects that are so close to Silicon Valley's heart. The second gallery on Life Tech: The Human Machine, which is backed mostly by the Valley Foundation, also technifies the human body with displays on human-powered vehicles (HPVs) for air, land, and water travel, DNA engineering, microsurgery, and medical imaging technology.

Strangely enough, the only place where The Tech toys with the ellipsis of capital in the entire museum is the connecting bridge to Silicon Valley and Beyond from Life Tech. This small space mainly deals with robotics. Here the panels extol the virtues of nonhuman steel-collar workers over those of human white-, pink-, and blue-collar workers. One display presents a worker wondering about his possible job loss to a robot, but others show experts talking up the job gains, productivity increases, and efficiency enhancements that should come from widespread robotization. Since this is The Tech, amazement must triumph over disenchantment. If old low-tech jobs are lost, then high-tech jobs will be gained. When you discover the innovator in yourself, then the message is you may be at peace with losing your job. Indeed, The Tech shows a path of permanent labor reconciliation and corporate redemption from job loss owing to constant innovation.

This zone in The Tech also recasts the human body in the lean and mean registers of performativity so favored now by transnational businesses.[18] Rather than serving as the temple of the soul or crowning glory of natural creation, bodies become another kind of economic and technical performance center. The individual body and all bodies in any given society must be kept up and running. Performativity demands healthy, happy, and hungry people eager to have the good things transnational capital brings to life. Life Tech: The Human Machine essentially reduces corporeality to biocapital: everyone gets some, and anyone can add to its powers as well as preserve its capabilities with the right tools. Similarly, biotechnologies are explored in a few pods devoted to The Digital Body. As a means of obviating one need for biostructural prostheses or therapies, the use of gene therapies is touted to advance genetic engineering or cellular reconstruction as solutions for good health.

While all of this is quite fascinating its subtext remains clear: performativity is everything. Like the studies of HPVs for water, land, and air in the Life Tech gallery, the human body itself is reduced by these displays to "tech." The embodied human is no longer the corporeal shell of an eternal soul; instead it becomes a power source, guidance system, or time-share in the service life of things. All technologies, as the subtext in all these displays indicates, are human-powered vehicles for capital's continuous revalorization, and the Life Tech gallery focuses visitors' minds on the necessity and legitimacy of this economistic application of their existence to the market's ongoing evolution. Consequently, human DNA should be mapped to help redesign animals and plants, medical imaging must be used to document collective biopower, and individuals ought to accept biomechanical prosthetics to maintain their performative edge as iterations of "the human machine."

Real Technology/Technological Realism

Technology at The Tech essentially is presented in the form of devices—boxes and wires, chips and disks, scanners and routers. The social construction of technology is not a far-fetched academic thesis in this environment. On the contrary, contemporary technologies for constructing the social are front and center in the exhibits.[19] High technology, in turn, is a complex, rapidly changing cluster of such devices. This is what really works, affects our lives, and changes the world by means of such things. A vast collective of devices has coevolved over time with human beings, and their interactions in the economy and environment, state and society, city and country are how human innovation constantly changes things and their users. Doing things with other things in new ways is redefined as humanity's most transcendent telos at The Tech. Consequently, technology is cast almost entirely as in itself and for itself with no higher purpose than self-regeneration and self-expansion in the endless circuits of planned obsolescence. Each innovation becomes a new link in an evolutionary chain of autogenic change that cascades through human communities in waves of new social change borne by the newest models, latest breakthroughs, freshest approaches.

The Tech's conceit of display—similar to that at the Exploratorium in San Francisco since 1969—is that its interactivity repositions the visitor, shifting him or her from the role of an observer of technology to that of an (inter)actor with technologies. By using some technical implements and processes like a scientist or technician would, museum patrons are made to believe they are participating in science, doing technology, or practicing at innovation. This maneuver, as the Exploratorium's founder, Frank Oppenheimer, argued, might "make it possible for people to believe that they can understand the world around them."[20] Yet this claim is in many ways a very limited approach to understanding, centered on technical implements, physical processes, and manufacturing tools. Such "understanding" is a make-believe vision of science, and it utterly ignores many of the economic, political, and social connections embedded in the technology on display.

Moreover, these dynamics of interactivity, in fact, often are not where "the tech" of innovation lies. Those forces are instead found in the autodestructive self-justification of corporate commodity chains as they create new markets through competition and collaboration. The missing link at The Tech between all of its devices, which mars each of its galleries, is an explicit treatment of technology as commodity. The relentless pursuit of perfection is today as much, or even more, about increasing corporate profits as it is engineering solutions. Nonetheless, this dynamic of devalorization and revalorization in the secret life of things as new commodities, which are worthy of purchase, suitable for desire, and pitched at need, is occluded in the booming buzzing confusion of The Tech's many displays. If The Tech presumes to make the technical world around its visitors understandable, then it does so by mostly masking what social and economic forces actually remake the world as technology.

Interactivity, therefore, must not be mistaken for genuine independent action. Interactivity assumes that individuals with certain agendas and assets will collaborate with other comparable individuals or institutional forces that share their goals to maximize their rational use of scarce resources. Social life is what is created out of their common efforts. Self-managing individuals must develop the enterprise and experience to organize their own existence, but they largely do this in cooperation/collaboration/coordination with larger institutions that steer these managed selves down the productive paths endorsed by governments, private firms, markets, and scientific disciplines. Much of this is not independent agency but rather sets of interactive decision making, choice-fulfillment, and activity-assessment routines conducted by individuals within, for, and even because of the larger institutions they interact with.

For people whose lives outside the museum must be more self-regulated and self-directed, interactive museum exhibitions, like those at

The Tech, provide methods well suited to educating the members of to-day's neoliberal civil society. Just free enough to support the collective choice of mass publics, interactive museums also do not evince com-plete freedom of action or true individual autonomy. To interact is to act between, with, because, and for others, which is the decisive lesson that neoliberal markets must impart to their clients in order to adduce the freedom to choose. And The Tech's most obvious subtext for all of its textualizations of technical virtuosity is that real "innovation" is co-operative, collaborative, or even collusive in its everyday workings on the high-tech frontier.

The Tech Museum of Innovation, then, is also a study in commercial illusion. Technology is found in "devices" whose positive effects are to make the big businesses controlling most technology into the undis-puted source of good work. Bad outcomes, poor effects, and evil works are neither shown as what can be just as pervasively true about technol-ogy nor as something that could be ultimately intrinsic to technical ac-tion. Pollution, contamination, destruction, which have been inevitable by-products of technical production, are glossed over almost entirely. The Tech's presentations of technology in action only trade on good works that work well. The bad effects, poor outcomes, and useless goods produced by many technological innovations do not get through the museum's door. Positive benefits rather than negative costs are the ped-agogical bottom line at The Tech, just as they are inside the public rela-tions departments of all the corporations which support it.

The Tech clearly desacralizes technology. It brings it down into every-day life as something whose relations, actions, and environs are fully in-vested in the ordinary comings and goings of the profane subjects who benefit from them. Technology at The Tech is upbeat in tempo and on the upside in tone. Engaging, effervescent, efficacious—this is what char-acterizes technology in The Tech's flashy and fun displays.[21] Like the films at Hackworth IMAX Theater, the performances commanded from The Tech's displays are those that optimize a "you are there" experience. Visitors are put into, on top of, around, under, and alongside the ma-chines or models of machines as coproducers of their performativity and efficiency. The phenomenological script behind each display is play; hence, the exhibitions' captions and aesthetics are pitched intellectually at the sensibilities of a ten- or twelve-year-old boy. Technology here even moves beyond being fixated on "know-how." Instead, it is far more focused on "do-something." To innovate at The Tech is to manage, manipulate, move, and make things.[22] The reality of "know-how," implying also "own-how," is completely reduced to the marginal facts in the small print about sponsorship, support, and strategy detailed on the galleries' entrances. Inducing workers to move inside the machines also may adduce the natural outcomes of labor alienation and subjection, but The Tech underscores that there are no better inducements than the allure of control over objects to turn human subjects into traffic controllers, thing managers, and machine operators.

The Tech celebrates *technē,* but its exhibits also implicitly are set up to serve as enrollment networks for an ethics and politics organized by corporate enterprises around agendas of permanent revolution, perpetual change, and persistent reorganization. While interactivity presumes to make the world understandable to museum visitors, those who truly understand how technology brings good things to life recognize that museum visitors also become more educable, once they leave The Tech, after mastering this kind of interactivity. The subpolitical dimensions of life, in which the momentum of business imperatives and technological dynamics sets the agendas of actual politics and ethics, are quite obvious in most displays at The Tech, but they also are mostly ignored in the museum's narratives.[23] Without being shackled with the ponderous worries of serving as "The Eth" or "The Pol," The Tech captures much of the implied ethics and tacit politics buried in the always ongoing innovations of capital. In its unending cycles of revalorization, "discovering the innovator in you" also becomes a means of normalizing "the you" made by/for/with innovations in science and technology. The artifices of newness constantly are being co-modified by, while working to attain greater commodifications with, the incessant flows of newness rising from the technical branches of corporations. Tech here becomes things, not capital; and capital always operates, in turn, not as a force for destructive exploitation but rather only as a source of constructive innovation. The symbolic registers of innovation here are meant to bring better living through chemistry, engineering, and physics, while staid accounts of exploitation only would tally up something depressing, like horrendous deaths from chemical pollution or the tremendous loss of natural habitat through chemical accidents.

In this regard, The Tech definitely reimagines the science museum in terms of the latest philosophies of science, namely, those tied to scientific realism.[24] The unending search for new natural laws in traditional philosophies of science obviously has been displaced by a much more performative fascination with focused searches for replicable mechanisms of explicable operation in nature, which can, in turn, be exploited with new technical devices. Discovering and affirming scientific laws is all right, but this sort of "basic research" or "pure science" rarely leads to innovations. On the other hand, seeking out, and then sharing under some financially rewarding conditions, any new, application-rich processes tied to physical, biological, electrical, and cybernetic phenomena that have openly discernible mechanisms leads to "commercial research" or "applied science." This outcome is the essence of corporate performativity, especially under today's conditions of transnational production. The juridical concerns of positivistic science are not forgotten, but the merchandising possibilities in scientific realism for higher corporate profits are what truly constitute the narrative anchors for The Tech's philosophies of science.

Most importantly, The Tech is a concrete testament to the collaborative qualities of contemporary corporate innovation. As William Baumol argues, innovation rather than pure competition is the driving force behind modern markets, because many firms increasingly share their technological innovations in joint ventures, technical collaboration agreements, and industrial standards accords that virtually guarantee that competing rivals will share key technologies.[25] The alliances represented by corporate donations to The Tech for the mutual construction of a memorial to the high-tech business world of Silicon Valley also essentially mirror the technology-sharing compacts out in the Valley that assure that one PC maker will soon share in any other PC maker's technological advances. Innovation is suited up in the wolves' clothing of raw competition for The Tech's displays, but most everyone in the Valley, in fact, dresses like sheep on the job as they flock together to keep innovations rolling out of their factories and shops.

The invitation to "be amazed," and "do amazing things" represents capital's allure to clever people who want to join in its construction of the new. Innovation is brought to life as things that collectively can constitute fresh mazeways of consumption, collaboration, and coproduction, first, for corporate growth, and second, for general social change. By pitching technology at the enthusiasms of precocious preteenage boys, The Tech also casts corporate "know-how" as an unending maze of delight inasmuch as corporate "own-how" at The Tech closely modulates the nature of wealth as delightful effects in the various display performances contained by its galleries. Discovering who the great innovators are, and then inspiring the wannabes to become future great innovators along with all the other current innovators, is the normative script embedded at the core of its narratives about technology. At The Tech Museum technicians are, first and foremost, change agents and their innovative technologies are the vital agencies we all are led to believe we need to continue changing. And this mostly will happen at bright, entertaining sites of corporate control and public vision out in so many colorful business parks not entirely unlike The Tech Museum itself. Thus, The Tech strives to advance such collaboration by continuously organizing new linkages for many networks in support of technical innovation, and it is open for enthusiastic enrollment six days a week.

CHAPTER ELEVEN

Channeling the News Stream:
The Full Press of a Free Press at the Newseum

Sitting just across the Potomac River from the Kennedy Center for the Arts, and next to Arlington National Cemetery and the Pentagon in Virginia, the Newseum strangely presumes to deputize Hermes to serve as one humanity's most important Muses. Along with Astronomy, Comedy, History, Music, or the other Muses, we are asked by the Freedom Forum to believe that "News" must reside in the Temple of the Muses, if not have its own special building. Because it is a long way to Mount Parnassus, the Newseum is devoted to Hermes, and it is conveniently sited in Arlington, Virginia, at the headquarters of the Freedom Forum. This Washington-based trade association of print, radio, television, and Web media outlets is dedicated to protecting a vision of "the free press" shared by these industries so that they might continue a full press for their sort of freedom, along with their version of Greek mythology, against the world's media viewers, readers, and users.

Oddly enough, for an exposition devoted to celebrating the media spectacle, the Newseum defends its muse by pretending to demystify the news gathering and reporting process. In this chapter, I will re-examine the Newseum's apparent dedication to revealing what goes on behind the studio curtains or beyond the banner heads at big news production sites. Print media are shown through their computer-based compositing cycles, and their text is envisioned as passing through a WWW-centered regeneration. In turn, a great many of the Newseum's displays focus on the elementary technics of broadcast media. One peers into the TV control room, pops by the TV talk-show studio, and pushes into a simulated TV broadcast.

This fascination with the tools and trades of TV technics, however, does not demystify news production. Instead, it occludes what "the news" truly is to the extent that it fails to demonstrate how and why news services have been produced by corporate sponsors, state regulators, and business interests to create markets for products, the subjects of government, and audiences for capital. Discussing how objects that bear "the news" are made does not truly demystify why the news commodity is produced. The goals of news production, like the goals of museum display, are to produce mass audiences and broad publics with particular needs and specific attitudes. Benedict Anderson argues that print capitalism, and now broadcast capitalism, are the soft armatures of national identity in every territorial state.[1] Because people who read similar newspapers or monitor shared radio/television broadcasts, as Ulrich Beck observes, become one nation or a unified public, the key media effect of effective media is the communicative unification generated by the mode of information.[2]

As a result, one probably should not separate print tools and broadcast trades from capitalist markets or nationalist sentiments. Nevertheless, this elision is precisely how the Newseum organizes its representation of "the news" by fixating on the cables, cameras, and control arms of studio technics. The Newseum, in fact, unveils the complex processes of news production only up to certain limits, namely, technical or operational ones. While the pretext of these displays is to show how much these machines contribute to the "invention of communication," a more pertinent subtext would be to reveal how they actually help to invent psychosocial identity and difference in the collective life of modern societies.[3] At that turn, however, the Newseum would have to push far beyond the commonsense view of news as a communications practice that imparts some novel awareness of something previously unknown to free people. It rather would need to explore how the news also is always a commercializing practice, producing ads for products, producing products for ads, and producing audiences for ads to buy products.

Instead of showing how the media are commercial or state organs to cogenerate the new forms of culture and styles of progress with mass publics in the invention of communication between massed communicants, the Newseum chooses to cast the news as a collective consciousness or memorialization machine. The Newseum suggests Hermes should be the preeminent Muse, because our psychosocial identities are cast in the control rooms or forged on the front pages of media markets in the acts of bringing us "the news." Moments of our lives, according to the Freedom Forum, are now history on videotape or in news photo layouts.[4] All that we "are" comes from the rush of the news stream out in the daily news cycle, which leaves traces of its fusion in memory or fission with practice every new daily cycle. As Mattelart and Mattelart assert, it is difficult to construct critical studies of television images or print discourses in the media, because their ephemerality, immediacy, and spontaneity wash away so much of their influence even as the influencing occurs. "For the majority of people," they maintain, "promotional and advertising discourse on new products is the main mode of access to knowledge about this novel dimensions of these technologies."[5] So theoretical reflection and studied criticism can slip away into time-urgency and journalistic exuberance. The Newseum, in turn, does not create a space for reflective critique or theoretical study. Instead it simply provides an archive of past moments of televisual exuberance and hot copy from deadlines now long gone, which only reinforce this depthlessness of media memories. Print capitalism produces acts and artifacts of a print capitalist subjectivity in objects of print-capitalist commerce, and broadcast capitalism also generates broadcasting acts and artifacts on tape as master reels for broadcast subjects to organize their broadcast-bound lives. The Newseum hopes to provide an overview of these dynamics amidst its artifacts; but, more importantly, I will argue that it mystifies the social relations of cultural conjunction that are expressed in the technical effects of the news.

The Newseum Site

A common conceit used by the editors and owners who run the contemporary mass media sees the world as a place that is made and remade by their constant coverage. This presumption of world-making power is rendered concrete with an immense geodesic globe on the Newseum's second floor. As visitors enter from the Freedom Park outside or ascend from the ground floor on the escalator in the museum building, they confront this metal world modeled out of three-sided, engraved, pewter-colored bars: The News Globe. It is, in turn, encircled by a continuous electronic headline readout. On each side of the bars, banners from hundreds of local, regional, national, and international newspapers mark their locality on this symbol of media globalism.[6] From *Die Zeit,*

The Guardian, and *New York Times* to the *Akron Beacon, San Jose Mercury News,* and *Kansas City Kansan,* the bars symbolically allude to the zones of coverage, areas of circulation, and regions of influence in which the press generates its powers. Identical in form, uniform in process, and formative in effect, these newspaper-publishing operations, along with the electronic broadcast media, have made and do remake the world every day in the mediascape of this daily, weekly, and monthly planet.

The physical layout of the Newseum mimics the inverted pyramid of well-written wire copy: the highest floor, like the top of the story, holds most of this news museum's content, and tapers down through the second floor to rest on its smallest point of the first floor where the visitor enters.[7] In the entry foyer, a dictionarylike definition on the wall details the meanings of "news" and "newseum" for patrons: *news:* (1) a report of recent events, especially unusual or noble ones; (2) information from a newspaper, news periodical, or newscast; (3) anything previously unknown; and *newseum:* (1) the world's first museum devoted to the past, present, and future of the news; (2) an institution that fosters free press, free speech, and free spirit. The narrative thematic of the Newseum from the entry foyer to the last exit, then, is simple. "News" in senses one and three should be understood through the media mentioned in sense two. All communication in all places at all times is captured by this lead, allowing the Newseum's curators to reconstruct all of human history in terms of the technics for message mediation attaining more, better, faster, wider coverage.[8] The means evolve, but the content is more or less the same from prehistoric cave paintings and ancient Egypt to today's CNN cable feed and Murdoch newspapers.[9] The human need to know simply reduces the knowing of needy humans wanting information to an acceptance of their "formation" through the media. With these insights on their minds, visitors then pass through an airport-grade metal detector and bag search to gain access to the level 1 lobby—an explicit reminder that the operating broadcast studio and control room on levels 2 and 3 are part of a fully functional power center in today's modes of information. Anyone seeking illegal control of the mode of information is a criminal, and the rituals of criminal detection by electromagnetic body scans must be performed even here in the Newseum.

On level 1, the News Byte Cafe offers refreshments and access to the Internet through a sectioned site that cuts the WWW into twelve targeted slices: Internet Generation, General Newspapers, International,

Sports, Comics and Features, Radio, Television, Magazines, Politics, Money and Business, Inside Story of the News, and Cafe Favorites. At the information desk on the other side of the partition, "news" is spelled in many languages and several alphabets, but the real world news is constantly flying past visitors on all sides on the terminals in the News Byte Cafe.

An escalator or elevator ride up to level 2 brings visitors before the News Globe, which carries nameplates from 1,841 newspapers—small locals, larger regionals, and major national newspapers—from all over the world and the United States. On one wall, a staircase winds around the News Globe to level 3, and on the opposite side the Second Amendment of the Constitution of the United States is reproduced in full. A high-definition video theater on this level runs a short film on great moments in history as represented in the news media, where individual psychosocial identities might be recharged by clips of major media moments in the dark. Visitors then can enter the Interactive Newsroom area. In this space, interactive computer workstations invite visitors to be "a reporter," be "an editor," be "a photographer" in a series of hands-on video simulations of such media labor. Other workstations invite patrons to act out little professional journalistic morality plays in the Ethics Center. Bigger simulation bays allow visitors to perform "real" stand-ups as White House reporters, newscasters, weathercasters, and sportscasters on camera, which gives the Newseum a unique visitor service to sell back to its users. This display reinforces the naturalization of the ordinary ritualized dramaturgy in such broadcasting discourses to average viewers who here can be extraordinary producers of them, if only for fun.

Another elevator ride brings visitors up to level 3 where an elaborate frieze of case displays and multimedia exhibits seeks to recount "the history of the news."[10] It concludes at another wall, bearing a simple caption: "the human need to know, growing, changing, boundless, forever pushes the frontiers of news." This potted history of "the media" begins with Paleolithic cave paintings and progresses through the centuries to CNN in the 1990s and the early twenty-first century. Because human beings communicate, the Newseum presumes that the intent and content of all their different forms for communication always has been about sharing "news." Hence, both primitive petroglyphs and today's televisions are fitted neatly into a single linear evolutionary scheme.

The extraordinary influence of the news media today, in turn, is naturalized by this narrative frame, which presumes there always has been, will be, and is the presence of the media in our lives. In the Newseum's focus on the material devices used for communication in every stage of the news in its historical evolution, the TV broadcast simply becomes the broadest band for communicating messages whose content is not unlike those carried by Egyptian scribes, Greek runners, Roman roads, and medieval towncriers.[11] This assumption, however, is quite problematic. The primitive petroglyphs' audience was not the same as CNN's today, and there are tremendous differences in the power/knowledge being fabricated in broadcasting to modern mass publics that monochrome pictographs daubed on rocks by Paleolithic nomads simply cannot approach. This attempt to normalize almost every form of communication into a news message occludes who messages whom and why as well as who controls the communicative conveyances and how they operate in each distinctive context. These garbled truths, in turn, steer visitors past the Broadcast Studio Control Room to the Video News Wall— a 126-foot-long continuous collage of media retrospectives, edited news programs, and unedited news video from around the world captured through the Newseum's control room from what is called "the news stream."

As the *Self-Guided Tour* assures us, "the news changes daily" so "no two visits to the Newseum are the same," and the Video News Wall proves this by naturalizing "the news stream" as a force, not unlike the Gulf Stream or Jet Stream.[12] As visitors enter the loft gallery to view it, the Freedom Forum puts the full court press on them to be swept away in "the news stream":

> Every few seconds, millions of words, sounds, and images flash around the globe.
>
> This is the news stream—the endless flow of fresh data, events, issues and ideas that gives us our picture of the world.
>
> In the digital age, the news stream is growing beyond measure. News comes faster, from all directions.
>
> In this gallery, the Video News Wall lets you look at the news stream to see today's news as it happens.
>
> This 126-foot-long mural of the Global Village shows dozens of simultaneous feature television feeds. Special programs at the Video News Wall help you understand the decisions shaping today's news.

This awesome media experience, in turn, provides canned retrospectives on the mass media, daily unedited newsfeed from the world's major TV media concerns, and heavily edited news programming.[13]

There is a very palpable sense of political power and cultural authority at the Newseum. From the metal detectors at the entry points to the direct unedited broadcast feed coursing across the News Wall on the third floor, one is helped to understand "the decisions shaping today's news." In a cozy, albeit incomplete, effort to display the mechanics of mass media power, the Newseum explores the aesthetic production of modern communication: the cool command of high-tech control rooms, the rushed discourse of sound-bite exchanges, the endless flow of raw newsfeed from around the world, the aura of celebrity around on-air media personalities are all cut into simulation-sized bits on the second floor, allowing Newseum patrons to fill the simulated shoes and seats of their favorite famous TV figures as they tape themselves on screen at the Newseum for repeat performances back home. Power here reaches a perfect pitch as every little capillary and eddy is permitted to recirculate its effects on itself and others.[14] "The news stream" is that "endless flow of fresh data, events, issues and ideas that gives us our picture of the world," and the Newseum underscores this fact in these ontologues about the media. The press of the free press becomes quite concrete in "millions of words, sounds, and images" flashing around the globe to fix our knowledge about how power "comes faster, from all directions."

Mapping the Postmodern/Naming the System

In its new cognitive mapping for the mediascape, the Newseum disputes the understanding of political borders in space and the cultural boundedness of place as these phenomena have been positioned in the spaces drawn by commerce, diplomacy, and geography. Defying these conceptual boundaries, however, also requires the media to tell alternative stories, to elaborate their own culture for boundary creation, space definition, or state formation as an interconnected set of media practices. Jameson asserts that all existing discourses have failed to adequately map or effectively name ongoing processes of postmodern globalism like those portrayed on the Newseum's Video News Wall. He issues a new imperative: "we have to name the system."[15] The politics most suited to these postmodern times, therefore, "will have as its vocation the invention and projection of a global cognitive mapping, on a social as well as a spatial scale."[16] "The news stream" described by the Newseum clearly has this power. It is a map that creates its own terrain, and the terrain conforms closely to the media's televisual map.

As Vattimo argues, "the society in which we live is a society of generalized communication. It is a society of the mass media."[17] The setting of life here is shaken and stirred completely as it dissolves into pixels and bits. Power shifts focus, speed overcomes space, orders become disordered, time moves standards, community loses centers, values change denomination. Mediascapes, at this juncture, assume their current forms of corporate rationalization to the degree that "in the production of nature that use-value and exchange-value, and space and society, are fused together."[18] Mediascapes recombine society and space by producing new exchange-values in many unprecedented ways from the use-values of the electromagnetic spectrum, the industrial era's telecommunication infrastructures, and the contemporary restructuring of labor and leisure.

"As a social product," the spatiality of these mediascapes still remains "simultaneously the medium and outcome, presupposition and embodiment, of social action and relationship."[19] Digital emissions, analog waves, image streams, and information currents, which swirl through new televisual/telegraphic/telephonous flows, now become features to be taped/recorded/transcribed as virtual geographies of the mediascape. With this eruption of change, the conflicts of humans against nature, other humans, and themselves are recast in new unforeseen directions. Most importantly, the setting of space, the character of power, and the structure of order need more elaborate interpretations to mark the differences in the present as it is formed by mediascapes.

The perspectival space and neutral time created by print, however, slip away into the televisual with its more postperspectival visions of place and new simultaneous markings of time.[20] The oral, particular, local, and timely agendas of extrastatist social forces, set loose by minicams and uplink trucks, are contesting the written, general, universal, and timeless line of power born from print. Even though the Newseum pretends to provide one consistent narrative, the continual pluralizing of the subjects and objects of communication in today's proliferating networks of information "renders any unilinear view of the world and history impossible."[21]

From the televisual fuzz of "the news stream," modern representational differences between true and false, concept and object, real and representation can easily be lost. Baudrillard claims that one must see everything anew on such hyperreal mediascapes: "No more mirror of being and appearances, of the real and its concept. No more imaginary coextensity: rather, genetic miniaturization is the dimension of simulation. The real . . . no longer has to be rational, since it is no longer measured against some ideal or negative instance. It is nothing more than operational. In fact, since it is no longer enveloped by an imaginary, it is no longer real at all. It is a hyperreal, the product of an irradiating synthesis of combinatory models in a hyperspace without atmosphere."[22]

Baudrillard, in turn, rearticulates what the Newseum posits in its vision of the news: "we must think of the media as if they were, in outer orbit, a sort of genetic code which controls the mutation of the real into the hyperreal, just as the other, micro-molecular code controls the passage of the signal from a representative sphere of meaning to the genetic sphere of the programmed signal."[23] Simulation in the global news flow goes far beyond the old print divisions of space and time, sender and receiver, medium and message, expression and content as the world's complex webs of electronic media generate new hyperspaces with "no sense of place." Yet these ambiguous sites are always recognized in replays and reprints as "the moments of our lives." These fast capitalist transformations started during the 1950s and 1960s, when the impact of mass telecommunications, electronic computerization, cybernetic automation, and rapid transportation first began to be experienced broadly around the world; yet they accelerate with each passing year. Jameson claims this is a global change "which is somehow decisive but incomparable with the older convulsions of modernization and industrialization, less perceptive and dramatic somehow, but more permanent precisely because it is more thorough going and all-pervasive."[24]

As the Newseum asserts, communications systems can reorder the structures of social action as well as the institutional sites of cultural process in several different ways. Frequently in the past, these informational networks have buttressed the power of nation-states. Now, however, their effect "has been the opposite: breaking state monopolies of information, permeating national boundaries, allowing peoples to hear and see how others do things differently."[25] The logic of informational commodification demands constant expansion, turning everything into an object of communication. More and more national subcultures, local personalities, fundamentalist sects, and ethnic groups can gain a voice and presence in the mass media. Thus, "the West is living through an explosive situation, not only with regard to other cultural universes (such as the 'third world'), but internally as well, as an apparently irresistible pluralization renders an unilinear view of the world and history impossible."[26]

These transformations tend to fractalize cultures, economies, and societies, dividing them between demands made by nominal nationality in old "in-stated spaces" and the pull from actual transnationality in new "un-stated spaces" as both local and regional communities patch into truly transnational rather than essentially national modes of production. In such global economic changes, as Robert Reich maintains, "barriers to cross-border flows of knowledge, money, and tangible products are crumbling; groups of people in every nation are joining global webs."[27] Sovereignty is displaced or supplanted in the flows by performativity, or, as Lyotard claims, "the best possible input/output equation."[28] These shifts toward the performative provide new criteria on the air for determining what is strong, what is just, and what is true in the operational workings of informational flows. The normativity of laws in statist jurisdictions, then, gradually is supplanted by the performativity of styles, images, or procedures taken from the polydictive buzz of "the news stream."

More complex communities also can develop within the operational areas of these many new global flows as the imagination of mediatized communities defines their very loose limits and quite constrained powers. From the global flows of informational capitalism, "the world of generalized communication explodes like a multiplicity of 'local' rationalities—ethnic, sexual, religious, cultural, or aesthetic minorities—that finally speak up for themselves. They are no longer repressed and cowed into silence by the idea of a single true form of humanity that must be realized irrespective of particularity and individual finitude, transience, and contingency."[29] Emancipation in the informational order "consists in *disorientation*, which is at the same time also the liberation of differences, of local elements, of what generally could be called dialect."[30] Through the multiplicity of dialects and their different cultural universes, living in this unstable, pluralistic world "means to experience freedom as a continual oscillation between belonging and disorientation."[31]

Gaining access to these disorienting but connecting transnational flows with their flexible sites of operationalization eclipses the importance of fixing control of national space with rigid borders of organization. Again, as Manuel Castells asserts, "there is a shift, in fact, away from the centrality of the organizational unit to the network of information and decision. In other words, *flows, rather than organizations,* become the units of work, decision, and output accounting. Is the same trend developing in relation to the spatial dimension of organizations? Are flows substituting for localities in the information economy? Under the impact of information systems, are organizations not timeless but also placeless?"[32] The diversity, depth, and direction of these flows constitute a new dimension of thought and action. Flows in many ways represent *capital in motion,* circulating money, labor, products, and technology (as well as information in audio, video, and data form about them) throughout the global economy. Partly local, partly global, such flows are developing a telesphere/cybersphere of artificial spaces created by these streams of data, audio, and video.

In mediascapes there are innumerable new areas of operation, regions of action, spheres of simulation, and zones of performativity that are "un-stated" rather than "in-stated." Such hyperreal domains, as the Newseum shows, provide new centers, margins, and grids of power with the options to test their own agendas, interests, and values beyond, beside, and beneath the nation-state. With these changes there is a general mediatization of the world as "the images of the world we receive from the media and human sciences, albeit on different levels, are not simply different interpretations of a 'reality' that is 'given' regardless, but rather constitute the very objectivity of the world."[33]

At this juncture, as Jameson notes, "the nation-state itself has ceased to play a central functional and formal role in a process that has in a new quantum leap of capital prodigiously expanded beyond them, leaving them behind as ruined and archaic remains in the development of this mode of production."[34] National economies are increasingly nominal, while transnational economies now are quite fully determinate systems of organization. Areas of operation, above and below the nation-state, now frame the critical zones of corporate and social performativity, and "the news stream" carries signs of its success everywhere. Nation-states that remain closed, inaccessible economic spaces, attempting to control capital, labor, technology, and markets on a strictly national basis, are doomed to anachronistic stagnation, as in the cases of Cuba, the former Soviet Union, Myanmar, or North Korea. This constant enhancement of the forms and sources of information remakes "reality" entirely as image: "It may be that in the world of the mass media a 'prophecy' of Nietzsche's is fulfilled: in the end the true world becomes a fable."[35]

Mattelart argues that communication is simultaneously a system for imparting progress, instilling culture, and instigating war among the expansive populations of modern nations and markets.[36] The news is simply the narrow leading edge of broader cultural transformations being carried along as progress with all mass media. The Freedom Forum is, in large part, about celebrating the foundation of freedoms of a certain kind and in a particular fashion inside this strange kind of forum. In turn, it stands for forum freedoms of the press, assembly, conscience, or association that mass media communicate to mass publics.[37] News of this freedom—of its progress, of its culture, and of its war—is inescapable. Indeed, the Newseum naturalizes the news by recasting it as a natural force of the universe in its narrative visions for "the news stream."

The bricolage of mediated moments assembled here as print traces, photo glimpses, and historical relics is done to represent the impact of mediascapes in weaving the fabric of our lives. These televisual terrains and print places are contemporary society's critical conjunctures of communicative interaction. When broadcaster/broadcast/broadcasted/broadcastee intermesh hour-by-hour, day-by-day, week-by-week on the mediascape—a fact the Newseum seeks to commemorate to all of its visitors—shared realities can be socially constructed, operationally circulated, and historically contained in the audiences' reception of words and images. While there are prefigurations of these relations in early modern Europe with the newsbooks of the thirteenth century or the gazetteers of the eighteenth century, the Newseum underscores how powerful and pervasive these mediascapes become after the invention of Morse telegraphy or the proliferation of urban dailies in the nineteenth century.[38]

Only by the coupling of quick electromechanical means of communication and high-speed linotype printing presses in urban industrial areas can "the major media event" come into being. And with it come new human beings tied to their continuous creation in mediated events as the floating new majorities of media buyers, readers, listeners, watchers, users. Information previously unknown but now culled from a newspaper, news periodical, or newscast, remakes human beings into "news people." News, as discrete moments from our news-generated lives, also can become more distantly old news, history, and nostalgia, which can be revisited again and again as those "history-making events" of our lives at the Newseum. Such information is what "news peoples" are always formed within as agents. Mediascapes are the ranges where newspeople roam, while the watchers and watched, in turn, are made in large part out of these technological means for watching.[39]

By pretending merely to document the historical evolution of communications through changes in various technical instruments needed to communicate, the Newseum deflects attention from the ever-increasing commodification of information throughout these same processes of technological change. What might have been a truly social process of communicating information about distant new events in premodern communities has become a highly privatized and mostly deregulated business in the global capitalist marketplace. The growth of the news business with its resplendent panoply of fresh news commodities also evolves hand-in-hand with the globalizing world economy. The production of world news products today, then, cannot be easily disentangled from the reproduction of the worlds made by/for/with news. As Mattelart and Mattelart suggest, these relations of informational production embody the modes of producing informational economies, polities, and societies: "the new technologies of communication have not only assumed a central place in the industrial network—they are at the very heart of the strategies for reorganization of the relations between the state and citizens, local and central powers, producers and consumers, workers and managers, teachers and students, experts and those who execute their plans."[40] As the sphere of cultural transparency, media reactions now provide many people with their most definitive means of gauging political success, ethical possibility, and social conflict.

The repetitive rushing riffs of channel logos and news bureaus' trademarks at the Newseum's News Wall confirm how profoundly the media interweave sign and substance from everywhere at many distinct somewheres to transnationalize hitherto more closed national societies. These delocalizing tendencies create shared mediascapes in which Mother Theresa, Sophia Loren, Princess Diana, Celine Dion, Carolyn Bessette Kennedy, and Hillary Rodham Clinton all coexist dead and alive as audiovisual specters, with one's neighbors and local notables in the equally intermixed realms of work and leisure, entertainment and education, culture and kitsch. While the Newseum's central location near the heart of the metropolitan Washington area is prestigious, it obviously obscures the decentralized modality of such media networks.[41] Any single node of production and reception can simultaneously send out and pull in the powerful flows of newsfeed from anywhere to anywhere, which underscores how fluid the terrains of the general mediascape have become, even as they deconstitute the fixed localities in specific territories.

The Newseum has accumulated, and does display, many interesting artifacts from previous modes of communication. Yet more importantly, its displays are the best case in point of how so many electronic technologies now are used to mediate communicative interactions. The news thematic suggests these technologies only convey content from point to point, but the Newseum's genealogical reconstruction of how the United States and other industrial democracies have been changed by the workings of these communications illustrates how the news media operate as engines of continuous cultural reengineering by uniting states and democratizing industries. Ironically, then, the Newseum's display of communications technology actually documents something far more extensive than "the news," namely, how and why "communication now occupies a central place in strategies whose object is to restructure our societies."[42]

In this regard, the Newseum commemorates the growing ability of the broadcast, print, and now Web-centered media to exercise fluid forms of cultural, intellectual, and political leadership over many societies. In times marked by culture war, the Newseum depicts how culture wars are now a full-time job in most societies and states. This becomes "particularly evident in the introduction of telematics technology"; as Lyotard suggests, "the technocrats see in telematics a promise of liberalization and enrichment in the interactions between interlocutors; but what makes this process attractive for them is that it will result in new tensions in the system, and these will lead to an improvement in its performativity."[43] The media are a new site for political alliances and competitions to organize. There one finds shifting blocs of individual experts, partisan groups, social classes, corporate entities, and government agencies struggling to mediate their interests, resolve their conflicts, and coordinate their teamwork in the definition, circulation, and analysis of the news. Hegemony is constantly under construction, and relentlessly subjected to deconstruction, in the daily news cycle as these shifting coalitions of ideology and interest vie to organize democratic decision making to deliver something these operatives will accept. The new "net-war" that has broken out in the aftermath of the September 11, 2001, ter-rorist attacks in New York and Washington, D.C., has been fought, in part, on this terrain as a networked transnational "anti-terrorist" West-ern alliance struggles for the hearts and minds of global audiences with an equally transnational "terrorist" anti-Western network.[44] For better or worse, the visions of social progress, class compromise, individual success, and political harmony generated by the news media now are the hegemonic forms of intellectual understanding that statesmen and spinmeisters mobilize to succeed culturally and politically. While the Newseum does seem to be lacking most of the Muses, many other more intriguing spirits, like public opinion, national consciousness, class con-sciousness, and mass awareness, are all to be found in great numbers with Hermes amidst its historical and contemporary displays.

CONCLUSION

Piecing Together Knowledge and Pulling Apart Power at the Museum

This book has traced out my interpretations of how different types of museums work in the public life of the United States. By indicating how culture, history, nature, and technology are constructed as clusters of meaning and value by social institutions connected to museums in particular locales, I have suggested how their exhibitions can influence other beliefs and practices for America's population in general. In some ways, this might not be the best of times to take on museums as sites of cultural contestation. Over half of all households own stock, big SUVs are the nation's favorite automobile, and the average family house is more than 2,000 square feet, but few believe the boom will last, drive their SUVs without guilt, or enjoy bigger living space with much smaller families. Plainly, there was an authentic unease about the nation's cultural values in the fat times of the 1990s, which the photo finish in the 2000 presidential elections directly underscored and the economic slowdown in 2000–2001 definitely aggravated. These existential anxieties have become much greater in the aftermath of the September 11, 2001, terrorist attacks on the United States and the general slowdown in the world economy.

Still, the ongoing cultural war is about these contradictions, and the anxieties they engender allow politicians to cultivate mass publics to support new governmental actions. To fill their spiritual emptiness, some people turn to museums, at least in part, for greater enlightenment and more ethical direction. So, as I indicated in the introduction, modern museums are "permanent tools" of education for the communities they serve. Public intellectuals and interested politicians show up at the same museums to score ideological points—for the left and the right—or to define a new collective consensus—in favor of either comfortable traditions or progressive challenges. As entertainment increasingly saturates every corner of American life, however, it is no surprise that museums now have become almost fully invested in the entertainment industry.

Museum curators and media pundits wring their hands about how most Americans vote "no" with their feet when it comes to high culture, but the figures show something else. On the one hand, the top twenty-five theme parks in the United States drew nearly 130 million visitors during 1998. On the other hand, 865 million visited a museum, which represents a 50 percent increase from 1988.[1] Still, this comparison might be somewhat specious. Entertainment values have so saturated museums that one cannot assume that the theme parks provide only amusement while museums generate only enlightenment. Thanks to TV, visitors appear at museums with a vast archive of knowledge culled from the major networks as well as niche cable channels like Arts & Entertainment, Bravo, The History Channel, The Learning Channel, Discovery, and Animal Planet. Museums, in turn, provide relics and specimens from "real life" to affirm and anchor images and stories taken from "reel life" during screen time with TV, movies, and now the worldwide Web.

Museum exhibitions are bolted together out of rhetorical fragments taken from more specific discourses and practices that have not always been fabricated with objective detachment, passive gazing, and dispassionate consideration. Objects on display in museums are disembedded from their social contexts, and the viewing subjects are kept back from the social sites of their origin as they visit and view these objectified museum representations inside a museum's spectacular halls of exhibition. As Foucault suggests, the positioning of power here cycles through a complex set of simultaneous equations that must interoperate closely and correctly through many intellectual discourses and technical disciplines in order to be effective.[2] Therefore, entertainment values often provide the easiest, most satisfying solution for building an audience, a donor list, or a public. Such indirect systems of legislation operationalize themselves by identifying the key nodes of knowledge, critical regimes of rules, and important spaces of subjectivity to underpin our ontologies. Museums help to forge reality, and then they organize the collective rites of this unstable reality's reception that will write authoritative accounts of the past, present, and future in their displays.

By doing this, museums serve as ontologues, telling us what reality really is. Their often sophisticated narrative indirection orders social and personal behavior from below by steering inclinations tacitly or implicitly through amusing diversion, making this sort of knowing often far more powerful than direct legislation by sovereign agencies attempting to impose order from above through coercive acts.[3] Many social institutions are involved in activating and closing these educational processes, and it is quite apparent that all cultural institutions, like art, science, and history museums, are important centers of such power-expressing and knowledge-articulating activity.

The cultural war in museums is fought over power and knowledge. Intellectuals fret about aesthetics, identity, and morality, but they recognize that entertainmentality represents a new regime of rule in which sublime insights or lofty truths often get displaced by thrills and chills. Conservatives fume about postmodern degenerates running down America and imposing pornography on innocent communities, but they also recognize that entertainmentality will always push fun over sobriety. Liberals fulminate about government interference and blue-nosed conservatism, but they also accede to the imperatives of the culture industry's entertainmentality. As mass markets continue bridging Hollywood, Madison Avenue, and Las Vegas, something flashy comes front-and-center into our public life, and it can lessen the significance of civic purpose and enlightened rationality. Still, the collective sense of moral outrage sparked in the days after the September 11, 2001, terrorist attacks suggests that something deeper and more enduring persists amidst the showbiz. All of these contradictory tendencies are well worth fighting over, and the culture war, history war, nature war, and science war points toward how naturally many people have come to the same conclusion, even in times of considerable prosperity.

The moment of personal awe taken from the aura of genuine art rarely, if ever, occurs in the realm of entertainment, because art is aimed at individuals and entertainment focuses on collectives. The emergence of populations, which must be managed as data, markets, and tastes, redirects the practices of government, as I argue in this book, toward the more astute administration of people and things. One of the most effective techniques for governing these populations today is entertainment;

and, as I assert here, some of the most powerful public performances to interest and amuse people are museum exhibitions. To "amuse" people, one imparts some sense of "the Muses" to them, and museums can pull together publics and their knowledge of culture, history, nature, or technology in ways that artfully remediate the power of those governing the people and their things. Of course, currents of awareness run in many directions in the workings of museums. Everyone is not unaware of these dynamics, but most still are not fully conscious of the political positions being pushed in museums. This critical survey has tried to bring that point home by reexamining an array of different museum sites, exhibitions, and types from one analytical perspective in a single, thematically unified critique.

As Weber suggests, in any act of interpretation, the thematizing of an interpretive center for authoritative explanation, always is a considerable project in itself. It must begin somewhere, somehow, at some time to construct a contingent and contestable particularization of reality. For various museum practices, whether thematizations of culture, history, nature, or technology, this move represents selecting "a finite segment of the meaningless infinity of the world process" and then transforming it into "a segment on which *human beings* confer meaning and significance."[4] While all human beings are "endowed with the capacity and the will to take a deliberative attitude towards the world and to lend it *significance*," the knowledge practices in place at each museum, as Weber observes about cultural interpretation in general, rarely admit that "all knowledge of cultural reality is always knowledge from *particular points of view*."[5] Generalizing particular points of view with the inert facticity of certain artifacts and narrative texts in an actual display provides the curators of museums with their special powers to confer global meaning and eternal significance simply by exhibiting things and texts in displays. With the obvious powers resting in this rarely contested authority, however, issues of alleged impurity or purity easily can cause new cultural conflicts to arise, and these battles of reinterpretation have become much more common in the United States after the collapse of the Soviet Union.

Accordingly, museums serve decisively as a useful means of manufacturing the historical a priori underpinning our existing cultural understandings. Foucault argues that all "frameworks of thought" correlate with some historical a priori that "delimits in the totality of experience a field of knowledge, defines the mode of being of the objects that appear in that field, provides man's everyday perception with theoretical powers, and defines the conditions in which he can sustain a discourse about things recognized to be true."[6] By shaping the exhibition-as-a-world separate and apart from the external reality of society beyond its walls, each museum contributes to casting the world-as-an-exhibition in its renderings of culture, history, nature, or technology. By detaching their rhetorical operations further through additional rituals of objectivity from what is represented as materialized external reality, museums can animate political subjects with many values.

On the one hand, some citizens can gain an objective detachment toward their collective life that is meant to legitimize their learning as viewers and visitors at the museum. Museums divide political subjects from material objects as they separate their privileged collections of artifacts from the greater material lifeworld out of which each collected object is selected. And, once the division is made, they can try to purify their visitors' reverent understanding of these chosen material objects. Their highly particularized cultural representations of that outside world often pretend as if it were a domain of universality resting at complete ease beyond the scope of any human intervention. On the other hand, many approach these ritual acts of separation (here is the active objectness of another external reality as depicted with relics, there is the passive subjectness of visitors inside museum walls permitted to stroll by, inspecting objects) and modes of mediation (here are detached forms of objective awareness gained at exhibitions in intramuseum viewing; there are attached practices of subjective activity exhibited as some sort of extra-museum doing) as diverting moments of spectacular amusement. This ritual also solidified a separation between the things on display and the external historic realities they represent as museum presentations. In effect, such separation practices try to purify the past, distancing it from both the present-day realities outside the museum's walls and the long-gone past populations now dead and departed from the spaces and times conjured up by this reified past of relics. Finally, out of all these amused interactions, museum visitors and curators coproduce their loosely shared knowledge of the exhibition-as-a-world within the world-as-an-exhibition.

Although some have believed that museums should be culturally pure enterprises, they clearly are very important political structures for at least three reasons. First, culture, history, nature, and technology museums are involved integrally in concentrating and compounding many discrete domains of knowing into the compact nodes of specific knowledge. Such knowledge often is represented as being totalistic, but of course it is not. New knowledges are always developing in society, but few are cumulative or conclusive. Many diverse cultural interpretations of the same bodies of ever-changing knowledge are constantly seeking ratification in museum institutions.

Second, culture, history, nature, and technology museums are effectively embedded in establishing certain rules to stabilize regimes of artistic, historic, or scientific interpretation. The social ontologies of the how, what, where, when, who, and why constituting "technology," "nature," "history," and "culture" often find their first and most accessible articulation in the material displays exhibited at museum settings. The archival preservation of technological objects, the accumulative ordering of historic artifacts, and the authoritative regime of scientific discourse staged by museums all offer vital opportunities to express and stabilize the truths in many of America's everyday social ontologies.

And, third, these museums script their ongoing shows of force in projects that fashion fresh patterns of subjectivity in which individuals and collectivities can affirm themselves as individual or collective subjects with particular identities and peculiar values. Knowledge and power compound each other's effects at these cultural sites by granting access to the sights of knowing recognition as well as giving out the cites of powerful guidance through museum amusements. Entertainmentality supports the endless reenculturation of acculturated subjects who need to know the latest about what the authorities in American society sanction as being "the technical," "the natural," "the past," and "the culture."

Down these three paths of ideological practice—nodes of knowledge, regimes of rules, spaces of subjectivity—power operates productively within a regime of entertaining governmentality by giving art, nature, science, history, and technology a much more entertaining face.[7] Even so, these domains also open many other zones for contragovernmental contestation at the museum. Nodes of knowing can be challenged in terms of their material connections, political development, or intellectual derivations by pointing out other less obvious, or maybe more insidious, linkages. The regimes of discursive interpretation used to define these knowledge domains, in turn, can be questioned, refunctioned, or overturned as each context for their justification is identified. And the scripts of subjectivity these rule regimes and knowledge nodes elaborate also might steer the play of discursive power toward unanticipated or unintended outcomes, which many do not want. In this regard, as Foucault maintains, "there are manifold relations of power which permeate, characterize and constitute the social body, and these relations of power cannot themselves be established, consolidated nor implemented without the production, accumulation, circulation and functioning of a discourse. There can be no possible exercise of power without a certain economy of discourses of truth which operates through and on the basis of this association."[8]

If this economy of truth sputters, as has happened in today's culture wars, then many will ask who is remembering what for whom and for which purposes? Cultural conservatives pretend cultural life is not political and that knowledge or morality are not social constructions. Yet their anxieties over how museum displays are sometimes questioned by their audience indicates that these same cultural conservatives know full well that culture is always politicized, which shapes, in turn, knowledge and morality to suit particular social constructions. This outcome is what cultural warriors seek to control. Any astute reading of the museum recognizes its modes of remembering are also necessarily always manners of forgetting. We do remember how quality, truth, reality, and beauty are attained at museums, but cultural conservatives hope everyone will forget at the same time how political their social construction and maintenance really are. Still, the museum experience in the United States over the past generation has become less of an intellectual event tied to a person's cognitive development and more of a completely packaged ensemble of amusing consumer choices. Building new markets among the visiting public and then capturing the potential traffic in these new markets is what many museum planners are now trying to attain. Almost all major museums, as Hughes notes about art museums in particular, have adopted "partly by osmosis and partly by design, the strategies of the other mass media: emphasis on spectacle, cult of celebrity, the whole masterpiece-and-treasure syndrome."[9] Consequently, we find "it is now de rigueur for museums to promote their big exhibitions by arranging discount packages at hotels, planning related musical and other performing arts events, offering special meals at their own or nearby restaurants and, of course, selling related items in their shops."[10] Here is the social experience of entertainment that visitors seek; and, if such amusement has an educational element in it, then so much the better. However, museum curators are trying to promote their show as well as the allure of the associated consumer packages, so truly serious intellectual challenge usually will be downplayed as an attendance killer.

Therefore, the museum increasingly serves as another critical link in the means of production for the new global economy along with other privileged sites for culture, leisure, or sport. As factories pull their production lines out of older industrial cities, informational centers of production, like financial houses, stock brokerages, tourist attractions, sports stadiums, and museums, now are picked to provide employment, build traffic, and maintain status. Museums then become the anchor point of many visitors' personal self-images as well as a critical mechanism for economic development. "The museum plays an incredible role in American cities," according to Anna Somers Cocks, editor of *The Art Newspaper;* "it's a focal point, a place for entertainment, for shopping."[11] The city might not be functional any longer in its industrial forms, but people live there, government has invested in it, and the economy must continue growing. If cultural experiences rather than manufactured goods can become the product, then all of the necessary adjustments will be made. At the museum, consumer tastes, subjective preferences, and market dynamics are increasingly granted free rein in support of these economic, political, and social goals. Nonetheless, the discriminant functions of knowledge-preservation and power-confirmation at the museum remain in place, keeping alive American society's enduring economies of relative value by affirming the differential worth of the museum's objects in order to rightly train the human subjects who visit and benefit from each museum's operations.

John Stuart Mill's liberal account of intellectual exchange as a marketplace of ideas has undergone a radical transmutation in these times of transnational corporate capitalism. Today, culture, history, nature, and technology are turned into tools for the marketing of other ideas. Once cultural production becomes a full-fledged consumer product, then even once-privileged sites of extraordinary value are no longer exempt from the corrupting influences of consumer culture. Ideas circulate increasingly to build markets rather than minds, and the notion that some ideas will fail the test of open debate, critical exposure, or serious counterexamination is tempered by a sense of product cycle that perhaps needs all ideas to rotate in tight turns of rising favor and sinking disfavor.

Museums as informational centers, then, serve to center bigger collectives of people, who form up into certain working, learning, and co-operating social formations via the amusing remediation of ideas. Becoming "informed" is to accept the never-ending roles of being in social forms meant to serve the ends of informationalizers and support the means of the informationalized. The blossoming diversity of different museums in many distinctive niches and varied ranges only underscores the depth of these diversified and segregated markets that sort consumers and clients into an ever-changing array of psychodemographic segments for commerce and government. And from this kind of market momentum, we get one or two new museums a week in North America joining the thousands already in operation.

One must be extremely cautious about either being too critical of any museum's exhibits or becoming coopted too fully by any museum's power play. By criticizing how power works, one must not simply critique one limited set of political engagements by the established social formations in order to substitute his or her own apparently different, but also quite limited, ends to the service of these same means. All too often, the means for always being in control of the power plays simply erase the substantive agendas of any alternative set of critical ends. So the would-be cultural revolutionary merely becomes, in effect, a new political establishmentarian. Nonetheless, there are many political dynamics at play in the displays presented by any museum exhibition. Technical devices and historic artifacts are positioned to play out specific performances, and their aesthetic impact may, in turn, move both individual and collective subjects to repattern their behaviors to conform to the models and norms tagged by the exhibition with the artifacts on display.[12]

Museums, as my hometown museum's mission statement from the early 1960s asserts, give people the opportunity to see and understand objects from our colorful past, which becomes a way to color more fully the present and future. When those displays are made with such interpretive authority, they are always already shows of force that articulate new plays of political power in their presentations of "culture," "history," "nature," or "technology" for the museum. Which images and objects are mobilized, how they are displayed, where they are situated, and why they are chosen all constitute powerful rhetorical strategies for governmentalizing maneuvers, especially at those sites, like the Smithsonian Institution or the American Museum of Natural History, where the authoritative pretense is maintained that these sites are where "the nation tells its story."

Yet the nation apparently cannot tell what many see as "the whole story." Showing Hiroshima's rubble in a museum display as evidence of America's racist dark side instead of its purified superpower, which the Smithsonian show discussed in chapter 2 presumed to do, is a discursive countermove against the American state's ordinarily normalizing impulses. Shrewd curatorial vision, when coupled with a well-scripted narrative in an elegantly crafted exhibit, can leverage entertaining force in ways that might rewrite civic lessons against the prevailing regime of rules. When individual viewers or exhibition audiences encounter such displays and discourses, real conflict over their civic identities may well unfold at the show site. Therefore, my critical reexamination of these museum practices has sought, as Foucault asks, "to define the way in which individuals or groups represent words to themselves, utilize their forms and meanings, compose real discourse, reveal and conceal in it what they are thinking or saying, perhaps unknown to themselves, more or less than they wish, but in any case leave a mass of verbal traces of those thoughts, which must be deciphered and restored as far as possible to their representative vivacity."[13]

In the practices of cultural consumption fostered by museums, every museum visitor reaffirms how well the mode of production operates in each act of his or her personal consumption. Such acts, however, do not happen randomly without any foresight or preparation. On the contrary, a great deal of instruction about what to consume, why to acquire it, and how it works in the larger scheme of things is directed at the self-managing individual through advertising, government information, and formal school instruction. The amusements given to many by museum institutions cannot be separated from this complex of guidance-giving practices.[14] As sites of civic entertainment, museums are also increasingly implicated in the workings of commerce as their collections and displays become retooled to feed certain niche markets. At the same time, an ethic of entertainment, interactivity, and accessibility now thoroughly suffuses the rhetorics of museum display, as curators and designers find new ways to embed an appreciation for their exhibitions in the everyday routines of their visitors.

Every museum tries to present an artful display of artifacts and ideas to entertain and educate its visitors. At the same time, it also is a materialized ideological narrative, fabricating its own focalized normative code of practices and values out of peculiarly arranged displays with historical artifacts, corporate products, natural organisms, technological devices, or art works. While their public pose most frequently is one of cool detached objectivity, museums are unavoidably enterprises organized around engaged partisan principles. Increasingly, this pose can be toyed with, or even ironically exposed, by curators to create another layer of narrative complexity that pluralizes the positioning of their exhibits' play with multiperspectival narratives, inconclusive discourses, and do-it-yourself interpretations. Nevertheless, those tactics still express particular ideological commitments and assumptions, which now are tucked even deeper down in the interstices of curatorial discretion as tacit knowledge of what otherwise may have been articulate and direct.

The material on display in museums no longer is simply a cache of curiosities for the intellectual edification of autonomous rational subjects. Instead these evocative spectacles of knowledge serve as rhetorical relays, conceptual capacitors, and ideological integers for the virtual circuits of command/control/communication and intelligence that develop stable social interactions sustainably and successfully—as the visions of the Southwest at the Heard Museum, the sense of nature propounded at the Arizona–Sonora Desert Museum, the notion of high technology spread at The Tech, and the feel for information given at the Newseum all illustrate. As these connections are made, corporate sponsors, state cultural offices, and civic associations use museum spaces to insert the peculiar directions favored by their managers and members—which the Missouri Botanical Garden, the National Gallery, and Pima Air and Space Museum very well typify. Power, then, produces many effects through museum visitations as patrons view what has been legitimized as knowledge, even though this knowing usually serves as subtle advertisements for firms, governments, and special interests—as The Tech Museum or the Holocaust museum both suggest in their own different ways.

At The Tech and the Newseum, the computer industry and the media business are doing much more than staging objective accounts of how information-processing innovations or global news cycles happen. Likewise, the government of Japan at the National Gallery of Art in Washington, D.C., and the aged American airmen of World War II at the Pima Air and Space Museum or the curators of the National Air and Space Museum are seeking to represent different eras in history in a fashion that "opens the minds" of museum visitors to some facts while occluding other facts for these same audiences. Similarly, the nature of nature is fabricated in different forms for various publics at the American Museum of Natural History, the Arizona–Sonora Desert Museum, and the Missouri Botanical Garden to stabilize a chosen vision of what is enduring and what is transitory in humanity's dealings with the environment.

The culture war of the past decade explicitly underscores the significance of my arguments.[15] And my critical concerns about how culture, history, nature, and technology are represented at museums continue to preoccupy both sides of the culture war. George Will reminded President George W. Bush in January 2001 that "culture is the incubator of character,"[16] urging the newly inaugurated president to listen to Vice President Cheney's wife if he truly was worried about the national character of America. Slamming President Clinton's appointees to the National Endowments for the Arts and the Humanities, Will asserted that "what government should do first is define culture, for policy purposes, the way critic Allen Tate did, as 'the study of perfection, and the constant effort to achieve it.'"[17] Doubting that democracy could create such a cultural policy, Will called upon Lynne Cheney for a cultural warrior's intervention. The problem for everyone else is who gets to define the ideals of perfection, achieve perfectibility, and then display the perfected to the same democracy that seeks to learn these lessons. Others in this democracy would not trust either Will's or Cheney's answers.[18] How the problem of perfection is posed, the possibilities presented, and the policies then produced cannot be fully understood apart from the rhetorical battles fought out, as they have been discussed here, in the power play of museum exhibitions.

Museums are not merely a dusty domain for memorializing cultural genius or lionizing scientific progress: they also are, as a group of pioneer women in rural Arizona proclaimed at their museum nearly four decades ago, "permanent tools to supplement the educational system for adults and youth of the community." The efforts by major corporations and private entrepreneurs to insinuate their agendas and presences into the exhibit halls and food courts of the Smithsonian Institution's many museums in the early twenty-first century can only reiterate their point. Who takes the tools, who uses the tools, who ensures their permanence, and who is educated in this system by whom are always political processes in addition to being educational. Museums will remain salients of cultural struggle, because a people's visits to them, and the aesthetic/ethical/philosophical lessons that those individuals learn there, can transform their consciousness as well as alter their actions. Will is right: culture is an incubator of character, and museums are central nodes in the narrative networks that states and societies develop to cultivate national character. Most museums, then, are brimming with unresolved cultural contradictions and social conflicts that deserve to be studied more carefully. In their artistic depictions of culture, history, nature, and technology, there are many trails in museums leading back to the contested ground of politics. Much can be learned there about the trials of power and tests of knowledge, which many regard as legitimate and true, and others see as corrupt and mistaken, by following these paths wherever they may lead.

Notes

Introduction

1. A great deal of this conflict was sparked by battles over the proliferation of multiculturalism in American educational institutions and intellectual debates. For additional analysis, see Homi K. Bhabha, *The Location of Culture* (New York: Routledge, 1994); David A. Hollinger, *Postethnic America: Beyond Multiculturalism* (New York: Basic Books, 1995); and Nathan Glazer, *We Are All Multiculturalists Now* (Cambridge: Harvard University Press, 1997).

2. See Michael Belcher, *Exhibitions in Museums* (Leicester: Leicester University Press, 1991), xiii.

3. Judith Dobrzynski, "Art Museum Attendance Keeps Rising in the U.S.," *New York Times*, 1 February 1999, E1.

4. Jacqueline Trescott, "Natural History Trumpets Expansion," *Washington Post*, 11 May 1999, C1.

5. For a discussion of the early battles in the culture wars at museums, see Richard Bolton, ed., *Culture Wars: Documents from Recent Controversies in the Arts* (New York: New Press, 1992). Much of this struggle reflected anxieties about the identity and purpose of the United States after the demise of the Soviet Union. For thoughts about where the United States now stands as well as what some believe will be the major geopolitical divides of the future, see Francis Fukayama, *The End of History and the Last Man* (New York: Free Press, 1992); and Samuel Huntington, *The Clash of Civilizations and the Remaking of World Order* (New York: Simon and Schuster, 1996). Alan Wolfe argues that the nation itself, and particularly the middle class, is not greatly troubled by the culture wars. Instead, these battles either have been intramural struggles between intellectuals or attention-getting media events in a slack time following the end of the Cold War. See Alan Wolfe, *One Nation, After All* (New York: Viking, 1998). As the twenty-first century begins, Gertrude Himmelfarb sees American fracturing in another culture war between a now-establishmentarian elite culture of secularist liberation from the 1960s and a dissident culture of traditionalists. See her *One Nation, Two Cultures* (New York: Knopf, 1999). This theme of a new

elite hegemony forged in the rebellions of the 1960s is also articulated in Hilton Kramer and Roger Kimball, eds., *The Betrayal of Liberalism: How the Disciplines of Freedom and Equality Helped Foster the Illiberal Politics of Coercion and Control* (New York: Ivan R. Dee, 2000); and Roger Kimball, *The Long March: How the Cultural Revolution of the 1960s Changed America* (New York: Encounter Books, 2000).

6. See Robert William Fogel, *The Fourth Great Awakening and the Future of Egalitarianism* (Chicago: University of Chicago Press, 2000), Lawrence W. Levine, *The Opening of the American Mind: Canons, Culture, and History* (Boston: Beacon, 1996); and Russell Jacoby, *Dogmatic Wisdom: How the Culture Wars Divert Education and Distract America* (New York: Doubleday, 1994).

7. See Lynne V. Cheney, *Telling the Truth: Why Our Culture and Our Country Have Stopped Making Sense—and What We Can Do about It* (New York: Simon and Schuster, 1995), 144. Also see Sharon MacDonald, ed., *The Politics of Display: Museums, Science, Culture* (London: Routledge, 1998), 2–19. As David Brooks notes, however, many of these rebukes rarely stray from a professionally correct complacency that alternates between sentiments of calling for greater community or more control. Brooks calls this odd mix of attitudes "bourgeois bohemian," or "Bobo" culture. See his *Bobos in Paradise: The New Upper Class and How They Got There* (New York: Simon and Schuster, 2001).

8. Mohave Pioneers Historical Museum, *The Mohave County Story* (Kingman, Ariz.: Mohave Pioneers Historical Society, 1965), 19–20. Again, this pedagogical purpose is not unique to small local museums out in rural Arizona. In 2001 the National Museum of American History accepted a pledge of $38 million from the Catherine B. Reynolds Foundation. An innovator in the financial services industry, Reynolds also is closely tied through marriage to the director of the American Academy of Achievement. This nonprofit organization is set up to inspire America's youth, in part, by bringing high school students together with famous individuals at its International Achievement Summit. For her $38 million, Reynolds wanted an interactive hall of fame, which will be called "The Spirit of America," to feature a select group of contemporary celebrities like skater Dorothy Hamill, basketball star Michael Jordan, or lifestyle designer Martha Stewart. Exposure to these figures' courage, integrity, vision, and education, Reynolds believed, could do much to foster new achievements by today's youth to solve the nation's current problems. See Bruce I. Friedland, "$38 Million Gift Inspires Debate: Jacksonville Native Funds Smithsonian Exhibit," *The Florida Times-Union*, 30 July 2001, A-1. Upset about the public outcry over her donation, and frustrated by the curators' reactions to her designs, Reynolds pulled back most of her Smithsonian donation on February 4, 2002. See Jacqueline Trescott, "Catherine Reynolds, The Giver Who Gave Up," *Washington Post*, 6 February 2002, C1–2.

9. Mohave Pioneers Historical Museum, *The Mohave County Story*, 20. The current curators of the museum distribute a leaflet to visitors and prospective donors asking them "Are You Aware?" that, among other things, more than 30,000 people a year visit this museum, many of them are area residents, and businesses can profit from these local and out-of-town museum patrons seeking to familiarize themselves with the area at the museum. Once again, even this small museum shows what I argue throughout this book: economic development is rarely divorced from personal *Bildung* in today's museum management philosophies. One could dismiss these declarations as insignificant noises made from the edge of nowhere, but they echo

today in the deeds and words of donors to the Smithsonian Institution in Washington, D.C. Kenneth E. Behring, a California real estate developer, gave $20 million in 1997, and another $80 million in 2000, to the Smithsonian's National Museum of American History. While he wanted "The Behring Center" put on the building, Behring also is cultivating the Smithsonian to serve as a permanent tool to supplement the nation's education system as an influential public service organization. Indeed, $20 million of $100 million donation is already designated to pay for "a 'thematic hall' that will focus on 'American legends and legacies' in a 'tribute to deceased individuals who made great contributions to our country' and who truly epitomize 'the American spirit.'" See Elaine Sciolino, "Smithsonian Must Exhibit Ingenuity in the Face of Overlapping Gifts," *New York Times*, 6 August 2001, 1.

10. Milton Albert, "Art as an Institution," *American Sociological Review* 33, no. 3 (1968): 385.

11. Raymond Williams, *Marxism and Literature* (Oxford: Oxford University Press, 1977), 8–9. This same recognition about the political unity of art and culture is made on the right as well. See, for example, Lawrence E. Harrison and Samuel P. Huntington, eds., *Culture Matters: How Values Shape Human Progress* (New York: Basic Books, 2000).

12. Jean Baudrillard, *For a Critique of the Political Economy of the Sign* (St. Louis: Telos Press, 1981), 11. Because museums are a permanent tool to supplement the education of the young and the old, major corporations, like General Motors or McDonald's, are very interested today in performing what appear to be civic-minded acts in support of major national museums. On the one hand, General Motors has pledged $10 million to help the Smithsonian Institution update its transportation exhibits, which could be renamed the "GM Hall of Transportation," and, on the other hand, McDonald's agreed to a ten-year partnership with the Smithsonian to bring its food services to the nation's most popular museum, the National Air and Space Museum. See Paul Farhi, "McNuggets Join Moon Rocks at Air and Space," *Washington Post*, 29 August 2001, A1.

13. Christa Bürger, "The Disappearance of Art: The Postmodernism Debate in the U.S.," *Telos* 68 (summer 1986): 102.

14. In this respect, I am drawn to museums, like everyone else, in search of entertainment and enlightenment. So, at the western end of Route 66 in Los Angeles, I enjoy both the Autry Museum of Western Heritage and the Museum of Tolerance. And, at the eastern beginning of Route 66, I try never to miss the Museum of Science and Industry in Chicago. On my first trip to Washington, D.C., in the time of Nixon and Kissinger, I visited the National Air and Space Museum. And I try not to miss the National Gallery of Art on any visit to the capital. I was a resident of Tucson for almost five years, and the Arizona–Sonora Desert Museum and Pima Air and Space Museum still are some of my favorite places. I also lived for nearly three years in the Tower Grove and Shaw neighborhoods of south St. Louis, which encircle the Missouri Botanical Garden. And I now live in Virginia, where the Newseum has drawn me for repeated visits before I cross over the Potomac to experience, once again, the United States Holocaust Memorial Museum or the National Museum of American Art. For additional discussion of Route 66 as a core element in a nostalgia-based tourist industry, see Michael Wallis, *Route 66: The Mother Road* (New York: St. Martin's Press, 1990), and Quinta Scott and Susan Croce Kelly, *Route 66: The Highway and Its People* (Norman: University of Oklahoma Press, 1988).

15. Fredric Jameson, *The Political Unconscious: Narrative as a Socially Symbolic Act* (Ithaca: Cornell University Press, 1981), 20. For some more conservative counterpoint that questions such interpretive moves, see Richard J. Evans, *In Defense of History* (New York: Norton, 1999), 165–92.

16. See David Ricci, *The Tragedy of Political Science* (Princeton: Princeton University Press, 1984), 209–48.

17. For a parallel argument, see Bradley Macdonald, *William Morris and the Aesthetic Constitution of Politics* (Lanham, Md.: Lexington Books, 1999).

18. See Jacqueline Trescott, "The Arts Agency in Perspective: On the NEA's 35th, Leaders Discuss Future," *Washington Post,* 9 February 2000, C9.

19. A chronicle of these contradictory tensions can be found in an interesting public service autobiography; see Jane Alexander, *Command Performance: An Actress in the Theater of Politics* (New York: Public Affairs Press, 2000).

20. See Russell Jacoby, *The End of Utopia: Politics and Culture in an Age of Apathy* (New York: Basic Books, 1999), for additional consideration of the latest wrinkles in America's collective imagination of what is worth fighting over in the culture wars.

21. For more detailed discussion of culture war, see Rhys H. Williams, ed., *Cultural Wars in American Politics* (Hawthorne, N.Y.: Aldine de Gruyter, 1997); Todd Gitlin, *The Twilight of Common Dreams: Why America Is Wracked by Culture Wars* (New York: Henry Holt, 1995); and James Davidson Hunter, *Culture Wars: The Struggle to Define America* (New York: Basic Books, 1991). A useful analysis of how various academics and public intellectuals have organized their battle lines in the culture wars can be found in John Michael, *Anxious Intellects: Academic Professionals, Public Intellectuals, and Enlightenment Values* (Durham, N.C.: Duke University Press, 2000). These enduring cultural divisions also were expressed sharply again by the demography of the 2000 presidential elections. Vice President Gore won more than 60 percent of the vote only in a few highly populated urban regions, Texas Governor George W. Bush took more than 60 percent in mostly less populated rural territory and many suburban areas. Fifty-four percent of those making less than $30,000 a year voted for Gore; 54 percent of those earning $100,000 a year or more voted for Bush. Fifty-seven percent of all single people, 90 percent of blacks, and 36 percent of gun-owning households went for the Democrats, while 53 percent of all married people, 9 percent of blacks, and 61 percent of gun-owning households endorsed the Republicans. Internet users split more evenly 47 to 49 percent against Gore for Bush as did college graduates, who went 45 percent Democratic versus 51 percent Republican. See Matt Bal, "Red Zone vs. Blue Zone, Two Americas: The Urban-Rural Divide Was Starker Than Ever in Election 2000," *Newsweek,* 22 January 2001, 38–39.

1. Politics at the Exhibition

1. Richard Bolton, ed., *Culture Wars: Documents from the Recent Controversies in the Arts* (New York: New Press, 1992).

2. Michel Foucault, *The Order of Things: An Archaeology of the Human Sciences* (New York: Vintage, 1973), 354.

3. National Museum of American Art, "The West as America: Reinterpreting Images of the Frontier, 1820–1920" (exhibition brochure) (Washington, D.C.: National Museum of American Art, 1991), 1, 2.

4. William H. Truettner, ed., *The West as America: Reinterpreting Images of the Frontier, 1820–1920* (Washington, D.C.: Smithsonian Institution Press, 1991). The neglect of the American Indian in the major national museum institutions of the Smithsonian will remedied soon by the new National Museum of the American Indian. As the tenth and last major museum on the Mall in Washington, D.C., this institution will depict the history of Native Americans in the Western Hemisphere. Two-thirds paid for by the federal government, and one-third by a public/private trust fund tied in part to a profit stream from tribal casinos from across the nation, this museum also "promises to set the record straight" about the European invasion of the Americas. See Francis X. Clines, "Smithsonian Making Room for Indian Museum," *New York Times*, 29 September 2000, A14.

5. National Museum of American Art, "The West as America: Reinterpreting Images of the Frontier, 1820–1920" (public programs brochure) (Washington, D.C.: National Museum of American Art, 1991), 1.

6. Ibid., 1.

7. Cited in *Newsweek*, 27 May 1991, 70.

8. Cited in *Village Voice*, 25 June 1991, 99.

9. See *Washington Post*, 3 October 1998, B4.

10. Ibid.

11. Autry Museum of Western Heritage, *Your Maps to the Galleries* (Los Angeles: Autry Museum of Western Heritage, 1996), 1. This metaphysical quality in many Americans' spiritual feelings about the West is captured in the tenth anniversary celebration of the Autry Museum. See Brian W. Dippie, *West Fever* (Seattle: University of Washington Press and the Autry Museum of Western Heritage, 1998).

12. Autry Museum of Western Heritage, *Membership Information* (Los Angeles: Autry Museum of Western Heritage, 1996), 2. In March 2000, the Autry Museum brought an elaborate show for its first North American stop from the Royal Armouries Museum in Leeds. Titled "Buffalo Bill's Wild West," this exhibition carefully detailed how William F. Cody became an international superstar by representing the cowboys and Indians of the Old West in theatrical extravaganzas that were performed all over the world. Without Buffalo Bill, neither "the Western Heritage" nor "Gene Autry, the Singing Cowboy," would have been possible. See Martin Pegler and Graeme Riner, *Buffalo Bill's Wild West* (Leeds: Royal Armouries Museum, 1999). The power that film has to freeze notions of time and culture is examined closely by Philip Rosen, *Change Mummified: Cinema, Historicity, Theory* (Minneapolis: University of Minnesota Press, 2001).

13. Autry Museum of Western Heritage, *Gene Autry Western Heritage Museum* (Los Angeles: Autry Museum of Western Heritage, 1996), 2.

14. Autry Museum of Western Heritage, *General Information* (Los Angeles: Autry Museum of Western Heritage, 1996), 3–4.

15. Ibid., 5–6. While the parts of the museum devoted to the movie cowboy take up only a small amount of the facility's floor space, the Autry Museum's first curator, James Nottage, proudly noted that "the museum is a mix of scholarship and showmanship . . . enhancing our ability to inform and instruct." Cited in Dave Cunningham, "A Cowboy's Dream: The Gene Autry Western Heritage Museum," *Halo* 3, no. 7 (1988): 13.

16. Lawrence M. Small, the Smithsonian Institution's eleventh Secretary, admits as much when he declares that "the Smithsonian is the center of our cultural her-

itage—the repository of the creativity, the courage, the aspirations and the ingenuity of the American people." See his "America's Icons Deserve a Good Home," *Washington Post,* 26 June 2000, A19. For more discussion, see Benedict Anderson, *Imagined Communities: Reflections on the Origin and Spread of Nationalism,* rev. ed. (London: Verso, 1991). Small's quest to find a "good home" for America's icons has led him to seek problematic corporate tie-ins with big firms, like General Motors and McDonald's, and ego-boosting legacies from wealthy entrepreneurs, like Kenneth Behring and Catherine B. Reynolds. See Michael Kilian, "Small Appears to Be Selling Bits of Smithsonian to Top Bidder," *Chicago Tribune,* 6 September 2001, T7. For a thorough examaination of Lawrence Small's leadership at the Smithsonian, see Bob Thompson, "History for Sale," *Washington Post Magazine,* 20 January 2002, 14–22, 25–29.

17. National Museum of American Art, "The West as America" (exhibition brochure), 2.

18. Ibid.

19. See Timothy W. Luke, *Shows of Force: Power, Politics, and Ideology at Art Museums* (Durham, N.C.: Duke University Press, 1992).

20. See Todd Gitlin, *The Twilight of Common Dreams: Why America Is Wracked by Culture Wars* (New York: Henry Holt, 1995).

21. Michael Berenbaum, *The World Must Know: The History of the Holocaust Museum as Told in the United States Holocaust Museum* (Boston: Little, Brown, 1993).

22. Neil Asher Silberman, "The Battle Disney Should Have Won," *Lingua Franca: The Review of Academic Life* 5, no. 1 (November/December, 1994): 24–28.

23. John Stuart Mill, *The Essential Works of John Stuart Mill* (New York: Bantam Books, 1965), 269.

24. Ibid., 271.

25. Ibid., 297–98.

26. For an exhaustive analysis of this mythos, see Richard Slotkin, *Gunfighter Nation: The Myth of the Frontier in Twentieth-Century America* (Norman: University of Oklahoma Press, 1998).

2. Nuclear Reactions

1. Richard Bolton, ed., *Culture Wars: Documents from the Recent Controversies in the Arts* (New York: New Press, 1992).

2. James Davidson Hunter, *Culture Wars: The Struggle to Define America* (New York: Basic Books, 1991), 34, 42 (emphasis in the original).

3. Ibid., 173, 52.

4. Ibid., 52.

5. Paul Goldberger, "Historical Shows on Trial: Who Judges," *New York Times,* 11 February 1996, 21, 26.

6. Cited in Goldberger, "Historical Shows," 2, 26. A quite complete record of the entire controversy at the National Air and Space Museum, with all of its ideological dimensions, can be found in *Hiroshima's Shadow: Writings on the Denial of History and the Smithsonian Controversy,* ed. Kai Bird and Lawrence Lifschultz (Stony Creek, Conn.: Pamphleteer's Press, 1998).

7. Bruno Latour, *We Have Never Been Modern* (London: Harvester Wheatsleaf, 1993), 1–5, 30. Also see his *Science in Action* (Cambridge: Harvard University Press,

1987). At the same time, Latour believes that hybrids always have existed as quasi-objective, quasi-subjective (con)fusions of nature/culture, human/nonhuman, object/subject, present/past, being/nonbeing, inside/outside elements. However, the discursive rules of museums conform to the three guarantees of the modern constitution. That is, first, "even though we construct Nature, Nature is as if we did not construct it"; second, "even though we do not construct Society, Society is as if we did construct it"; and, third, "Nature and Society must remain absolutely distinct: the work of purification must remain absolutely distinct from the work of mediation" (93).

8. Martin Harwit, *An Exhibit Denied: Lobbying the History of the Enola Gay* (New York: Springer-Verlag, 1996), 427–28.

9. Ibid., 409–26.

10. Michael J. Hogan, *Hiroshima in History and Memory* (New York: Cambridge University Press, 1996), 200–31.

11. Cited in Philip Nobile, ed., *Judgment at the Smithsonian: Smithsonian Script by the Curators at the National Air and Space Museum* (New York: Marlowe and Company, 1995), xxxiii.

12. See William H. Truettner, ed., *The West as America: Reinterpreting Images of the Frontier, 1820–1920* (Washington, D.C.: Smithsonian Institution Press, 1991).

13. Harwit, *Exhibit Denied,* 50–65.

14. Cited in Arthur Hirsch, "Deadly Courier Retains Its Place in History," *Baltimore Sun,* 9 June 1994, A1.

15. See Michael J. Hogan, ed., *Hiroshima in History and Memory* (Cambridge: Cambridge University Press, 1996), 200–32.

16. Ibid.

17. *New York Times,* 5 February 1995, E5.

18. Cited in Nobile, *Judgment at the Smithsonian,* xliii.

19. For more discussion, see Gar Alperovitz, *The Decision to Use the Atomic Bomb and the Architecture of an American Myth* (New York: Knopf, 1995).

20. See Nobile, *Judgment,* xiii–xcvii, and Hogan, *Hiroshima,* 211–28. Harwit ultimately resigned as the National Air and Space Museum's director after the controversy; see *New York Times,* 3 May 1995, A9, 19.

21. Paul W. Tibbets, "Our Job Was to Win," *American Legion* 103 (November 1994): 28. The *Enola Gay* will be displayed in the National Air and Space Museum Center at Dulles International Airport, which should open in December 2003, with 15 million cubic feet of space and 177 other aircraft. Of its $238 million cost, $94 million was raised from private sources, including $60 million contributed from Steven Udvar-Hazy (See Jacqueline Trescott, "Smithsonian 'Too Shabby,'" C10, and, "Reflections on an Institution," C2). Nonetheless, as the Air and Space Museum's newest director, John Dailey, notes, the Smithsonian still needs to raise $95 million more for the Dulles Center. "What I did not realize until I came here," Dailey says, "is that we have to raise our own money for almost everything we do." Congressional appropriations pay for staff and maintenance, he says, but almost everything else—some 45 percent of the museum's funding—comes from nonfederal donors. Ken Ringle, "With Feet Firmly Planted in the Air: For Air and Space Museum Director John Dailey, the Sky's the Limit," *Washington Post,* 25 May 2000, C1, C5.

22. William Garvey, "The Shame of *Enola Gay,*" *Popular Mechanics,* August 1995, 45–49. Also see *New York Times,* 6 August 1995, 5–23; and *Washington Post,* 1 March

1995, A21. See Bird and Lifschultz, *Hiroshima's Shadow,* 377–409, for more op-ed treatments of the Smithsonian controversy. Much of the delay in this restoration could be attributed to shortfalls in funding during the 1980s. When Secretary I. Michael Heyman assumed office in late 1994, he found the Smithsonian Institution severely underfunded; then Congress shut down the government during November 1995 in a budget struggle with President Clinton. Heyman boosted the inflow of private donations to $92 million in 1999 from $51.8 million in 1995, but his successor, Lawrence Small, reported in March 2000 that the Smithsonian Institution's building and facilities still needed more than $250 million in repairs. See Jacqueline Trescott, "Reflections of an Institution: I. Michael Heyman Leaves the Smithsonian," *Washington Post,* 7 December 1999, C1, C2; and Smithsonian "'Too Shabby': Chief Seeks More Repair Funds," *Washington Post,* 9 March 2000, C1, C10.

23. *Washington Post,* 26 September 1994, A11.

24. Garvey, "The Shame of *Enola Gay,*" 49.

25. *Washington Post,* 26 September 1994, A10.

26. Cited in James Webb, "Was It Necessary?," *Parade,* 30 July 1995, 5.

27. Cited in *Washington Post,* 26 September 1994, A10.

28. Ibid.

29. Ibid.

30. Garvey, "The Shame of *Enola Gay,*" 49.

31. Charles Krauthammer, "World War II, Revised," *Washington Post,* 19 August 1994, A27.

32. John Correll, "Airplanes in the Mist," *Air Force Magazine* 77 (December 1994): 2.

33. *Washington Post,* 26 September 1994, A10.

34. See Hogan, *Hiroshima,* 80–142.

35. *Washington Post,* 31 January 1995, A12.

36. Ibid.

37. Ibid.

38. Ibid.

39. Ibid.

40. See Garvey, "The Shame of *Enola Gay,*" 49; and *Washington Post,* 9 July 1995, B2.

41. *Washington Post Weekend,* 14 July 1995, 30.

42. *Washington Post,* 9 July 1995, B2.

43. Ibid.

44. *The Wall Street Journal,* 29 August 1994, A10.

45. *The New York Times,* 7 June 1995, A1, 6. Also see *Washington Post,* 29 June 1995, A32.

46. Cited in Hogan, *Hiroshima,* 213.

47. See *Village Voice,* 25 June 1991, 99–100; and *Newsweek,* 27 May 1991, 70.

48. For more discussion, see Sharon MacDonald and Gordon Fyfe, eds., *Theorizing Museums: Representing Identity and Diversity in a Changing World* (Oxford: Blackwell, 1996). Lawrence M. Small, Secretary of the Smithsonian Institution, underscores this vital role played by the Smithsonian Institution's museums for the American people. More than 90 percent of the Smithsonian's visitors are American citizens, and they travel great distances "on a pilgrimage to the nation's secular shrines... they're the physical manifestation of our shared sense of national identity." *Washington Post,* 26 June 2000, A19.

49. Webb, "Was It Necessary?," 4. In contrast to the *Enola Gay*, the *Bockscar* B-29 has had a far less visible postwar presence. It too was put into storage during 1946 at Davis-Monthan Air Force Base in Tucson, Arizona, until the Air Force refurbished it during 1961. On 26 September 1961, it was flown to Wright-Patterson Air Force Base in Dayton, Ohio, where it was given a place of honor at the United States Air Force Museum located there. Displayed next to SAC's B-36, B-47, B-52, B-57, B-58, B-70, and B-1A bombers, it has engendered very little controversy since 1945. See *New York Times*, 26 March 1995, 1-11.

50. See Paul Fussell, *Thank God for the Atomic Bomb, and Other Essays* (New York: Summit Books, 1988), 23.

51. In my judgment, Fussell here is much too glib. One need not buy into this bazaar of stereotypes. I was born in 1951 to a father who was drafted into the U.S. Army in 1945 right out of high school. Having completed basic training in July 1945, he had been issued, as he recalls, tropical khakis for assignment to the Pacific in preparation for the invasion of Japan. After the atomic bombs were dropped, he returned that uniform to the quartermaster and was reissued woolen olive drab kit for his reassignment to the Allied occupation forces in Berlin. Despite what Paul Fussell or the *Wall Street Journal* claims about the implacability of "60s-type professors," I cannot help seeing both sides of the Hiroshima and Nagasaki story. For more on patriotism and the generational divide, also see Edward T. Linenthal and Tom Englehardt, *History Wars: The Enola Gay and Other Battles for the American Past* (New York: Henry Holt, 1996), 97–114.

52. Harwit, *Exhibit Denied*, 428.

53. Ibid., 428–29.

3. Memorializing Mass Murder

1. For critical readings of such museum practices, see Daniel J. Sherman and Irit Rogoff, *Museum/Culture: Histories, Discourses, Spectacles* (Minneapolis: University of Minnesota Press, 1994); Robert Harrison, *Eccentric Spaces: A Voyage through Real and Imaginary Worlds* (New York: Ecco Press, 1994); Ivan Karp and Steven Lavine, eds., *Exhibiting Cultures: The Poetics and Politics of Display* (Washington, D.C.: Smithsonian Institution Press, 1991); Peter Vergo, *The New Museology* (London: Reaktion Books, 1989); Warren Leon and Roy Rosenzwieg, eds., *History Museums of the United States: A Critical Assessment* (Urbana: University of Illinois Press, 1989); Robert Lumley, ed., *The Museum Time-Machine: Putting Cultures on Display* (London: Routledge, 1988); and George W. Stocking Jr., *Objects and Others: Essays on Museums and Material Culture* (Madison: University of Wisconsin Press, 1985).

2. See Timothy W. Luke, *Shows of Force: Power, Politics, and Ideology at Art Museums* (Durham, N.C.: Duke University Press, 1992).

3. Michel Foucault, "Governmentality," in *The Foucault Effect: Studies in Governmentality*, ed. Graham Burchell, Colin Gordon, and Peter Miller (Chicago: University of Chicago Press, 1991), 87–104.

4. *United States Holocaust Memorial Museum Newsletter: Special Issue* (Washington, D.C.: United States Holocaust Memorial Museum Foundation, 1993), 2. For a thorough discussion of those who continue to deny that the Holocaust happened, see

Michael Shermer and Alex Grobman, *Denying History: Who Says the Holocaust Never Happened and Why Do They Say It?* (Berkeley: University of California Press, 2000).

5. For additional discussion of these political dynamics, in analyses of the Holocaust, see Raul Hilberg, *The Destruction of the European Jews: Revised and Definitive Edition* (New York: Holmes and Meier, 1985); Michael Marrus, *The Holocaust in History* (Hanover, N.H.: Brandeis University Press, 1987); Richard L. Rubenstein and John Roth, *Approaches to Auschwitz* (Atlanta: John Knox, 1987); Benno Müller-Hill, *Murderous Science: Elimination by Scientific Selection of Jews, Gypsies, and Others, Germany 1933–1945* (Oxford: Oxford University Press, 1988); and Leni Yahil, *The Holocaust: The Fate of European Jews* (Oxford: Oxford University Press, 1991).

6. *United States Holocaust Memorial Museum Charter Membership Application Forms* (Washington, D.C.: United States Holocaust Memorial Museum Foundation, 1993), 2.

7. Ibid.

8. Ibid., 9.

9. For some sense of these discursive frameworks and pictorial rhetorics, see the exhibition's catalogue: Michael Berenbaum, *The World Must Know: The History of the Holocaust Museum as Told in the United States Holocaust Memorial Museum* (Boston: Little, Brown, 1993).

10. See Henry Friedlander, *The Origins of Nazi Genocide: From Euthanasia to the Final Solution* (Chapel Hill: University of North Carolina Press, 1995).

11. *Where: Los Angeles* (September 1996), 96–97. Operating as part of The Simon Wiesenthal Center, the Museum of Tolerance officially opened 8 February 1993 after breaking ground for its construction on 7 December 1986. At the groundbreaking, the museum's experiential tenor was given full rein as hundreds of Holocaust death camp survivors participated in the ceremonies by spreading soil gathered from World War II death camps and recounting their life stories. The Wiesenthal Center is a Jewish human rights agency supported mostly by private donations from more than 400,000 members all around the world. This striking eight-level, 165,000-square-foot complex houses its organizational headquarters as well as the museum space.

12. The Simon Wiesenthal Center, *Beit Hashoah: The Museum of Tolerance* (Santa Barbara: Albion Publishing Group, 1993), 8.

13. Ibid., 24.

14. Leaving the Museum of Tolerance's Holocaust section, one passes close by the Wiesenthal Center's Global Situation Room, where "researchers compile up-to-the-minute data on human rights violations around the world" (*Museum of Tolerance*, 43) from electronic research networks, newswires, and international press services. As the nerve center of the Wiesenthal Center's human rights watch, the room suggests how conscientious concern for intolerance might check future acts of genocide. Yet this glimpse at such a moral panopticon raises as many questions as it answers. On the one hand, it is commendable that the Center performs this service, because as the museum's curators assert, "monitoring the activities of human rights violations links the atrocities of the past with those of the present and reminds us of our continuous need to be on the alert for acts of injustice and intolerance where they occur" (*Museum of Tolerance*, 43). On the other hand, being on the alert since 1993 in a tiny West L.A. neighborhood has done nothing to stop genocide in Burundi, Chechnya, Rwanda, Brazil, or Kurdistan.

15. In this sense, the Holocaust Museum serves many significant cultural ends as

a system of simulation. See Jean Baudrillard, *Simulations* (New York: Semiotext(e), 1983), 23–26.

16. Hannah Arendt, *The Origins of Totalitarianism* (New York: Harcourt Brace, 1951). To prove the banality of its evil, the Holocaust Museum mobilizes banal traces of the Holocaust's destruction. The museum's powers of hyperreal persuasion, for example, often reside in the concentration of ordinary material traces embedded in everyday life within industrial societies—toothbrushes, combs, shoes, suitcases, razors, photographs. In many ways, these personal accoutrements are more tangible signs of personhood for the museum's visitors than even the names and numbers of the death camps' victims. These are the odds and ends accumulated by the Reich at the moment of their owner's death, but not cremated or buried as historic evidence of that death. The telltale piles of thousands, tens of thousands, hundreds of thousands of them are awesome indicators of an efficient horror. They represent the abnormal deaths of normalized urban consumers, like ourselves, people who acquire, use, and accumulate goods to anchor our peculiarly privileged forms of subjectivity. For those rural victims of the Holocaust caught out on the farm, however, who were not transported with personal effects into the death camp system, their deaths seem much less real. The only trace of them are ghastly photos of SS troopers shooting anonymous peasants on the rocky lips of vast trenches, clinical log entries listing names and occupations of those consigned to mass graves on the Russian steppes, or Gestapo communiques boasting of good hunting in the East. These displays also uncomfortably echo similar images from the American West, British India, French Africa, or Portuguese East Indies, in which one sees colonists standing amidst piles of dead natives confident that every murdered indigenous person advanced the white man's enlightened progress around the world. These earlier holocausts, like those of so many Lithuanian, Russian, or Ukrainian Jews, happened in a world unmarked by the traces of industrial life. Such peoples left behind no toothbrushes, street shoes, combs, or family photos. Their deaths are mostly anonymous, permitting their demise not to be ennobled as a "holocaust" or maybe even valorized as genocide. They were simply lost, becoming the "lost American," the "lost African," or the "lost civilization." Even though they were not yet normalized urban beings, they too were expunged in genocide.

17. *Museum Newsletter: Special Issue,* 6.

18. Berenbaum, *The World Must Know,* 233.

19. See Reinhard Rürup, *Topography of Terror: Gestapo, SS, and Reichssicherheitshauptamt on the "Prinz-Albrecht Terrain"—A Documentation* (Berlin: Willmuth Arenhövel, 1987). In June 1999 the Bundestag approved Peter Eisenman's ambitious design for more than 2,000 stone pillars to be built in Berlin between the Brandenburg Gate and Potsdamer Platz not as a museum, not rather as a "documentation center" for the Holocaust. With another vote just prior to the ballot that gave approval to Eisenman's design, Germany's Parliament also decided the memorial would be specifically dedicated to the Jews instead of all Hitler's many victims. See Roger Cohen, "A Berlin Holocaust Memorial Approved," *New York Times,* 26 June 1999, A3. This installation will be joined by the new Jewish Museum, which focuses on 2,000 years of German-Jewish history. Designed by the American architect Daniel Liebeskind, it did not open until August 2001, even though its construction was largely completed in 1998. See Roger Cohen, "A Jewish Museum Struggles to Be Born," *New York Times,* 15 August 2000, E1, 3.

20. See Michael Goldberg, *Why Should Jews Survive? Looking Past the Holocaust Toward a Jewish Future* (New York: Oxford University Press, 1995). Yet the Holocaust's meaning is not univocal, even in Israel. Some ultraorthodox Jews boycott the Israeli state's Holocaust Day rites, protest Holocaust news clips, and dispute official narratives about anti-Nazi Jewish resistance—all on religious grounds. See Deborah Sontag, "More Than One Way to Remember the Holocaust," *New York Times,* 3 May 2000, A4.

21. For an example of this kind of cross-national, comparative Holocaust analysis, see Yehuda Bauer, *The Holocaust in Historical Perspective* (Seattle: University of Washington Press, 1978). While the Holocaust Museum's displays do not go systematically into these sorts of issues, its community outreach programs have taken some of them under consideration. One outreach program made available to the public during fall 1995 provided an eight-week overview of "genocide and state murders" from Armenia, Ukraine, and China to Cambodia, Rwanda, and Burundi. Still, the tenor of these programs, as one scheduled presentation suggests, centers on "why genocide must be distinguished from, yet related to crimes of war, state terror, and gross violations of human rights; and how the Holocaust sensitizes us, but is misleading as a paradigm." United States Holocaust Memorial Museum: Public Programs, "Genocide and Mass Murder in the Twentieth Century: A Historical Perspective," (Washington, D.C.: United States Holocaust Memorial Museum, 1995), 2. The Holocaust is a misleading paradigm for classifying genocide inasmuch as its uniqueness must be protected against loosely misapplying its symbolic powers to serious, but allegedly less evil, instances of war crimes, state terror, or human rights violations.

22. For an analysis of how the Holocaust became "The Holocaust" in the United States, see Peter Novick, *The Holocaust in American Life* (Boston: Houghton Mifflin, 1999). A more strident discussion of the Holocaust as a globally circulating bundle of ideological representations can be found in Norman Finkelstein, *The Holocaust Industry: Reflections on the Exploitation of Jewish Suffering* (New York: Verso, 2000).

4. Signs of Empire/Empires of Sign

1. See Roland Barthes, *Empire of Signs* (New York: Hill and Wang, 1982), 3–8.

2. See *Washington Post,* 15 November 1998, G1–G4; and *Washington Post,* 30 October 1988, G1. Also see, for additional discussion, Yoshiaki Shimizu, *Japan: The Shaping of Daimyo Culture, 1185–1868* (Washington, D.C.: National Gallery of Art, 1988). This discussion draws from my *Shows of Force: Power, Politics, and Ideology in Art Exhibitions* (Durham, N.C.: Duke University Press, 1992).

3. For several classic predictions about this presumed course of events, see William Ouchi, *Theory Z: How American Business Can Meet the Japanese Challenge* (Reading, Mass.: Addison Wesley, 1981); Ezra Vogel, *Japan as Number One: Lessons for America* (Cambridge: Harvard University Press, 1979); Herman Kahn, *The Emerging Japanese Superstate: Challenge and Response* (Englewood Cliffs, N.J.: Prentice Hall, 1970); and Zbigniew Brzezinski, *The Fragile Blossom: Crisis and Change in Japan* (New York: Harper and Row, 1972).

4. *The Wall Street Journal,* 30 January 1989, A8.

5. This show opened at the Sackler Gallery on 27 May 1990 and ran through 9 September 1990 before moving on to exhibition dates in San Francisco and Los An-

geles. See, for more detailed consideration, Ann Yonemura, *Yokohama: Prints from Nineteenth-Century Japan* (Washington, D.C.: Arthur M. Sackler Gallery, 1990).

6. *Washington Post*, 21 February 1989, A19.

7. See, for example, *Washington Post*, 12 January 1989, A16.

8. *Washington Post*, 21 February 1989, A19.

9. Ibid.

10. See Purnendra Jain and Takashi Inoguchi, eds., *Japanese Politics Today: Beyond Karaoke Democracy?* (New York: St. Martins, 1997).

11. See Mike M. Mochizuki, ed., *Toward a True Alliance: Restructuring U.S.-Japan Security Relations* (Washington, D.C.: Brookings Institution Press, 1997).

12. See Robert T. Singer et al., *Edo: Art in Japan 1615–1868* (Washington, D.C.: National Gallery of Art, 1998).

13. *Washington Post*, 7 January 1989, G10. Also see *New York Times*, 13 November 1998, B37.

14. Ibid.

15. Eve M. Ferguson, "'Edo' Exhibit Offers First Major Survey of This Japanese Art," *The Washington Diplomat* 5, no. 1 (January 1999): B4.

16. Singer et al., *Edo*, 13.

17. Ibid., 15.

18. Ferguson, "'Edo' Exhibit," B4.

19. Mochizuki, *True Alliance*, 29.

20. Jain and Inoguchi, *Japanese Politics Today*, 1–29.

21. For more discussion of the salaryman's demise along with that of the firms that sustained him, see Stephanie Strom, "In Japan, From a Lifetime Job to No Job at All," *New York Times*, 3 February 1999, A1, A6.

22. Joan Warner, Pete Engardio, and Thane Peterson, "The Atlantic Century?" *Businessweek*, 8 February 1999, 64–67.

23. See Sharon Macdonald, ed., *The Politics of Display: Museums, Science, Culture* (London: Routledge, 1998).

5. Inventing the Southwest

1. See The Heard Museum, "Inventing the Southwest: The Fred Harvey Company and Native American Art" (Phoenix: Heard Museum, 1995); and Marta Weigle and Barbara A. Babcock, eds., *The Great Southwest of the Fred Harvey Company and the Santa Fe Railway* (Phoenix: Heard Museum, 1996).

2. See *Fodor's Arizona '95* (New York: Random House, 1994), 178.

3. Ibid., 179.

4. See *Frommer's Arizona '95* (New York: Simon and Schuster, 1995), 106.

5. *Valley Guide Quarterly*, vol. 6, no. 3 (fall 1995): 47.

6. Ibid., 4.

7. For more discussion of the curiosity cabinet and its relations to modern museums, see Sharon Macdonald, "Exhibitions of Power and Power of Exhibition: An Introduction to the Politics of Display," in *The Politics of Display: Museums, Science, Culture*, ed. Sharon Macdonald (London: Routledge, 1998), 1–24.

8. For more discussion of Phoenix and its early years as a city, see Bradford Luckingham, *Phoenix: The History of a Southwestern Metropolis* (Tucson: University of Arizona Press, 1989).

9. Ann E. Marshall and Mary H. Brennan, *The Heard Museum: History and Collections* (Phoenix: Heard Museum, 1995), 2–7.

10. T. C. McLuhan, *Dream Tracks: The Railroad and the American Indian* (New York: Harry Abrams, 1985), 16.

11. Ibid., 19.

12. Marshall and Brennan, *The Heard Museum,* 12.

13. Ibid., 10–12.

14. "Inventing the Southwest," 1.

15. Weigle and Babcock, *The Great Southwest,* 25–33.

16. Ibid., 67–85.

17. Ibid., 67.

18. The Heard Museum, "Gallery Guide and Map" (Phoenix: Heard Museum, 1995), 3.

19. The Heard Museum, "Native Cultures and Art" (Phoenix: Heard Museum, 1993–94), 2.

20. The Heard Museum, "Following the Sun and Moon: Hopi Kachina Dolls" (Phoenix: Heard Museum, 1995).

21. Margaret Archuleta, *Sixth Annual Native American Fine Arts Invitational* (Phoenix: Heard Museum, 1994), 3.

22. Margaret Archuleta, *Fifth Annual Native American Fine Arts Invitational* (Phoenix: Heard Museum, 1991).

23. See Theresa Harlan, *Watchful Eyes: Native American Women Artists* (Phoenix: Heard Museum, 1994).

24. *The Statistical Abstract of the United States,* 114th edition (Washington, D.C.: U.S. Department of Commerce, 1994), 28.

25. *Valley Guide Quarterly,* 12.

26. Ibid.

27. The Heard Museum, "Heard Museum North" (Phoenix: Heard Museum, 1995), 1.

28. *Frommer's Arizona '95,* 199.

29. Ibid.

30. See John Urry, *The Tourist Gaze: Leisure and Travel in Contemporary Society* (London: Sage, 1990).

31. See Timothy W. Luke, *Screens of Power: Ideology, Domination, and Resistance in Informational Society* (Urbana: University of Illinois Press, 1989).

32. A recent exception to this vision at the Heard Museum is a powerful new display that opened during 2000 devoted to government-run Indian boarding schools, like the now-defunct Phoenix Indian School in the heart of metropolitan Phoenix. "Remembering Our Indian School Days: The Boarding School Experience" is a powerful study of the cultural-assimilation practices that were forced on the Native Americans that the Heard Museum has romanticized for so many decades.

33. For a parallel account, see Richard W. Hill Sr., "The Museum Indian: Still Frozen in Time and Mind," *Museum News* 79, no. 3 (May/June 2000): 40–67.

6. Museum Pieces

1. Edward O. Wilson, "Foreword," in Lyle Rexer and Rachel Klein, *American Museum of Natural History: 125 Years of Expedition and Discovery* (New York: Harry Abrams/American Museum of Natural History, 1995), 18.

2. Michel Foucault, *The Archaeology of Knowledge and The Discourse on Language* (London: Tavistock, 1972), 140.

3. See T. R. Adam, *The Civic Value of Museums* (New York: American Association for Adult Education, 1937).

4. Benedict Anderson, *Imagined Communities: Reflections on the Origin and Spread of Nationalism* (London: Verso, 1983).

5. See T. R. Adam, *The Museum and Popular Culture* (New York: American Association for Adult Education, 1939).

6. For a parallel discussion of museums as ontological anchors, see Timothy Mitchell, *Colonizing Egypt* (Berkeley: University of California Press), ix–xvi.

7. Michel Foucault, "The Order of Discourse," in *Language and Politics,* ed. Michael Shapiro (Oxford: Blackwell, 1984), 127.

8. David Campbell, *Writing Security: United States Foreign Policy and the Politics of Identity* (Minneapolis: University of Minnesota Press, 1992), 6.

9. O. Impey and A. MacGregor, eds., *The Origin of Museums* (Oxford: Clarendon, 1985).

10. Douglas J. Preston, *Dinosaurs in the Attic: An Excursion to the American Museum of Natural History* (New York: St. Martin's, 1986), 8–9.

11. Ibid., 16.

12. Ibid., 8, 11. For a fascinating discussion of Paleozoic life-forms and their hold on the American imagination, as well as the special place of the American Museum of Natural History in creating these myths, see W. J. T. Mitchell, *The Last Dinosaur Book: The Life and Times of a Cultural Icon* (Chicago: University of Chicago Press, 1998).

13. Ibid., 14–15.

14. Ibid., 19.

15. Donna Haraway, *Primate Visions: Gender, Race, and Nature in the World of Modern Science* (New York: Routledge, 1989), 26–89.

16. Preston, *Dinosaurs in the Attic,* 22–23.

17. Lyle Rexer and Rachel Klein, *American Museum of Natural History: 125 Years of Expedition and Discovery* (New York: Harry Abrams/American Museum of Natural History, 1995), 29.

18. Ben Agger, *Socio(onto)logy: A Disciplinary Reading* (Urbana: University of Illinois Press, 1989).

19. Rexer and Klein, *American Museum,* 25.

20. American Museum of Natural History, *Seven Continents on Central Park West: Visitor's Brochure* (New York: American Museum of Natural History, 1995), 1.

21. Ibid., 2.

22. Quetzil E. Castañeda, *In the Museum of Maya Culture: Touring Chichén Itzá* (Minneapolis: University of Minnesota Press, 1996), 103.

23. Michel Foucault, *Discipline and Punish: The Birth of the Prison* (New York: Vintage, 1979), 170.

24. Preston, *Dinosaurs in the Attic,* x–xi.

25. Michel Foucault, *The Order of Things: An Archaeology of the Human Sciences* (New York: Vintage, 1970). My observation plays off Foucault's preface to *The Order of Things,* in which he claims: "This book first arose out of a passage in Borges, out of the laughter that shattered, as I read the passage, all the familiar landmarks of my thought—*our* thought, the thought that bears the stamp of our age and our geography—breaking up all the ordered surfaces and all the planes with which we are

accustomed to tame the wild profusion of existing things, and continuing long after-
wards to disturb and threaten with collapse our age-old distinction between the Same
and the Other. This passage quotes a certain Chinese encyclopaedia in which it is
written that 'animals are divided into: (a) belonging to the Emperor, (b) embalmed,
(c) tame, (d) sucking pigs, (e) sirens, (f) fabulous, (g) stray dogs, (h) included in the
present classification, (i) frenzied, (j) innumerable, (k) drawn from a very fine camel-
hair brush, (l) *et cetera,* (m) having just broken the water pitcher, (n) that from a
long way off look like flies.' In the wonderment of this taxonomy, the thing we apprehend in one great leap, the thing that, by means of the fable, is demonstrated as
the exotic charm of another system of thought, is the limitation of our own, the
stark impossibility of thinking *that*" (xv).

26. Preston, *Dinosaurs in the Attic,* xi.

27. American Museum of Natural History, *Seven Continents,* 3.

28. Preston, *Dinosaurs in the Attic,* xii.

29. Ibid., xi.

30. Carolyn Merchant, *The Death of Nature* (New York: Harper and Row,
1980).

31. American Museum of Natural History, *Seven Continents,* 3.

32. Michel Foucault, *The History of Sexuality,* vol. 1, *An Introduction* (New York:
Vintage, 1980), 138.

33. Ibid., 139–40.

34. Preston, *Dinosaurs in the Attic,* 5.

35. Ibid., 6.

36. Ibid., 6–7.

37. Ibid., 6.

38. Ibid., 16.

39. Ibid., 24.

40. American Museum of Natural History, *Seven Continents,* 3.

41. Haraway, *Primate Visions,* 26–58.

42. Preston, *Dinosaurs in the Attic,* 81.

43. Ibid., 81. Contemporary aesthetics often turns this quest for verisimilitude
into an attempt to efface with art. See Michael Kimmelman, "Trompe L'Oeil on Nature's Behalf," *New York Times,* 7 January 2000, E39, E42.

44. Preston, *Dinosaurs in the Attic,* 81.

45. Ibid., 84.

46. Foucault, *Discipline and Punish,* 170–71.

47. Ibid.

48. Ibid.

49. Ibid., 172.

50. Ibid., 173.

51. Ibid., 186–87.

52. Ibid., 170.

53. J. Fabian, *Time and the Other* (New York: Columbia University Press, 1983),
31, 67.

54. Castañeda, *In the Museum,* 101.

55. American Museum of Natural History, *Seven Continents,* 3.

56. Foucault, *History of Sexuality,* 142.

57. Ibid.

58. American Museum of Natural History, *Official Visitor's Guide* (New York: American Museum of Natural History, 1993), 1–2.

59. Foucault, *History of Sexuality,* 143.

60. Ibid., 146.

61. Ibid., 141.

62. Ibid.

63. American Museum of Natural History, *Official Visitor's Guide,* 2.

64. Foucault, *History of Sexuality,* 141.

65. See Timothy W. Luke, "Liberal Society and Cyborg Subjectivity: The Politics of Environments, Bodies, and Nature," *Alternatives: A Journal of World Policy* 21 no. 1 (1996): 1–30.

66. American Museum of Natural History, *Seven Continents,* 1.

67. Preston, *Dinosaurs in the Attic,* 15.

68. Wilson, "Forward," 18. This big thinking is still advanced in the museum's operations, in the new Rose Center for Earth and Space as well as the new Hayden Planetarium, which explore astrophysics and cosmology in these impressive display spaces. See Tina Kelley, "A Place Where the Big Bang Often Produces Puzzled Silence," *New York Times,* 7 March 2000, B1, B4; and Herbert Muschamp, "It's Something New Under the Stars (And Looking Up)," *New York Times,* 13 February 2000, AR1, 38.

7. The Missouri Botanical Garden

1. R. W. Apple Jr., "St. Louis: The River Runs by It, History through It," *New York Times,* 16 April 1999, B29.

2. See L. U. Reavis, *St. Louis: The Future Great City of the World* (St. Louis: C. R. Barus, 1876); and Walter B. Stevens, *Saint Louis: The Fourth City* (St. Louis: S. J. Clarke Publishing Company, 1909).

3. "Preface," Dr. Peter H. Raven, Director, Missouri Botanical Garden, in *The Unseen Garden: Research at the Missouri Botanical Garden* (St. Louis: Missouri Botanical Garden, 1993), 1.

4. See, for more discussion, Klaus Eder, *The Social Construction of Nature: A Sociology of Ecological Enlightenment* (London: Sage, 1996); and Kate Soper, *What Is Nature?* (Oxford: Blackwell, 1997).

5. See William Barnaby Faherty, S.J., *A Gift to Glory In: The First Hundred Years of the Missouri Botanical Garden* (Ocean Park, Wash.: Harris and Friedrich, 1989), ix–xxi.

6. William Barnaby Faherty, S.J., *Henry Shaw: His Life and Legacies* (St. Louis: Missouri Botanical Garden/University of Missouri Press, 1987), 80. For Kew's leading place in British imperialism, see Linda Brockway, *Science and Colonial Expansion: The Role of the British Royal Botanic Garden* (New York: Academic Press, 1979).

7. Flaherty, *Henry Shaw,* 163.

8. Ibid.

9. Ibid.

10. Ibid., 195.

11. See Heather Angel, *Kew: A World of Plants* (London: Collins and Brown, 1993); Nigel Harper, ed., *Kew: Royal Botanic Gardens* (London: Stemmer House,

1982); and Ronald King, *The World of Kew* (London: Macmillan, 1976). For Kew's role in colonial agribusiness, see David Headrick, *Tentacles of Progress: Technology Transfer in the Age of Imperialism* (Oxford: Oxford University Press, 1988).

12. Royal Botanic Gardens Kew, "Friends" (Richmond: Friends of the Royal Botanic Gardens, 1994), 6.

13. Courtaulds, "Courtaulds and Kew" (London: Courtaulds, 1994), 3–7.

14. See F. Nigel Hepper, ed., *Plant Hunting at Kew* (London: Her Majesty's Stationery Office, 1989), xiii–xv.

15. Missouri Botanical Garden, *Guidebook* (St. Louis: Missouri Botanical Garden, 1988), 9.

16. Ibid., 32–38.

17. Ibid., 17–29.

18. Ibid., 26.

19. Ibid., 25–28.

20. Ibid., 38–41.

21. Michel Foucault, "Governmentality," in *The Foucault Effect: Studies in Governmentality,* ed. Graham Burchell, Colin Gordon, and Peter Miller (Chicago: University of Chicago Press, 1991), 97.

22. Ibid., 100.

23. Ibid., 102.

24. Ibid.

25. Missouri Botanical Garden, *Visitor's Guide* (St. Louis: Missouri Botanical Garden, 1998), 4.

26. Michel Foucault, *The History of Sexuality,* vol. 1, *An Introduction* (New York: Vintage, 1980), 146.

27. Michel Foucault, *The Order of Things: An Archaeology of the Human Sciences* (New York: Vintage, 1970), 158.

28. Ibid.

29. Foucault, *History of Sexuality,* 138–42.

30. Ibid., 145.

31. Ibid., 142.

32. Ibid.

33. Ibid., 143.

34. Ibid.

35. Ibid., 143–44.

36. See Faherty, *Henry Shaw,* 160–75. In particular, Shaw believed viniculture and wine making promoted both the taming of nature and the civilization of society.

37. See Michel Foucault, "Truth and Power," *Power/Knowledge: Selected Interviews and Other Writings, 1972–1977* (New York: Vintage, 1980), 133.

38. Bruno Latour, *We Have Never Been Modern* (London: Harvester Wheatsleaf, 1993), 32.

39. Ibid.

40. Foucault, "Governmentality," *The Foucault Effect,* 93.

41. Ibid., 102.

42. Ibid., 100, 102.

43. The statistical surveillance regime of states, as Foucault maintains, emerges alongside monarchical absolutism during the late seventeenth century. Intellectual disciplines, ranging from geography and cartography to statistics and civil engineer-

ing, are mobilized to inventory and organize the wealth of populations in territories by the state. For additional discussion, see Graham Burchell, Colin Gordon, and Peter Miller, eds., *The Foucault Effect: Studies in Governmentality*, 1–48. A very useful example of sustainability thinking conjoined with professional-technical environmentality can be found in Thaddeus C. Trzyna, *A Sustainable World: Defining and Measuring Sustainable Development* (IUCN/California Institute of Public Affairs, 1995).

44. For a typical expression of sustainability discourse as a legitimation code, see John Young, *Sustaining the Earth* (Cambridge: Harvard University Press, 1990).

45. Michel Foucault, *Discipline and Punish: The Birth of the Prison* (New York: Vintage, 1979), 29.

46. Missouri Botanical Garden, *Visitor's Guide*, 3.

47. Ibid., 4–5.

48. John Cairns, Jr. "Achieving Sustainable Use of the Planet in the Next Century: What Should Virginians Do?" *Virginia Issues and Answers* 2, no. 2 (summer 1995): 3.

49. W. E. Westmen, "How Much Are Nature's Services Worth?," *Science* 197, (1978): 960–64. Also see WWF-World Wide Fund for Nature, *The Vital Wealth of Plants* (Gland: WWF-World Wide Fund for Nature, 1993).

50. Cairns, "Sustainable Use," 3.

51. Missouri Botanical Garden, *Visitor's Guide*, 4.

52. Cairns, "Sustainable Use," 6.

53. Missouri Botanical Garden, *Visitor's Guide*, 4–8.

54. Barry Commoner, *Making Peace with the Planet* (New York: Pantheon, 1990), 8.

55. Missouri Botanical Garden, *Visitor's Guide*, 7.

56. Commoner, *Making Peace*, 9.

57. Ibid., 11.

58. Missouri Botanical Garden, *Visitor's Guide*, 4.

59. Faherty, *Henry Shaw*, 194.

60. Ibid.

61. Michel Foucault, "Afterword: The Subject and Power," in *Michel Foucault: Beyond Structuralism and Hermeneutics*, ed. Hubert L. Dreyfus and Paul Rabinow (Chicago: University of Chicago Press, 1982), 214–15.

62. Ibid., 215.

63. Foucault, *History of Sexuality*, 25.

64. For more elaboration of why state power must guarantee environmental security, see Norman Myers, *Ultimate Security: The Environmental Basis of Political Stability* (New York: Norton, 1993).

65. See Timothy W. Luke, "Worldwatching as the Limits to Growth," *Capitalism Nature Socialism* 5, no. 2 (June 1994): 43–64.

66. Foucault, *History of Sexuality*, 139.

67. Ibid., 141.

68. Ibid.

69. Ibid.

70. Ibid.

71. Fredric Jameson, *Postmodernism, or the Cultural Logic of Late Capitalism*, (Durham, N.C.: Duke University Press, 1992), ix.

72. Foucault, *History of Sexuality*, 142.

8. Southwestern Environments as Hyperreality

1. See Kate Soper, *What Is Nature? Culture, Politics, and the Non-Human* (Oxford: Blackwell, 1995).

2. A good discussion of these tendencies can be found in Catriona Sandilands, *The Good-Natured Feminist: Ecofeminism and the Quest for Democracy* (Minneapolis: University of Minnesota Press, 1999); and Neil Evernden, *The Social Creation of Nature* (Toronto: University of Toronto Press, 1992).

3. See Michel Foucault, *The History of Sexuality*, vol. 1, *An Introduction* (New York: Vintage, 1980).

4. See Michel Foucault, *Discipline and Punish: The Birth of the Prison* (New York: Vintage, 1979).

5. Timothy W. Luke, *Shows of Force: Power, Politics, and Ideology in Art Exhibits* (Durham, N.C.: Duke University Press, 1992).

6. Daniel J. Sherman and Irit Rogoff, *Museum Culture: Histories, Discourses, Spectacles* (Minneapolis: University of Minnesota Press, 1994).

7. Carol Duncan, *Civilizing Rituals: Inside Public Art Museums* (London: Routledge, 1995).

8. David Harvey, *Justice, Nature, and the Geography of Difference* (Oxford: Blackwell, 1996), 316.

9. See Eilean Hooper-Greenhill, ed., *Museum, Media, Message* (London: Routledge, 1995).

10. *Frommer's Arizona '95* (New York: Simon and Schuster, 1995), 179.

11. *Tucson Lifestyle*, February 1996, 110.

12. William H. Carr, *Pebbles in Your Shoes: The Story of How the Arizona–Sonora Desert Museum Began and Grew* (Tucson: Arizona–Sonora Desert Museum, 1982), 20. For additional discussion of the area around the Arizona–Sonora Desert Museum, see Gary Paul Nabhan, *Saguaro: A View of Saguaro National Monument and the Tucson Basin* (Tucson: Southwest Parks and Monuments Association, 1986).

13. Ibid., 45.

14. Ruth Kirk, *An Inside Look at the Arizona–Sonora Desert Museum* (Tucson: Arizona–Sonora Desert Museum, 1989), jacket.

15. Cited in Carr, *Pebbles in Your Shoes*, 107.

16. *County and City Data Book*, 12th ed. (Washington, D.C.: U.S. Department of Commerce, 1994), 650.

17. Ibid.

18. *Statistical Abstracts of the United States*, 114th ed. (Washington, D.C.: U.S. Department of Commerce, 1994), 77. Also see Peter Wiley and Roger Gottlieb, *Empires of the Sun: The Rise of the New American West* (Tucson: University of Arizona Press, 1985).

19. William Claibourne, "Mojave Caught in Dispute Over Man's Relationship to Nature," *Washington Post*, 28 May 2000, A3.

20. Carr, *Pebbles*, 33–37.

21. Ibid., 35.

22. Joseph Wood Krutch, *If You Don't Mind Me Saying So* (New York: William Sloan Associates, 1964), 365.

23. *Visitor's Guide: Arizona–Sonora Desert Museum* (Tucson: Arizona–Sonora Desert Museum, 1993).

24. Carr, *Pebbles*, 185.

25. Kirk, *An Inside Look*, 18.

26. Michael F. Logan, *Fighting Sprawl and City Hall: Resistance to Urban Growth in the Southwest* (Tucson: University of Arizona Press, 1995), 72.

27. Margaret Regan, "Faking It," *Tucson Guide Quarterly* 12 (summer 1994): A8.

28. Jean Baudrillard, *Simulations* (New York: Semiotext(e), 1983), 32.

29. Ibid., 2.

30. Regan, "Faking It," 63.

31. Ibid.

32. R. J. Hoage and William A. Deiss, eds. *New Worlds, New Animals: From Menagerie to Zoological Park in the Nineteenth Century* (Baltimore: Johns Hopkins University Press, 1996).

33. Timothy W. Luke, *Screens of Power: Ideology, Domination, and Resistance in Informational Society* (Urbana: University of Illinois Press, 1989).

34. Regan, "Faking It," 64.

35. Baudrillard, *Simulations*, 26.

36. Ibid., 25.

37. Regan, "Faking It," 64.

38. See Michael Wallis, *Route 66: The Mother Road* (New York: St. Martin's, 1990); William H. Goetzmann and William N. Goetzmann, *The West of the Imagination* (New York: Norton, 1986); and, T. C. McLuhan, *Dream Tracks: The Railroad and the American Indian 1890–1930* (New York: Harry N. Abrams, 1985).

39. Baudrillard, *Simulations*, 4.

40. See Marta Weigle and Barbara A. Babcock, eds., *The Great Southwest of the Fred Harvey Company and the Santa Fe Railway* (Phoenix: Heard Museum, 1996).

41. "Zoo's New Primates: Fully Clothed Danes," *New York Times*, 29 August 1996, A8.

42. Sharon Zukin, *Landscapes of Power: From Detroit to Disney World* (Berkeley: University of California Press, 1991), 222.

43. *Tucson Lifestyle* 13 (June 1994): 75.

44. Ibid., 43.

45. Baudrillard, *Simulations*, 12.

46. Ibid., 25.

47. Carol Cochran, *Where the Desert Speaks: A Brief History of the Arizona–Sonora Desert Museum* (Tucson: Arizona–Sonora Desert Museum, 1995), 18.

48. *sonorensis* 16, no. 1 (spring 1996): 19.

49. *sonorensis* 15, no. 1 (spring 1995): 17.

50. Ibid., 17, 19.

51. *sonorensis* (spring 1996): 19.

52. *sonorensis* (spring 1995), cover.

53. Ibid.

54. *Arizona–Sonora Desert Museum: Visitor's Guide* (Tucson: Arizona–Sonora Desert Museum, 1995), 2.

55. *sonorensis* (spring 1995): 8.

56. Bill McKibben, *The End of Nature* (New York: Doubleday, 1989).

57. Carolyn Merchant, *The Death of Nature: Women and the Scientific Revolution* (San Francisco: Harper and Row, 1990).

9. Superpower Aircraft and Aircrafting Superpower

1. *Pima Air and Space Museum Album* (Tucson: Arizona Aerospace Foundation, 1995), 2.

2. Ibid.

3. See Bruno Latour, *We Have Never Been Modern* (London: Harvester Wheatsleaf, 1993).

4. Donald MacKenzie, *Knowing Machines: Essays on Technical Change* (Cambridge: MIT Press, 1996), 14–15.

5. See Bruno Latour, *Science in Action* (Cambridge: Harvard University Press, 1987).

6. Donna Haraway, *Simians, Cyborgs, and Women: The Reinvention of Nature* (New York: Routledge, 1991), 149–50.

7. Ibid.

8. *Tucson Official Visitor's Guide* (Tucson: Metropolitan Tucson Convention and Visitor's Bureau, 1996–1997), 50.

9. Arizona Wing: Confederate Air Force, "A Flying Museum" (Mesa: Arizona Wing CAF, 1997), 4.

10. Ibid., 2.

11. Ibid., 12.

12. *Pima Air and Space Museum Album*, 26–107.

13. Ibid., 138.

14. Bruno Latour, *We Have Never Been Modern*, 1–5, 30.

15. Ibid., 4.

16. Ibid., 6 (emphasis in the original).

17. Ibid., 4.

18. Latour, at the same time, believes that hybrids always have been evolving as quasi-objective, quasi-subjective (con)fusions of elements drawn from nature/culture, human/nonhuman, object/subject, present/past, being/nonbeing, inside/outside elements. See *We Have Never Been Modern*, 93.

19. Ibid., 10–11.

20. See Ben Agger, *Socio(onto)logy* (Urbana: University of Illinois Press, 1989).

21. Latour, *We Have Never Been Modern*, 14–15.

22. Timothy W. Luke, *Shows of Force: Power, Politics, and Ideology at Art Museums* (Durham, N.C.: Duke University Press, 1992).

23. Carol Duncan, *Civilizing Rituals: Inside Public Art Museums* (London: Routledge, 1995), 7–20.

24. Eilean Hooper-Greenhill, ed. *Museum, Media, Message* (London: Routledge, 1995), 1–12.

25. Michel Foucault, "Governmentality," in *The Foucault Effect: Studies in Governmentality*, ed. S. Graham Burchell, Colin Gordon, and Peter Miller (Chicago: University of Chicago Press, 1991).

26. Latour, *We Have Never Been Modern*, 6.

27. Daniel J. Sherman and Irit Rogoff, *Museum Culture: Histories, Discourses, Spectacles* (Minneapolis: University of Minnesota Press, 1994).

28. Latour, *We Have Never Been Modern*, 15.

29. *Exhibit Guide* (Tucson: Pima Air and Space Museum, 1995), 1.

30. Ibid., 2.

31. Ibid. This level of volunteerism is high, but it is not uncommon. For every paid staff member at American museums, 2.5 people volunteer. See *New York Times,* 19 April 2000, H20.

32. Champlin Fighter Museum, "Champlin Fighter Museum: Home of the American Fighter Aces Association," (Mesa: Champlin Fighter Museum, 1996), 2. In 2000, this organization decided to relocate its collection to a new site in Seattle.

33. Ibid., 4.

34. Ibid., 10.

35. *Pima Air and Space Museum Album,* 2.

36. See *National Air and Space Museum,* (Washington, D.C.: Smithsonian Institution, 1989).

37. See *United States Air Force Museum* (Dayton, Ohio: Air Force Museum Foundation, 1996).

10. Strange Attractor

1. For more discussion of Silicon Valley and San Jose, see Everett M. Rogers and Judith K. Larsen, *Silicon Valley Fever: Growth of High-Technology Culture* (New York: Basic Books, 1984); and Elton B. Sherwin, *The Silicon Valley Way: Discover the Secret of America's Fastest Growing Companies* (Rocklin, Calif.: Prima Publications, 1998).

2. See Jim Bennett, "Can Science Museums Take History Seriously?," in *The Politics of Display: Museums, Science, Culture,* ed. Sharon MacDonald (London: Routledge, 1998), 173–82.

3. See Carmen McCann and Susan Wagemann, *What Goes Around* (San Jose: The Tech Museum of Innovation, 1998), 18. Also see *The Tech* (San Jose: The Tech Museum of Innovation, 2000), 4–14.

4. Ibid., 18–19.

5. Ibid., 19–20.

6. Peter Giles, "Message from Peter Giles," *What Goes Around,* 31.

7. Ibid., 29–54.

8. *School Field Trips* (San Jose: The Tech Museum of Innovation, 1998–1999), 6.

9. Ibid.

10. "Welcome to The Tech: Tips for Your Visit" (San Jose: The Tech Museum of Innovation, 1998), 1.

11. *Visitor Guide* (San Jose: The Tech Museum of Innovation, 1998), 2. Julius Rosenwald, the president of Sears Roebuck, had essentially the same inspiration about the technologies of smoke and steel when he commissioned the planning for Chicago's Museum of Science and Industry in 1926. That museum, however, did not really take off until Major Lenox Lohr invited major American corporations into its exhibition halls to show their products, recount their histories, and foot the bills for the Museum of Science and Industry. While this strategy worked as an attendance-builder by turning the museum into Chicago's biggest cultural attraction, it also locked this institution into a vicious cycle of corporations defining what is "science" and "industry" in allegedly cutting-edge displays that quickly dull, rapidly age, or basically underwhelm. In turn, the museum either must maintain out-of-date exhibits or invite more corporate sponsors to renew the same cycle. The Tech Museum ob-

viously has taken the same road to draw visitors to San Jose and maintain its exhibits, but it is far less grandiose than Chicago's impressive Museum of Science and Industry.

12. Ibid. To underscore this personalized potential in the innovation process, The Tech also runs with Microsoft Corporation a new interactive lecture series, titled "Masters of Change: People Whose Innovations Have Changed Our Lives."

13. *Discover Silicon Valley* 24, no. 11 (Redwood City, Calif.: Discover Magazine, 1998), 4.

14. *Visitor Guide*, 2.

15. Fredric Jameson, *Postmodernism, or, the Cultural Logic of Late Capitalism* (Durham, N.C.: Duke University Press, 1992).

16. Giles, "Message," 31.

17. *Discover Silicon Valley,* 5.

18. See Jean-François Lyotard, *The Postmodern Condition: A Report on Knowledge* (Minneapolis: University of Minnesota Press, 1984).

19. For more discussion of the social construction of technology, see Wiebe E. Bijker, Thomas P. Hughes, and Trevor Pinch, eds., *The Social Construction of Technological Systems* (Cambridge: MIT Press, 1989).

20. Cited in H. Hein, *The Exploratorium: The Museum as Laboratory* (Washington, D.C.: Smithsonian Institution Press, 1990), xv. Over time, this display aesthetic has become normalized. And it is being supplemented, even at the Exploratorium itself, with more expositive static forms of representation in shows like "Revealing Bodies," which deals with the interplay of science and art in anatomical knowledge. See Tessa DeCarlo, "A Science Museum Embraces Art through Anatomy," *New York Times,* 6 August 2000, AR 33, 34.

21. For a conventional reading of The Tech in this vein, see Tom McNichol, "The Geek Guide to Silicon Valley," *Washington Post,* 1 November 1998, E1, E5.

22. See, for example, The Tech's membership literature, which bids visitors to "Join today... and embark on an extraordinary journey all year long!" comprised of doing one thing after another in a series of doing things: visiting exhibits, sneaking a peek at new traveling shows, venturing into new worlds, experiencing the IMAX Dome Theater, discovering unique gift items, refreshing your energy, or entering "a world like no other at The Tech." *Membership: Join The Tech Today!* (San Jose: The Tech Museum of Innovation, 1998), 2.

23. For more discussion, see Ulrich Beck, *The Risk Society* (London: Sage, 1992).

24. See Roy Bhaskar, *A Realist History of Science* (London: Verso, 1997).

25. See Michael M. Weinstein, "Rewriting the Book on Capitalism: Now Cooperative Innovation Steals Competition's Thunder," *New York Times,* 5 June 1989, B7, B9. For more discussion about capitalism's hidden underside of corporate collaboration, see Joseph Schumpeter, *Capitalism, Socialism, and Democracy* (London: Allen and Unwin, 1943), as well as Tom Wolfe's critical celebration of Silicon Valley's collusive capitalism in *Hooking Up* (New York: Farrar Straus, 2000). Wolfe's satirical writing closely monitors where, why, and how such high-tech collusion occurs.

11. Channeling the News Stream

1. Benedict Anderson, *Imagined Communities: Reflections on the Origin and Spread of Nationalism,* rev. ed. (London: Verso, 1991).

2. Ulrich Beck, *The Reinvention of Politics* (Oxford: Polity Press, 1997), 72.

3. See Armand Mattelart, *The Invention of Communication* (Minneapolis: University of Minnesota Press, 1996), ix–xvii.

4. The Freedom Forum is an international foundation founded in 1991 by Allen H. Neuharth as a successor to the Gannett Foundation. That foundation was first established in 1935, and the Freedom Forum now is backed by more than $900 million in assets accumulated from Gannett newspaper chain profits since the 1930s. With offices in San Francisco, Cocoa Beach, Buenos Aires, Hong Kong, Johannesburg, and London, it is headquartered in Arlington, Virginia, where it runs the Newseum. In addition, the Freedom Forum operates the Media Studies Center in New York City and the First Amendment Center at Vanderbilt University in Nashville, Tennessee, in its efforts to push the merits of "free press, free speech, and free spirit for all people." (Newseum, *Self-Guided Tour: Newseum* [Arlington, Va.: The Freedom Forum, 1997], 10). Even though the Freedom Forum invested about $50 million in the Newseum, it has kept admission to the facility free. The attraction is powerful—more than 1.5 million visited the Newseum from 1997 to 2000. Yet its managers believe that even more would visit if the facility were in the District of Columbia. (See David Montgomery, "Newseum Eyes D.C. Sites," *Washington Post*, 2 March 2000, A1, A5.) Another view of "the freedoms" that this sort of foundation may represent is considered in the discussion of "the media-industrial complex" in *New Perspectives Quarterly* 15, no. 5 (fall 1998).

5. Armand Mattelart and Michele Mattelart, *Rethinking Media Theory* (Minneapolis: University of Minnesota Press, 1992), 4.

6. Newseum, *Self-Guided Tour*, 2.

7. Ibid.

8. Ibid.

9. Ibid., 1.

10. Ibid.

11. Ibid.

12. Ibid., 9.

13. As the *Self-Guided Tour* suggests, this display is "a living mural of the global village" (3). Unfortunately, the effect, once considered for a few hours, is one of how the global village uses electronic cultural power to muralize life in accord with entertainment values. The news, like everyday life in general, becomes a movie, reality TV, or a scripted kit of cinematic gesture and belief.

14. See Michel Foucault, *Discipline and Punish: The Birth of the Prison* (New York: Vintage, 1979), 40–43.

15. Fredric Jameson, *Postmodernism, or, the Cultural Logic of Late Capitalism* (Durham, N.C.: Duke University Press, 1992), 418.

16. Ibid., 54.

17. Gianni Vattimo, *The Transparent Society* (Baltimore: Johns Hopkins University Press, 1992), 1.

18. Neil Smith, *Uneven Development* (Oxford: Blackwell, 1984), 32.

19. Edward Soja, *Postmodern Geographies* (London: Verso, 1998), 129.

20. See Stephen Toulmin, *Cosmopolis: The Hidden Agenda of Modernity* (New York: Free Press, 1990).

21. Vattimo, *Transparent Society*, 6.

22. Jean Baudrillard, *In the Shadow of the Silent Majorities* (New York: Semiotext(e), 1983), 3.

23. Ibid., 55.

24. Jameson, *Postmodernism*, xxi.

25. Paul Kennedy, *Preparing for the Twenty-First Century* (New York: Random House, 1992), 333.

26. Vattimo, *Transparent Society*, 6.

27. Robert Reich, *The Work of Nations: Preparing Ourselves for Twenty-First-Century Capitalism* (New York: Knopf, 1991), 172.

28. Jean-François Lyotard, *The Postmodern Condition: A Report on Knowledge* (Minneapolis: University of Minnesota Press, 1984), 46.

29. Vattimo, *Transparent Society*, 9.

30. Ibid., 8.

31. Ibid., 10.

32. Manuel Castells, *The Informational City* (Oxford: Blackwell, 1989), 142.

33. Vattimo, *Transparent Society*, 24–25.

34. Jameson, *Postmodernism*, 412.

35. Vattimo, *Transparent Society*, 7.

36. See Armand Mattelart, *Mapping World Communication: War, Progress, Culture* (Minneapolis: University of Minnesota Press, 1993). This power was expressed very well in the Newseum's 2000 exhibit "Reflected Lives, Directed Lives: American Women's Magazines," which examined how the culture industry in the United States has engineered many different cultural models for "feminine" beauty and behavior over the past century.

37. For more elaboration of the public sphere as such a freedom forum, see Jürgen Habermas, *The Structural Transformation of the Public Sphere* (Cambridge: MIT Press, 1989).

38. Newseum, *Self-Guided Tour*.

39. See Timothy W. Luke, *Screens of Power: Ideology, Domination, and Resistance in Informational Society* (Urbana: University of Illinois Press, 1989), 3–58.

40. *Rethinking Media Theory*, vii.

41. Being on the outskirts of power in Virginia, however, has never been enough for the Freedom Forum. When the Gannett Company and *USA Today* announced their move out to more suburban Tysons Corner, Virginia, the Freedom Forum began searching for a downtown D.C. location during 2000 in anticipation of its current lease's expiration in 2003. In July 2000, the Forum made a bid for a high-visibility site on Pennsylvania Avenue next to the Canadian Embassy and across from the National Gallery of Art. See Jackie Spinner, "Newseum Bids for D.C. Site: City Offered $100 Million," *Washington Post*, 12 July 2000, A1, A13; and Kenneth Bredemeier, "A Foundation to Build On: Freedom Forum's Investments Gave It Means for D.C. Offer," *Washington Post*, 13 July 2000, E1, 17. In a December 11, 2001, press release, the museum's management announced the closing of its Rosslyn location on March 2, 2002, to move the Newseum and Freedom Forum into the District of Columbia for a 2005 reopening. "By moving to the District," Freedom Forum and Newseum president Peter Prichard claimed, "we will significantly expand our programming, reach a much greater audience and deepen our impact." For more, see http://www.newseum.org/newseum/pressroom/releases/newseumclosing_front.htm.

42. Mattelart, *The Invention of Communication*, xii.

43. Lyotard, *The Postmodern Condition*, 64.

44. See John Arquilla and David Ronfeldt, "Cyberwar Is Coming!," *Comparative Strategy* 12, no. 2 (spring 1993): 141–65, and Alvin and Heidi Toffler, *War and Anti-War: Survival at the Dawn of the Twenty-first Century* (Boston: Little, Brown, 1993).

Conclusion

1. See *USA Today*, 8 August 1999, 13A; and *New York Times*, 19 April 2000, H20. Museums, however, have seen huge drops in attendance after the September 11, 2001, terrorist attacks. This loss of interest in visiting museums also has really damaged many institutions' overall financial stability.

2. See Michel Foucault, *Power/Knowledge: Selected Interviews and Other Writings, 1972–1977* (New York: Pantheon, 1980).

3. See Michel Foucault, *The History of Sexuality*, vol. 1, *An Introduction* (New York: Vintage, 1980).

4. Max Weber, *The Methodology of the Social Sciences* (New York: Free Press, 1949), 81.

5. Ibid.

6. Michel Foucault, *The Order of Things: An Archaeology of the Human Sciences* (New York: Vintage, 1970), 158. The quest for entertainment in such frameworks for thought even percolates into display graphics, as evinced in the American Museum of Natural History's exhibit in 2000, "Fighting Dinosaurs: New Discoveries from Mongolia." As Michael Novacheck, its senior vice president and provost explains, "they [the visiting public] want dramatic visuals." See Robert J. Hughes, "Attack of the Killer Exhibits," *Wall Street Journal*, 30 June 2000, W12.

7. See Michel Foucault, "Governmentality," in *The Foucault Effect: Studies in Governmentality*, ed. S. Graham Burchell, Colin Gordon, and Peter Miller (Chicago: University of Chicago Press, 1991), 87–104. Also see Neal Karlen, "Displaying Art with a Smiley Face," *New York Times*, 19 April 2000, H1, H16–17.

8. Foucault, *Power/Knowledge*, 95.

9. Robert Hughes, *Nothing If Not Critical: Selected Essays on Art and Artists* (New York: Knopf, 1990), 389. Museums that are seen as stodgy are failures waiting to happen, and their governing boards are continuously pushed to find more astute, commercially minded curators to keep them afloat. See, for example, Bruce Weber, "How to Make a Museum More Fun to Visit," *New York Times*, 23 December 1999, E1, E5.

10. *New York Times*, 1 February 1999, E1, E3. Strangely enough, many museums are renting themselves out for parties. Since 1990, most museums have experienced a major decline in public funding, while their operating budgets have risen 60 percent. The San Francisco Museum of Modern Art rents its spaces out for all-night rave dance parties, and the Dallas Museum of Art brings in more than $2 billion annually for its $13 billion budget from parties. See Daniel Costello, "It's Party Time at Museums," *Wall Street Journal*, 2 June 2000, W4.

11. *New York Times*, 1 February 1999. Not surprisingly, then, there are around 15,000 museums in the United States, or one museum for every 16,500 Americans, and more than half of them charge no admission fees. See *New York Times*, 19 April 2000, H20.

12. Daniel J. Sherman and Irit Rogoff, *Museum Culture: Histories, Discourses, Spectacles* (Minneapolis: University of Minnesota Press, 1994). John Seabrook makes a similar point about how taste, sophistication, and culture can all be bought today. Consequently, museums provide what some still expect—a quasi-independent point of reference in the marketing of culture and culture of marketing to appraise cultural capital. See his *Nobrow: The Culture of Marketing—the Marketing of Culture* (New York: Knopf, 2000).

13. Foucault, *History of Sexuality*, 119. The Smithsonian's willingness to bend the truth has been more recently exemplified by its "authentication" of the costumes in Mel Gibson's film about the American Revolutionary War, *The Patriot*, which appeared in 2000. Many historians contested hotly the accuracy of the military uniforms in the movie, but the Smithsonian Institution signed off on the costumery through its new, and very aptly named, division: Smithsonian Entertainment. See Jonathan Yardley, "A Bit of Show Biz in the Mall," *Washington Post*, 21 February 2000, C2.

14. See Ben Agger, *Socio(onto)logy: A Disciplinary Reading* (Urbana: University of Illinois Press, 1989). Like entertainment conglomerates, museum managers see themselves as engaged in the project of building audiences for their displays as much as preserving their displays for all potential visitors. For a hard-nosed discussion of how audiences bring in more donors and dollars, see Judith H. Dobrzynski, "Hip vs. Stately: The Tao of Two Museums," *New York Times*, 20 February 2000, AR1, 50.

15. Again, see James Davison Hunter, *Culture Wars: The Struggle to Define America* (New York: Basic Books, 1991), for a sharp account of the "culture wars," along with Todd Gitlin, *The Twilight of Common Dreams: Why America Is Wracked by Culture Wars* (New York: Henry Holt, 1995), and John Michael, *Anxious Intellects: Academic Professionals, Public Intellectuals, and Enlightenment Values* (Durham, N.C.: Duke University Press, 2000).

16. George F. Will, "'Art' Unburdened by Excellence," *Washington Post*, 26 January 2001, A19.

17. Ibid.

18. See Michael Kimmelman, "Museums in a Quandary: Where Are the Ideals?" *New York Times*, 26 August 2001, AR1, AR26.

Index

Abbey, Edward, 160
Adam, T. R., 245n
Adams, Robert McCormick, 27
Afghanistan, 63, 183, 185
Agassiz, Louis, 104
Agger, Ben, 245n, 252n, 258n
Akron Beacon, 206
Albuquerque (N.Mex.), xvii, 88, 147
Alexander, Jane, 234n
Alperovitz, Gar, 237n
Americanization, xv–xxv, 1–18, 19–36,
    82–99, 100–123, 124–45, 146–64, 165–
    85, 203–17, 218–30. *See also*
    nationalism
American Museum of Natural History,
    xxvi, 100–123, 186, 229, 257n
American Southwest, xvi, xxv–xxvi, 82–
    99, 146–64
Anderson, Benedict, 204, 235n, 245n,
    255n
Angel, Heather, 248n
Angola, 58, 63
Arendt, Hannah, 55, 240n
Arizona, xvi–xxvi, 7, 82–99, 146–64
Arizona-Sonora Desert Museum, xxvi,
    123, 126, 146–64, 228, 229
Arlington (Vir.), xxvi, 203–17
atomic bomb, 19–36; "Fat Man," 29;
    Hiroshima, 19–36, 227, 239n; "Little
    Boy," 20, 23; Nagasaki, 24, 27, 31, 32,

33, 239n. *See also* bomber aircraft;
    Manhattan Project
Auschwitz, 45, 53
Autry, Gene, xxv, 9–12, 234n

Barthes, Roland, 66, 242n
Baudrillard, Jean, xxi, 154, 156, 158, 161,
    211, 233n, 239n, 240n, 250n–51n, 256n
Bauer, Yehuda, 242n
Baumol, William, 201
Beck, Ulrich, 204, 254n, 255n
Behring, Kenneth E., 232n, 236n
Belcher, Michael, 231n
Berenbaum, Michael, 240n
Berlin, 16, 239n
Bernhardi, Johann Jakob, 127
Bhabha, Homi, x, 231n
Bhaskar, Roy, 254n
Bickmore, Albert S., 104–5, 122
Bierstadt, Albert, 11, 13
Bijker, Wiebe E., 254n
Billy the Kid, 11
Bingham, George Caleb, 7, 13
Bird, Kai, 236n, 237n
Birmingham (England), xx
Bockscar, 29, 35, 238n. *See also Enola
    Gay*
Bolton, Richard, 1, 231n, 234n, 236n
bomber aircraft: B-1B, 36; B-2, 36;
    B-17, 169, 171, 172, 173, 179, 180, 181;

bomber aircraft *(continued)*: B-24, 171,
  172; B-25, 168, 171, 172; B-26, 171; B-29,
  xxv, 21, 23, 25, 28, 29, 36, 172, 238n;
  B-52, 36, 165, 238n. *See also* Atomic
  bomb
Boorstin, Daniel, 9
Bosnia, 55, 58, 59, 63, 183
Brezhnev, Leonid, 20
Brockway, Linda, 247n
Brooklyn (N.Y.), x, xiv
Brooklyn Art Museum, xiv
Brooks, David, 232n
Brzezinski, Zbigniew, 242n
Bürger, Christa, xxii, 233n
Bush, President George W., xv, 20, 229,
  234n
Bush, President George W. H., 8, 40,
  73–74
Businessweek, 79
Butler, Judith, x

Cambodia, 50, 58, 63
Camp Beale (Ariz.), xvii
Campbell, David, 103, 245n
Carr, William H., 149, 150–51, 152, 154
Carter, President Jimmy, 40, 57, 59
Castañeda, Quetzil, 107, 117, 245n, 246n
Castells, Manuel, 213, 256n
Catherine B. Reynolds Foundation,
  232n
Champlin Flight Museum, 178–79
Chechnya, 55, 59, 240n
Cheney, Lynne V., xv, xvi, 229, 232n
Cheney, Vice President Dick, xv
Chicago, xx, 10, 84–85, 100, 187–89, 191,
  192
Chicago Museum of Science and
  Industry, 187, 188, 189, 191, 192, 233n
Chin, Mel, 1
Churchill, Winston, 180
Cincinnati (Ohio), x
Clinton, President Bill, xv, 40, 59, 229,
  237n
Cochran, Senator Thad, 30
Cocks, Anna Somers, 225
Cody, William F. "Buffalo Bill," 235n
Cold War, xxiv, 1–18, 19–36, 37, 65–81,
  125, 165–85

Commoner, Barry, 141–42, 248n
Conable, Barber, 27
Confederate Air Force, 168–69, 178,
  252n
conservativism, xv, xxiii–xxvi, 4–18, 19–
  36, 82–99, 165–85, 218–30. *See also*
  liberalism
"Constructing a Peaceful World:
  Beyond Hiroshima and Nagasaki"
  exhibit, 31–35
Cuba, 214
cultural left, x, xvi–xxvi, 4–18, 19–36,
  218–30
cultural right, x, xvi–xxvi, 4–18, 19–36,
  218–30
culture war, ix–x, xiii–xxvi, 1–18, 19–36,
  82–99, 203–17, 218–30
Custer, General George Armstrong, 11
cyborgs, 105–85
Czechoslovakia, 14, 44, 46

Daimyo, 65–81
D'Amato, Senator Alphonse, 1
Davis-Monthan Air Force Base, 25, 165–
  85, 238n
Democratic party, xiv–xv, 1, 20, 40, 234n
Denver, 5, 34
Devine, Andy, xix, xxiii
Die Zeit, 205
Disneyfication, 11–12, 16, 55–64, 154–57,
  159
Duncan, Carol, 250n, 252n

Earp, Wyatt, 10, 11
Eder, Klaus, 247n
Edmonds, Kermit, xvii
Edo Japan, 65–81
Eisenhower, General Dwight D., 43
Engelmann, George, 127
Englehardt, Tom, 239n
Enola Gay, ix, xxv, 19–36, 65, 73, 237n,
  238n. *See also Bockscar*
entertainment, 2–18
entertainmentality, 2–4, 36, 133–45, 151–
  64, 218–30. *See also* governmentality
Ethiopia, 58
Evans, Richard J., 233n
Exploratorium, 197–98

Falcon Field (Mesa, Ariz.), 168–69, 178–79
fascism, 19–36, 37–64
Finkelstein, Norman, 242n
Finley, Karen, 1
Fleck, John, 1
Fogel, Robert William, 232n
Ford, Henry, 55
Ford, John, 14
Foucault, Michel, 2–4, 102–3, 107–8, 110, 114–15, 118–20, 133–45, 184–85, 219, 221, 227, 234n, 239n, 245n, 246n, 247n, 248n, 249n, 250nn, 253n, 255n, 257n, 258n. *See also* entertainmentality; governmentality
Fred Harvey Company, xxvi, 82–99
Friedlander, Henry, 239n
Fukuyama, Francis, 231n
Fuller, William, 6
Fussell, Paul, 35, 239n
Fyfe, Gordon, 238n

Gandhi, Mahatma, 50
Gannett Company, xxvi
Gast, John, 6
Gene Autry Museum of Western Heritage, xxv, 1–18, 96, 233n, 235n
General Motors, 233n, 236n
Germany, 27, 33, 37–64
Gestapo, 47, 61, 241n
Giles, Peter, 188, 193
Gingrich, Newt, 21–22
Gitlin, Todd, 234n, 236n, 258n
Giuliani, Rudolph W., xiv
Glazer, Nathan, 231n
Goetzmann, William H., 251n
Goetzmann, William N., 251n
Goldberg, Michael, 241n
Goldwater, Senator Barry, 171
Gore, Al, Jr., xv, 20, 234n
governmentality, 2–18, 38–39, 58–64, 100–110, 133–45, 218–30. *See also* Michel Foucault
Gray, Asa, 127, 132
Guardian, The, 206
Guatemala, 58
Gulf War, 178
Gypsies (Roma), 39, 44, 53, 56, 63

Haacke, Hans, 1
Habermas, Jürgen, 256n
Haraway, Donna, 105, 167–85, 245n, 246n, 252n
Harper, Nigel, 248n
Harrison, Lawrence E., 233n
Harrison, Robert, 239n
Harvey, David, 250n
Harwit, Martin, 23, 26, 27, 28, 30, 31, 34, 35, 237n, 239n
Headrick, David, 248n
Heard, Dwight B., 84–99
Heard, Maie Bartlett, 84–99
Heard Museum, xxv, 82–99, 186, 228
Hermes, 203–4
Heyman, I. Michael, 24, 30, 237–38n
Hilberg, Raul, 239n
Himmelfarb, Gertrude, xiv, 231n
Hiroshima, xxv, 19–36, 227, 239n. *See also* atomic bomb; Nagasaki
history wars, ix, xviii, 19–36, 37–64, 82–99, 165–85, 218–30
Hitler, Adolph, 37, 38, 50–51, 58, 60–61, 63, 64
Hobbes, Thomas, 137
Ho Chi Minh, 57
Hogan, Michael J., 237n
Hollinger, David, 231n
Hollywood, xix, xxiii, 10–12, 49–54, 60, 220
Holocaust, 37–64
Hooker, Sir William Jackson, 127, 128
Hooper-Greenhill, Eilean, 250n 252n
Hughes, Holly, 1
Hughes, Robert, 224, 257n
Hughes, Thomas P., 254n
Hughes Corporation, 167, 170–71
Hunter, James Davidson, 19, 2345n, 236n 258n
Huntington, Samuel, 231n, 233n
Hussein, Saddam, 57

Inoguchi, Takashi, 213n
"Inventing the Southwest: The Fred Harvey Company and Native American Art," 82–99
Iraq, 183, 185
Iron Curtain, xxiv

Israel, 37–64
Italy, xx
Ivey, Bill, xxiv

Jacoby, Russell, 234n
Jain, Purendra, 243n
Jameson, Fredric, xxiii, 145, 209, 213, 233n, 250n, 254n, 255n
Japan, xxv, 19–36, 65–81
Jehovah's Witnesses, 39, 44
Jews, 37–64

Kaczynski, Ted, 195
Kahn, Herman, 242n
Kansas City (Mo.), 87
Kansas City Kansan, 208
Karp, Ivan, 239n
Kassenbaum, Senator Nancy, 29
Kelly, Susan Croce, 233n
Kennedy, Paul, 256n
Kimball, Roger, 232n
King, Ronald, 248n
Kingman (Ariz.), xvi–xxi
Kollwitz, Käthe, 60
Korean War, 165–85
Kosovo, 58, 63, 67
Kramer, Hilton, 232n
Krutch, Joseph Wood, 150, 163, 251n
Kurdistan, 58, 59, 63, 240n

Larsen, Judith K., 253n
Larson, Merv, 154–57
Las Vegas, xvii, 147
Latour, Bruno, 167–85, 236n, 248n, 252n–53n
Laughlin (Nev.), xx
Lavine, Steven, 239n
Lebanon, 14
Legorreta, Richard, 187
Leon, Warren, 239n
Leutze, Emmanuel, 5–6, 13
Levine, Lawrence W., 232n
liberalism, xv, xxiii–xxvi, 4–18, 19–36, 82–99, 124–45, 186–202, 218–30
Libya, 186
Lifschultz, Lawrence, 236n, 237n
Linenthal, Edward T., 239n

Linnaeus, Carl, 128, 132
Lithuania, 45
Logan, Michael F., 251n
Los Angeles, xx, xxv, 1–18, 38, 48–54, 147
Lumley, Robert, 259n
Lyotard, Jean-François, 212, 216, 254n, 256n

MacDonald, Sharon, 238n, 243n
MacKenzie, Donald, 252n
Mandela, Nelson, 50
Manhattan Project, 21, 36. *See also* atomic bomb
Mao Tse-Tung, 50
Mapplethorpe, Robert, x, 1
Marrus, Michael, 239n
Marshall, General George C., 43
Marx, Karl, 118
Marxism, 63; Marxism-Leninism, 13; communists, 39, 41, 43, 44, 53, 56, 60–61, 63
Mattelart, Armand, 205, 215, 255n, 256n–57n
Mattelart, Michele, 205, 215, 255n
McDonalds, 233n, 236n
McKibben, Bill, 252n
McLuhan, T. C., 244n, 251n
McVeigh, Timothy, xx
Merchant, Carolyn, 109, 248n, 252n
Michael, John, 234n, 258n
Milan (Italy), xx
Mill, John Stuart, 17–18, 225, 236n
Milosevic, Slobodan, 58
Mississippi River, 6, 14, 124, 125
Missouri, 7, 124–45
Missouri Botanical Garden, xxvi, 123–45, 186, 228, 229, 233n
Missouri River, 124
Mitchell, Timothy, 245n
Mitchell, W. J. T., 245n
Mochizuki, Mike M., 243n
Mohave County (Ariz.), xvi
Mohave County Pioneers Historical Society, xvii–xxiii, 229–30
Mozambique, 58
Müller–Hill, Benno, 240n

Museum of Tolerance, xxv, 37–64, 233n, 240n. *See also* Wiesenthal Center

museums, xii–xiv; aesthetics and politics, 2–4, 12–18, 151–64; as cultural institutions, xiii–xxvi, 203–17; as educational institutions, xvii–xxvi, 186–202; normative roles, x, xiv–xxvi, 100–103, 165–85; political practices, 19–36, 79–81, 107–10, 133–45, 218–30

Mussolini, Benito, 50

Myanmar, 58, 214

Myers, Norman, 249n

Nagasaki, 24, 27, 31, 32, 33, 239n. *See also* atomic bomb; Hiroshima

NASA (National Aeronautical and Space Administration), 191

National Air and Space Museum, xxv, 19–36, 166, 168, 170, 178, 183, 233n

National Endowment for the Arts (NEA), xxiv, 1

National Endowment for the Humanities (NEH), xxiv

National Gallery of Art, xxv, 65–81, 228, 229

nationalism, xvi–xxv, 1–18, 100–123, 218–30; national identity, xiv–xvi, 1–18, 82–99, 165–85; nationalist conflict, xxiv–xxv, 4–9, 19–36, 203–17

National Museum of American Art, xxv, 1–18, 23, 233n

National Museum of American History, 232n, 236n

National Museum of Natural History, xv

Native Americans, xvii, xix, 1–18, 82–94, 146–64, 243n–44n. *See also* Americanization

Nazism, 27, 33, 37–64

Neufeld, Michael, 27, 28, 30, 34, 35

Newseum, xxvi, 204–17, 228, 229, 233n

New York City, x, xxvi, 100–123, 186, 217

New York Times, 124, 206

Nietzsche, Friedrich, 214

Nobile, Philip, 237n

Novick, Peter, 242n

Nuttall, Thomas, 132

Oakley, Annie, 10

Oklahoma City bombing, xx

Old West, xvi–xix, 1–18, 82–99

ontology, 22, 67, 80, 100–103, 176, 219–30; socio(onto)logy, 175, 252n, 258n

Ouchi, William, 242n

Pack, Arthur Newton, 149, 154

Pearl Harbor, 20

Pentagon, x

Phoenix (Ariz.), xx, xxv, 82–99, 147, 149–51, 153, 186, 244n

Phoenix Indian School, 244

Pima Air and Space Museum, xxvi, 21, 165–85, 228, 229, 233n

Pinch, Trevor, 254n

politics: cultural politics, xiii–xxvi, 19–36, 82–99, 165–85, 203–17; electoral politics, xv, 19–36; global politics, xxiv–xxv, 37–64, 65–81; museum politics, ix–x, xiii–xxvi, 19–36, 100–123, 218–30; symbolic politics, x, xix–xxiii, 1–18, 124–45, 146–64, 186–202

Pol Pot, 50

postmodernism, xiv, 13, 203–17

Purcell, Roy, xvii

Rawls, John, 137

Reagan, President Ronald, 29, 40, 68, 73, 74

Reavis, L. U., 247n

Reich, Robert, 212, 256n

Remington, Frederic, 7, 11, 13, 14, 90

Republican party, xiv–xv, 1,9, 20, 21, 29, 30, 35, 68, 85, 234n

Reynolds, Catherine B., 232n, 236n

Ricci, David, 234n

Riddle, Nelson, xx

Rogers, Everett M., 253n

Rogers, Roy, 10

Rogers, Will, 10

Roosevelt, President Franklin Delano, 50

Roosevelt, President Theodore, 85, 105, 112

Rosen, Philip, 235n

Rosenzwieg, Roy, 239n

Roth, Hohn, 240n
Route 66, xvii–xxiii
Route 66, xx–xxiii
Royal Botanic Gardens (Kew), 127–31
Rubenstein, Richard L., 240n
Russell, Charles, 7, 13, 90
Rwanda, 55, 58, 59, 240n

SA (Sturmabtielung), 43, 44
Saatchi, Charles, xiv
Saint Louis (Mo.), xxvi, 5, 34, 88, 124–45, 188
Salt River (Ariz.), 84, 91
San Diego (Calif.), 87, 88
Sandilands, Catriona, 250n
San Francisco (Calif.), 87, 88
San Jose (Calif.), xxvi, 186–202
San Jose Mercury News, 188, 191, 194, 206
Santa Fe Railroad, 84–99
Saudi Arabia, 40
Seattle (Wash.)
Schreyvogel, Charles, 7–8
Schumpter, Joseph, 255n
Schwartz, Carol, 187, 188
science war, ix, xviii, 100–123, 124–45, 148–64, 186–202, 218–30
Scott, Quinta, 233n
Seabrook, John, 258n
"Sensation" exhibition, x
September 11, 2001, x, 217, 218, 220
Serrano, Andres, 1
Shaw, Henry, 124, 127–33
Sherry, Michael, 35
Sherwin, Elton B., 253n
Silicon Valley, xxvi, 186–202
Simon Wiesenthal Center, 49, 240n. *See also* Museum of Tolerance
Slotkin, Richard, 236n
Small, Lawrence M., 235n, 238n
Smith, Neil, 256n
Smithsonian Institution, ix, 1, 4–9, 13, 15, 19–36, 166, 227, 232n, 233n, 235n, 237n, 238n, 258n
social science: history, xiii–xxvi; political science, ix–x, xiii–xiv, xxiii–xxiv; sociology, xxi
Soja, Edward, 256n

Sonoran Desert, 146–64
Soviet Union. *See* Union of Soviet Socialist Republics
Speer, Albert, 180
Sprinkle, Annie, 1
SS (Schutzstaffel), 45, 47, 48, 61, 241n
Stalin, Joseph, 20
Stevens, Senator Ted, 9, 30
Stevens, Walter B., 247n
Stewart, Jimmy, 10
Stocking, George W., Jr., 239n
Sudan, 58, 63
Sullivan, Robert, xv
Sweeney, General Chuck, 26, 34–35
Swift, Jonathan, 145

Tate, Alan, 229
Tech Museum of Innovation, xxvi, 186–202, 228, 229
television, xiii
terrorism, ix–x
Tibbetts, General Paul W., 25, 28, 32, 36, 237n
Toffler, Heidi, 257n
Toffler, Alvin, 257n
Tokyo, 16, 29, 33
Toulmin, Stephen, 256n
Trans-World Airlines, 167
Trelease, William, 128, 143
Troup, Bobby, xx
Truettner, William H., 234n, 237n
Trzyna, Thaddeus C., 249n
Tucson (Ariz.), xx, xxvi, 147–64, 165–85; Old Tucson, 158
Tucson Daily Citizen, 149
Tweed, William "Boss," 104–5

Union of Soviet Socialist Republics, xxiv, 8, 13, 14, 20, 21, 32, 33, 45, 57, 63, 75, 77, 79, 165, 174, 214, 221
United States Air Force Museum, 167, 170, 173, 178, 183
United States Congress, 1, 4–9, 16–18, 19–36, 40–41
United States Holocaust Memorial Museum, xxv, 15, 37–64, 228, 233n
U.S. presidential election (2000), xiv, 40, 73–74, 101

Universal Studios, 54, 63
Urry, John, 244n

Vattimo, Gianni, 210, 256n
Vergo, Peter, 239n
Vietnam, 25–27, 165, 183
Vietnam War, 165–85
Vogel, Ezra, 242n

Wallis, Michael, 233n, 251n
Wall Street Journal, 28
Walt Disney Company, 11, 16, 51, 54
Walzer, Michael, 35
Washington, D.C., x, xxv, xxvi, 1–18, 19–36, 38, 40–42, 47, 57, 65–81, 103, 203–17
Washington Post, 23, 26, 27, 66, 72
Wayne, John, 10, 29
Weber, Max, 221, 257n
"West as America, The," exhibit, ix, xxv, 1–18, 19, 28, 34, 96
Wiesel, Elie, 40, 59

Wiesenthal, Simon, 49, 240n. *See also* Simon Wiesenthal Center
Will, George, 229–30, 258n
Williams, Raymond, xxi, 233n
Wilson, Edward, O., 101, 244n
Wired, 195
Wolfe, Alan, 231n
Wolfe, Tom, 255n
World Trade Center, x
World War I, 165–85
World War II, 16, 19–36, 38, 40, 165–85
Wright-Patterson Air Force Base, 167, 183, 238n
Wyeth (N.C.), 11

Yahil, Leni, 240n
Young, John, 249n
Yugoslavia, 14, 183

Zukin, Sharon, 251n

Timothy W. Luke is University Distinguished Professor of Political Science at Virginia Polytechnic Institute and State University. He is the author of several books, including *Ecocritique: Contesting the Politics of Nature, Economy, and Culture* (Minnesota, 1997); *Shows of Force: Power, Politics, and Ideology in Art Exhibitions*; and *Capitalism, Democracy, and Ecology: Departing from Marx*. He is the coeditor (with Chris Toulouse) of *The Politics of Cyberspace: A New Political Science Reader*.